Stanley Cavell

Stanley Cavell

Skepticism, Subjectivity, and the Ordinary

Espen Hammer

Polity

First published in 2002 by Polity Press in association with Blackwell Publishers Ltd

Editorial office:
Polity Press
65 Bridge Street
Cambridge CB2 1UR, UK

Marketing and production:
Blackwell Publishers Ltd
108 Cowley Road
Oxford OX4 1JF, UK

Published in the USA by
Blackwell Publishers Inc.
350 Main Street
Malden, MA 02148, USA

ISBN 0-7456-2357-3
ISBN 0-7456-2358-1 (pbk)

A catalogue record for this book is available from the British Library.

Library of Congress Cataloging-in-Publication Data
Hammer, Espen.
    Stanley Cavell : skepticism, subjectivity, and the ordinary / Espen Hammer.
       p. cm. – (Key contemporary thinkers)
    Includes bibliographical references and index.
    ISBN 0-7456-2357-3 (alk. paper) – ISBN 0-7456-2358-1 (pbk. : alk. paper)
    1. Cavell, Stanley, 1926–   I. Title. II. Key contemporary thinkers (Cambridge, England)
B945.C274 H36 2002
191 – dc21

                      2001040617

Typeset in $10\frac{1}{2}$ on 12 pt Palatino by Best-set Typesetter Ltd., Hong Kong
Printed in Great Britain by MPG Books Ltd, Bodmin, Cornwall

This book is printed on acid-free paper.

Key Contemporary Thinkers

Published

Dennis Smith, *Zygmunt Bauman: Prophet of Postmodernity*
Nicholas H. Smith, *Charles Taylor: Meaning, Morals and Modernity*
Geoffrey Stokes, *Popper: Philosophy, Politics and Scientific Method*
Georgia Warnke, *Gadamer: Hermeneutics, Tradition and Reason*
James Williams, *Lyotard: Towards a Postmodern Philosophy*
Jonathan Wolff, *Robert Nozick: Property, Justice and the Minimal State*

Forthcoming

Maria Baghramian, *Hilary Putnam*
Sara Beardsworth, *Kristeva*
James Carey, *Innis and McLuhan*
Rosemary Cowan, *Cornell West: The Politics of Redemption*
George Crowder, *Isaiah Berlin: Liberty, Pluralism and Liberalism*
Thomas D'Andrea, *Alasdair MacIntyre*
Eric Dunning, *Norbert Elias*
Jocelyn Dunphy, *Paul Ricoeur*
Matthew Elton, *Daniel Dennett*
Nigel Gibson, *Frantz Fanon*
Keith Hart, *C. L. R. James*
Sarah Kay, *Žižek: A Critical Introduction*
Paul Kelly, *Ronald Dworkin*
Carl Levy, *Antonio Gramsci*
Moya Lloyd, *Judith Butler*
Dermot Moran, *Edmund Husserl*
Kari Palonen, *Quentin Skinner*
Steve Redhead, *Paul Virilio: Theorist for an Accelerated Culture*
Chris Rojek, *Stuart Hall and Cultural Studies*
Wes Sharrock and Rupert Read, *Kuhn*
Nicholas Walker, *Heidegger*

Contents

Acknowledgments

My thanks are due to the many friends and colleagues who have helped make the writing of this book possible. I am especially grateful to Simon Critchley, Peter Dews, Stephen Mulhall, and Michael Weston, as well as to my partner, Kristin Gjesdal, who carefully read the entire manuscript and suggested many vital improvements. Thanks should also go to Ståle Finke, Axel Honneth, Rupert Read, and Davide Sparti for the benefit I have received from discussing Cavell's work with them. I am indebted to the editors and the unnamed reviewers at Polity for their care and critical sympathy. Cavell himself has my deepest gratitude for his appreciation and enthusiasm, which has been an invaluable source of inspiration. A period of leave from the department of philosophy at the University of Essex enabled me to finish the project. I am grateful to Oxford University Press for permission to publish excerpts from Stanley Cavell, *The Claim of Reason: Wittgenstein, Skepticism, Morality, and Tragedy* (OUP, 1979). Finally, I thank my son, Mathias, for his untiring celebration of the everyday, as well as for the education he has provided me with over the years.

Abbreviations

Works by Cavell

CHU	*Conditions Handsome and Unhandsome: The Constitution of Emersonian Perfectionism*
CR	*The Claim of Reason: Wittgenstein, Skepticism, Morality, and Tragedy*
CT	*Contesting Tears: The Hollywood Melodrama of the Unknown Woman*
DK	*Disowning Knowledge: In Six Plays of Shakespeare*
MWM	*Must We Mean What We Say? A Book of Essays*
NYUA	*This New Yet Unapproachable America*
PH	*Pursuits of Happiness: The Hollywood Comedy of Remarriage*
PP	*Philosophical Passages: Wittgenstein, Emerson, Austin, Derrida*
POP	*A Pitch of Philosophy*
QO	*In Quest of the Ordinary: Lines of Skepticism and Romanticism*
SW	*The Senses of Walden*
TCR	*The Cavell Reader*
TOS	*Themes Out of School: Effects and Causes*
WV	*The World Viewed: Reflections on the Ontology of Film*

Other Works

PhP	John L. Austin, *Philosophical Papers* (Oxford: Oxford University Press, 1970)
PI	Ludwig Wittgenstein, *Philosophical Investigations*, tr. G. E. M. Anscombe (Oxford: Blackwell, 1958)

Preface

Cavell is one of the most significant and brilliant American philosophers writing today. He is also one of the most prolific and influential, though hardly in the sense that his books are easily accessible
and quickly made marketable in contemporary debate. Apart from
the challenges imposed by the immense scope of his textual references and the sheer number of topics under scrutiny, his work
has proven notoriously hard to categorize. More than most original
philosophers of his own generation, Cavell has resisted the pre-
given styles, camps, and orientations of current academic philosophy. And rather than accommodating himself to the professional
demands of analytic philosophy imposed by his educational
background and career, his pursuit of a uniquely individual voice
has translated into a huge body of work that not only traverses
the divide between analytic and continental philosophy but also
displays a dazzling literary quality. In the minds of readers unwilling, often from a suspicion of mystification, to make the effort to
respond to its verbal density and highly diagnostic character, his
writing, at times reminiscent of Derrida, has often been dismissed
as self-indulgent or even irresponsible. But for those who, like
myself, view it as a fascinating and rewarding outgrowth of post-
analytic thinking, it offers intellectual delights rarely equaled
elsewhere. If this book succeeds in encouraging and facilitating the
entry into some of the most consequential of its many dimensions
and vistas, it will have fulfilled its aim.

Unlike most philosophers in the Anglo-Saxon world, Cavell
places a lot of emphasis on notions of reading and responding, and

almost all of his work engages with other texts or expressive manifestations, whether literary, artistic, philosophical, psychoanalytical, or political. Thus any commentary such as this, seeking to present and reflect upon an author's ideas in a reasonably linear and manageable fashion, will be faced with the problem of textual proliferation: that for every move in Cavell there is another person's words that have provoked it. While it would be impossible to write on Cavell without taking his interlocutors into account, I have, in the interest of clarity, tried to limit the amount of secondary material to a minimum. In particular, since Cavell is a lot less interested in interpretation than in dialogue, I generally abstain from questioning the "validity" of his readings. Throughout, my focus will be on the ways in which his encounters with the tradition inform and determine his own views.

Cavell's early work was primarily concerned, as we shall see, with Austin's and Wittgenstein's turn toward ordinary language – the most abiding source of inspiration for his thinking. Soon ethics, aesthetics, epistemology, politics, film, drama, literature, music, painting, sculpture, romanticism, feminism, psychoanalysis, and transcendentalism were to become objects of his reflections on the ordinary. Following the 1979 publication of *The Claim of Reason*, his 500-page masterpiece, Cavell's output has shown an extraordinary acceleration, culminating in the many books and essays appearing in the late 1980s and early 1990s. In all these writings we find a genuine philosophical modernist at work – eagerly determined, like a modernist artist, to explore and question the conditions of his own practice.

My main difficulty in aiming to introduce Cavell to a wider audience is the apparent unsummarizability of most of his work. For those who primarily look to philosophy for theories, theses, and arguments in their support, it may have shockingly little to offer. The quickest way to register why this is so would be to notice the extent to which he shares Wittgenstein's vision of philosophy. For both thinkers, philosophy, rather than being a specialized academic discipline dealing with a limited number of relatively abstruse and abstract problems, arises within the context of everyday life, and there is no subject of human concern that in principle escapes the potential interests of philosophy. Moreover, the impulse to philosophize is seen as a constitutive function of the human, or rather of the way in which humans possess language. Constantly drawn between the skeptical desire to repudiate our habitation in language and the acceptance of our responsibility for maintaining it, or between metaphysics and the difficult peace of the ordinary, we are all, whether willfully or not, caught up in an inescapable dialectic for which there is no final resolution. Cavell follows Wittgenstein in thinking that strands of conceptual confusion can be untangled by clarifying our own linguistic practices. Yet faced with the tensions and temptations that mark the human mind, they both refuse the appeal to method. As opposed to both Kantianism and logical positivism, arguably the two most influential schools of philosophy in modern times, no single procedure is at hand that will be able to solve our intellectual quandaries. To think otherwise would be to relinquish the burden of articulating our position in language, the points and connections by means of which we make ourselves intelligible. Like Freudian therapy, philosophy must, rather, be tailored to a particular diagnosis involving the history of a specific individual. Aiming at the discovery and articulation of the self, it can thus be said to contain an ineradicable existential dimension. Cavell sometimes calls it education – the education of grown-ups. Though in search of commonality, such a process of self-authorization and self-authentication is hardly served by the major vehicles of philosophical transmission today, namely popularization and professionalization. In view of this consideration, my hope is to have written a book that invites, rather than forecloses, reflection, and which draws the reader (back) to Cavell's texts without removing the impetus to respond individually to them.

A central feature of Cavell's thought is that while adopting the techniques of clarification used in ordinary language philosophy, he explicitly avoids Austin's and more orthodox Wittgensteinians' belief that skepticism can be refuted. For Cavell, the skeptic is right in pointing out that our fundamental relation to the world and others is not one of knowledge or certainty. The ordinary links between words and world, since they are only human, based on nothing more than our fragile agreement in judgments, do not provide certainty and can easily be repudiated. Misleading, however, is the skeptic's sense of himself as having uncovered a fateful intellectual lack that once and for all cuts us off from the world and others. While metaphysically finite and separate, humans are able to transcend their own isolation and overcome privacy, though not on the basis of knowledge alone. What knowing presupposes is acceptance and acknowledgment – ways of responding that, though epistemically unassured, secure our habitation with things and others. Again, this is hardly what philosophers normally would think of as a *position* – nor is it meant to be. In its play of denial and peace, metaphysics and everydayness, it is as vulnerable as advanced philosophical reflection can ever be.

Since the everyday figures more as a promise of redemption than as the network of commonsense certainties and unproblematized practices it is often made out to be, it appears to us from the vantage point of an ongoing quest. And while configuring itself as a perfectionist journey of the actual toward the next self, this quest ultimately becomes an intrinsic dimension of moral and political judgment. In Cavell's vision of liberal politics, all citizens are engaged in articulating the extent and nature of their agreement and the content for which they are prepared to take responsibility. If their mutuality should turn out to be threatened or lost, they may, like Cavell's native heroes, Emerson and Thoreau, be forced, at least temporarily, to retreat in order to further rearticulate the terms on which their agreement is based. In part, this is the ambition of Cavell's peculiar brand of romanticism, which in addition to Emerson and Thoreau includes writers such as Wordsworth, Coleridge, Schlegel, and Heidegger. It can also be viewed as the condition of philosophical exploration in general.

This book is intended as a critical introduction to Cavell. In addition to addressing a philosophically trained audience, it is my hope that it may prove useful to other categories of reader, among them students of literature and film. The book is also meant to amend the fact that certain significant aspects of Cavell's writing, especially in his more recent period, have largely remained unexamined, at least in any detail.[1] Among these are his fascinating response to Levinas as well as his elaborate engagement with deconstruction, the contemporary philosophical endeavor most closely resembling, though also crucially diverging from, Cavell's own. I have not been able, however, to make much room in this book for Cavell's interesting relation to Heidegger. Nor is much time spent on the remarkable study of operatic self-revelation in the closing chapter of *A Pitch of Philosophy*. I say little about Cavell's biographical exercises, less than I would like about Thoreau, and very little about Nietzsche, a constant influence on Cavell's thought. To my abiding regret, the Marx brothers, Fred Astaire, and Beckett became impossible to fit in. On the other hand, I regularly return to Cavell's relation to Austin and Wittgenstein, which has proved absolutely vital to his now more than 40 years of ongoing philosophical inquiry.

Except where circumstances call for the introduction of material from a different context, the division of chapters roughly corresponds to the chronological development of Cavell's work. The first chapter considers his early effort to define and defend the practices of ordinary language philosophy. The status and implication of his highly idiosyncratic interpretation of both Austin and Wittgenstein are examined, as well as his reflection on the nature and aims of philosophy. The second chapter takes up his explorations of skepticism about the external world. The guiding interest here is in uncovering the differences between Cavell's handling of the skeptical challenge and more traditional Wittgensteinian approaches. For this purpose, the crucial notion of criteria will be brought to the fore. The third chapter discusses the problem of human minds – of how the existence of others and oneself can be accounted for. It also addresses the tragic ramifications of this issue as they make themselves felt in Cavell's interpretation of Shakespearean drama. The final part of the chapter applies the results obtained so far to his intervention in current debates within feminism. The fourth chapter turns to Cavell's understanding of art and aesthetics. What is an aesthetic judgment? How does it differ from other types of judgment? In addition to his formal aesthetics, it also deals with more material issues. An area of research that throws a lot of light on his project as a whole is the ontology of film: what is film's relationship to reality, and how does film, as an aesthetic object, relate to other forms of visual representation, such as photography and modernist painting? The final part of the chapter deals with Cavell's interpretation of the Hollywood comedy of remarriage as well as the so-called melodrama of the unknown woman, both of which study precisely the interrelation between denial and eventual acknowledgment which make up the dialectical core intuition of his thinking. The fifth chapter discusses the extension of Cavell's views to moral theory and politics. What is the logic and point of moral argumentation? What does it mean to speak for others? What is a democracy? The notion of perfectionism and his readings of Emerson and Thoreau are also of significance in this respect. The chapter ends with a comparison between Cavell and Levinas with regard to their handling of the ethical relation. The sixth and final chapter discusses Cavell's contribution to literary studies. The focus here will be on his recent interpretation of the late Wittgenstein as a romantic thinker, as well as the question of the voice, which he has defended against deconstructionist criticisms of the metaphysics of presence.

1

Ordinary Language Philosophy

Although it continues to exert influence, half a century after its heyday ordinary language philosophy (or Oxford philosophy) is no longer fashionable, having been replaced by intellectual currents such as deconstruction, hermeneutics, and more recent developments in analytical philosophy. Yet in the 1950s and early 1960s, though its actual practitioners were few and the representative contributions rather diverse in nature, it was commonly viewed as a major new movement in philosophy. Before encountering ordinary language philosophy, Cavell had co-authored two articles published in major philosophical journals, both of them in a spirit critical of logical positivism, the then dominant doctrine of American academic philosophy. However, it was not until he encountered the teaching of John Austin – the founder of ordinary language philosophy – at Harvard in 1955 that he started to find what he calls his own voice as a philosopher:

> Then I had the experience of knowing what I was put on earth to do. I felt that anything I did from then on, call it anything you want to, call it philosophy, will be affected by my experience of dealing with this material. It is not necessarily that in Austin I found a better philosopher than my other teachers had been, but that in responding to him I found the beginning of my own intellectual voice.[1]

This chapter will attempt to elucidate Cavell's early thinking about the nature and implications of ordinary language philosophy. Readers who are entirely new to the enterprise might find it somewhat demanding; yet since this engagement sets the trajectory of all his subsequent work, including the most recent, it is crucial at this stage to obtain as clear an understanding as possible of his initial reception of Austin's work. But in addition to the emphasis on Austin, Cavell strikingly blends his reconstruction of ordinary language philosophy with elements from Wittgenstein's *Philosophical Investigations* (a book to which Austin himself, from his conspicuous lack of references to it, seems to have been either indifferent or outright hostile). Although Cavell later recognizes profound differences between Austin's and Wittgenstein's approaches to skepticism, the focus in this chapter will be on how these two philosophers, each in their own way, shape Cavell's thinking about the ordinary.

The Philosophical Significance of What We Ordinarily Say

According to a widespread preconception, especially among philosophers in the Continental tradition, ordinary language philosophy, with its emphasis on what we ordinarily say and mean, is essentially expressive of a positivist attitude. On Herbert Marcuse's interpretation, which was instrumental in spreading this view, the appeal to the ordinary in these philosophers' writings is simply ideological: while failing to realize the constructed character of the social world, it views the social as a realm of brute "facts" before which critical thinking inevitably must halt.[2] It would be premature at this stage simply to brush Marcuse off as having entirely misunderstood what Oxford philosophy was all about. Yet for Cavell, such an assessment must seem very strange indeed. For one thing, as only scant knowledge of their work reveals, both Austin and Wittgenstein were deeply hostile to logical positivism. For example, Austin's *Sense and Sensibilia* is a sustained attempt to demonstrate the absurdity of some of positivism's central doctrines.[3] More importantly, however, much of the motivating force behind Cavell's early work consists precisely in liberating himself from the positivist climate (at Berkeley and Harvard) within which he received his training.[4] Like "friends who have quarreled," he writes, positivism and ordinary language philosophy "are neither able to tolerate nor to ignore one another" (MWM, 2).

As Cavell explains in one of his early attempts to clarify the difference between his own efforts and those of his mentors, the fundamental goal of leading American philosophers at the time was to logi-cally clarify the structure of (natural) science.[5] To the proponents of the hegemonic logical positivist program, it seemed evident that sat-isfactory theory-formation in science presupposes the achievement of a perfect formal perspicuity. This implied that natural language had to be replaced by formalized systems or be revised through logical unmasking of formal disorder. Whereas the structure of theories was held to be representable in purely logical notation, the answerability to the world was seen as occasioned by simple obser-vational statements, purporting to refer to sense-data. On this view, all we shall ever be in a position to know will necessarily be an inte-gral part of a natural science (or any investigation using its methods). Outside the rigorously defined domains of science, no claim can count as knowledge unless it gets analyzed and tested against a standing body of scientific belief. In an even more radical version, statements about the world for which the exact conditions of em-pirical verifiability cannot be specified in advance were regarded as simply meaningless. Since they presumably contain no empirical content, that is, since no observations of the world would be able to demonstrate their truth or falsehood, they are patently nonsensical.

Needless to say, the rise of logical positivism to intellectual prominence meant that the relationship between philosophy and the culture at large entered a phase of mutual suspicion. For, ac-cording to its most militant spokesmen, all ethical, aesthetic, meta-physical, and religious questions – in short, all the issues that traditionally have made philosophy relevant to its own culture – were ruled out as not worth pursuing. They should, rather, be viewed as pseudo questions, incapable of yielding anything but pseudo answers. (Notoriously, such a minimalist conception gen-erated problems for the propositions of positivism themselves, which seem not to pass the test of verifiability. Moreover, in the wake of criticisms made by Quine and others, many philosophers came to adopt naturalist positions, which were often felt to be more coherent.) But logical positivism did not just threaten the integrity of the 'higher' achievements of culture. Indeed, on this view, every-day life, with its endlessly intricate networks of expressions, reac-tions, and responses, could not function as a source of meaning and orientation to human existence. Appeals to the ordinary had to be viewed as pre-philosophical, unworthy of intellectual attention.

In "Must We Mean What We Say?", his first single-handedly written philosophical article, which was published in 1958, Cavell attempts to defend Austin's methods (and the Oxford philosophers in general) against criticisms leveled by Benson Mates, a well-known logical positivist.[6] In order to set the stage for his discussion, Cavell initially notes the uncontroversial point that philosophers who subscribe to the procedures of ordinary language philosophy usually deem it sufficient to solve – or at least make progress with – a philosophical puzzle by pointing out that words have been employed in a non-standard way, and then delineate their standard (or ordinary) employment. Such a practice, which Cavell refers to as the production of "categorial declaratives," typically involves (a) citing *instances* of what is ordinarily said in a language ("We do say . . . but we don't say . . ."; "We ask whether . . . but we do not ask whether . . ."); and (b) occasionally accompanying these instances by *explications* of what is performatively implied by their enunciation ("When we say . . . we imply (suggest, say) . . ."; "We don't say . . . unless we mean . . ."). In Austin's own formulation, proceeding in philosophy from ordinary language means to examine *"what we should say when*, and so why and what we should mean by it."[7] While objecting to this program, Mates's overall strategy consists in referring to an actual conflict between two philosophers who work by reference to such a procedure, and then argue that the nature of their disagreement bespeaks not only a fundamental lack of methodological soundness but a failure to indicate the rationale and relevance of such supplications.

The example Mates provides is a discussion between Gilbert Ryle and Austin in which Ryle had argued that saying that someone is responsible for some action implies that it in some sense is morally fishy, one that ought not to have been done, or someone's fault, to which Austin had replied by providing a counter-instance, namely that on special occasions we say "The gift was made voluntarily," which does not imply that the action of making the gift was morally fishy or in any sense blameworthy. According to Ryle, "It makes sense . . . to ask whether a boy was responsible for breaking a window, but not whether he was responsible for finishing his homework in good time."[8] While agreeing with this, Austin, by pointing out that making a gift is seldom something that ought not to be done, counters Ryle's generalization: it is not true that all cases of speaking about responsible action, though they inevitably have to make reference to some sort of irregularity with regard to the action, imply that somebody is *morally* at fault.

In Mates's account of it, all that this discussion reveals is two professors of philosophy each claiming about their own intuitions that only they express objective truths about language. In the absence of evidence, however, further discussion seems unlikely to settle the dispute; hence it is unclear, Mates continues, why such a debate, since it does not seem responsive to any objectively binding constraints, should even qualify as serious philosophy. According to Mates, the obvious way of establishing such responsiveness to evidence would be to take a poll. Philosophers of ordinary language should leave their armchairs and start doing empirical linguistics.

Cavell's initial response to this objection is quite simple. The production of instances of what we say when and its implications must be made by competent speakers of the language in question, in this case native English speakers. However, evidence is generally not needed in order for statements of this kind to be made; and in so far as it is needed, native speakers will necessarily be the *source* of such evidence. Obviously, a non-native speaker may be uncertain about what we say when and its implications, but such an uncertainty would exclude that person from doing ordinary language philosophy with the language in question. Moreover, in constructing the grammar of a specific language, a descriptive linguist is bound to rely on the intuitions of competent native speakers. No special information or counting of noses would then be relevant in telling the difference between correct and incorrect moves in that language. Indeed, if the native speaker's intuitions had not been sufficient for these purposes, then there would never be any linguistic data in the first place. Cavell is not thereby disclaiming the existence of cases of relevant empirical linguistic research on one's own native language, say on questions concerning its history or sound system. His point is, rather, that someone who tends to require special information in order to produce the instances that interest the philosopher would no longer count as a native speaker. Such a person would not be a master of the language in question. Finally, the procedures of the philosopher of ordinary language philosophy do not rely on memory. Someone may forget or remember certain expressions, or what expressions mean; but on the assumption that it is employed continuously, nobody forgets (or remembers) his or her own native language. Thus to speak a language does not require a tremendous amount of empirical information about its use, as if its possession were on a par with knowledge about objects in the world. Rather, "All that is needed is the truth of the proposition that a natural language is what native speakers of that language speak" (MWM, 5).

Relying on his competence as a native speaker, Cavell then goes on to offer his own reaction to the clash between Ryle and Austin. Although Ryle was right in resisting the view, common to many philosophers (in search of generality), that the term "voluntary" correctly applies to all actions that are not involuntary, what Austin's counter-example shows is that he failed to specify its applicability with sufficient precision. As philosophers of ordinary language, they were both in the business of undoing a too crude distinction ("all actions are either voluntary or involuntary"); but whereas Ryle narrowly construed the condition for intelligibly asking whether an action is voluntary (as opposed to involuntary) to be that it somehow is *morally* fishy, Austin viewed a whole variety of (real or imagined) cases of fishy actions – not only *morally* fishy ones – as liable to be described as voluntary. They both agreed that what we would call a *normal* action – an ordinary, unremarkable action, for example the making of a usual Christmas gift – does not call for the question whether it is voluntary or not; indeed, the question cannot meaningfully (competently) arise. But Austin differed from Ryle in correctly perceiving that the question whether it was voluntary or not can intelligibly be raised in a variety of cases of unusual or untoward actions, for example giving the neighborhood policeman a check for $3,000. As Cavell concludes, "Ryle's treatment leaves the subject a bit wobbly. Feeling how *enormously* wrong it is to remove 'voluntary' from a *specific* function, he fails to sense the slighter error of his own specification" (MWM, 8).

As this example involving action and freedom illustrates, part of the effort of a philosopher of ordinary language consists in showing up traditionally neglected differences. Both Austin and Ryle reproach their fellow practitioners for employing a metaphysically distorted picture of the mind, one according to which all actions are either voluntary or involuntary. Thus the negative purpose of such investigations is to repudiate, to quote Cavell,

> the distinctions lying around philosophy – dispossessing them, as it were, by showing better ones. And better not merely because finer, but because more solid, having, so to speak, a greater natural weight; appearing normal, even inevitable, when the others are luridly arbitrary; useful where the others are academic; fruitful where the others stop cold. (MWM, 103)

On the other hand, the positive purpose of Austin's distinctions consists in that they, like the work of an art critic, bring to attention "the capacities and salience of an individual object in question" (ibid). Indeed, ordinary language philosophy is about whatever (ordinary) language is about: the ordinary world. While excluding most of what mathematics and science, using constructed languages, refer to, the world of the ordinary includes all the objects, people, events, values, and ideals we encounter in our ordinary lives. Such a philosophy will have little or nothing to say about "quantum leaps" or "mass society," though it presents us with a procedure with which to clarify the nature of cultural phenomena such as morality, knowledge, love, art, religion, thinking, and so forth – as well as material ones such as trees or chairs. It should thus be able to relate to all aspects and corners of ordinary human concern; accordingly, it demands to be taken seriously as a "new philosophy" (MWM, 1), capable of challenging other schools of contemporary thought.

As these are obviously ambitious claims (to say the least), it seems necessary to look more in detail at the epistemic status of the knowledge Cavell claims to possess when siding with Austin in his discussion with Ryle (or Ryle when disagreeing with Austin). What exactly is achieved by the formation of such knowledge? Consider statements of the second type, that is, of what we say when together with an explication of what saying so implies. Austin's examples counter Ryle's claims because they make us realize that the statement (of the second type) "When we say, 'The gift was made voluntarily' we imply that the action of making the gift was one which ought not to be done, or was someone's fault," is false. So on the assumption that Austin produced the more plausible account, if someone for example asks (A) "whether you dress the way you do voluntarily," you will take him to imply or mean (B) "that there is something peculiar or fishy about your manner of dress." What is the nature of this implication? What might it be that warrants our sense that raising the question of voluntariness must mean or imply that something about one's actions is fishy? In Mates's account, the answer is obvious. Since the relation between A and B is not logical (not holding logically between propositions), it follows that its nature must be a matter of the contingent pragmatics of language (the way we happen to use it). A reply of this sort would be consistent with Mates's commitment to the positivist thesis that all non-logical relations between statements must be dependent on contingent facts about the world. The problem, though, with Mates's recourse to the distinction between the logical-semantic and the pragmatic levels of language is that, applied to examples such as the one just mentioned, it strikingly fails to do justice to the "hardness" of the implication, the *must* in "must mean." By raising, Cavell argues, the question of voluntariness, "he MUST MEAN that my clothes are peculiar" (MWM, 9). In this sense, then, *we must mean what we say*. Rather than being a matter of how we (contingently) happen to use language, the necessity involved is itself expressive of an unavoidable condition of linguistic intelligibility: *this* is how we must speak in order to make sense of ourselves, be intelligible – in short, to speak the language we speak (in this case, English). If a series of utterances betray a disregard for such implications, for example, if a person continuously turns out not to imply fishiness by the request for an answer as to whether or not an action of dressing has been voluntary, then that does not force us to revise our relevant linguistic intuitions. It only reveals something about this specific person – that she is different, indifferent, mad, or incompetent, in short that she is not taking responsibility, at least not in the same way as we do, for the implications of her utterances. Our linguistic responsibilities thus extend not only to explicit factual claims, that is, to abide, say, by the norms of logic, truth, and sincerity; they also, regardless of whether we heed them or not, require us to mean or intend the implications of what we say. To say something is to take up a particular position vis-à-vis others, one that encompasses obligations and expectations, and which allows the repositioning of oneself along certain routes, for example by apologies, excuses, clarifications – in short what Cavell, following Austin, calls elaboratives. As the next chapter will explore in further detail, it is precisely the refusal of this kind of responsibility (and therefore also burden) that in Cavell's view characterizes much traditional philosophy.

Having introduced the theme of philosophy's forgoing of responsibility, it is important at this stage to draw attention to the fact that Cavell, in "Must We Mean What We Say?", may seem to want to encourage a somewhat different vision of language from that which he defends only a few years later, i.e. in the early 1960s. In this very early essay, written before Cavell's encounter with Wittgenstein, the relevant sense in which we are held to be responsible for our utterances is in terms of observing and respecting the necessary implications of our utterances. You *must* imply fishiness by asking whether a person dresses the way he does voluntarily; if you want to make sense and speak a certain language, you have, as it were, no choice with regard to the commitments your speech involves:

the language makes the choice for you, it intervenes on your behalf. The commitment to such a strong necessity-thesis invites, in other words, a vision of language whereby speakers, in their production of strings of meaningful utterances, are guided along by impersonal rules of some sort. Indeed, for such a necessity-thesis to go through, it must be the case that speakers always encounter a definite number of possibilities as to how to correctly employ terms or concepts in given circumstances. In his later works, however, Cavell starts to reject such a view of language in favor of a conception of individual response and judgment within a shared form of life. As will soon be discussed in more depth, to be responsible for one's own utterances then becomes not simply a matter of being responsive to the material inferences provided by a given linguistic structure, but of accepting that the commitments and obligations we project in a given speech act are expressions of who we are, and that the position of authority ought not to lie with an impersonal body of rules, thus risking what Cavell calls "a subliming of language," but with the subject of the enunciation itself. Projecting and observing linguistic implications articulate who we are and hence what we take to be authoritative in our everyday practices. In this later account, then, the major "sin" of philosophy or metaphysics consists not in a disregard for the necessity of material inferences, but in a discounting of the self.

The emphasis on individual responsibility seems conspicuously at odds with the position outlined in "Must We Mean What We Say?", where Cavell is happy to align his notion of linguistic constraints with conceptions of the "quasi-logical," of the "necessary but not logical," or, as some Oxford philosophers, most notably Stephen Toulmin, have proposed, with "a third sort" of logic in addition to the inductive and deductive varieties.[9] All three alternatives would make sense, Cavell claims, as possible characterizations of the nature of such implications. In particular, what fascinates Cavell is that "something *does* follow from the fact that a term is used in its usual way: it entitles you (or, using the term, you entitle others) to make certain inferences, draw certain conclusions" (MWM, 11). Cavell further maintains that the process of learning what these implications are is part of learning the language. Although few speakers of a language ever utilize the full range of conversational implicatures that their native tongue provides, comprehensive knowledge of this "logic of ordinary language" is required for a native speaker to possess linguistic competence at all.

Hence there is generally no need to ask, as it were, for directions in language. Our knowledge of its performative logic remains largely implicit, constituting a "know how" rather than a "know that." But this is a condition of there being a shared language at all: if every implication of a word had to be made explicit, then communication would never get going. We would never get to the point.

We have seen that explications of instances of ordinary language are neither analytic nor synthetic. Their truth-value, which is not contingent but necessary, is constituted neither by virtue of formal logic nor by correspondence or non-correspondence with facts (native speakers, as opposed to a linguist describing English, do not know what would be the case for these statements to be false). While being tempted to call them a priori, Cavell's suggestion is that they should be viewed as a species of transcendental knowledge. The usefulness of Kantian terminology reveals itself in the analogy between Kant's effort to uncover the conditions of possibility of knowledge and the ordinary language philosopher's attempt to explore the conditions of possibility of phenomena in general.[10] Transcendental knowledge is knowledge of the conditions or constraints a phenomenon must satisfy in order to be what it is. It concerns the essence of the phenomenon – what the phenomenon is *as such*. As Wittgenstein, approvingly cited by Cavell, puts it, "our investigation . . . is directed not toward phenomena, but, as one might say, toward the '*possibilities*' of phenomena" (PI, §90). Applied to the debate between Ryle and Austin, this means that both philosophers explore the conditions of possibility of actions – the *essence*, as it were, of action. The concept of an action *überhaupt* entails that if fishy or conspicuous, then necessarily the question whether it is voluntary or not arises. For something X to qualify as an action for us, it *must* appear as constrained by that implication. In uncovering such tacit linguistic knowledge, then, the philosopher simultaneously reveals essential truths about phenomena. The possible configurations of the world necessarily accord with non-arbitrary yet human constraints. Hence the affinity between Cavell's account of ordinary language and Kant's transcendental idealism. Both aim at showing how the intelligibility of the world is conditional upon our practices and concepts.

So explications of what is implied by the said serves to illuminate both language and the world. The debate between Austin and Ryle brings to light not only what the concept of action essentially means; it also tells us something essential about actions themselves. The same can be said to hold true for statements that produce instances of what is said. In Cavell's example, someone comes across the word "umiak." Upon finding out what the word means, i.e., when it would be correct to say of something X that "this is an umiak," one simultaneously realizes what an umiak *is*. Knowing the word "umiak" means knowing the object umiak – the small boat used by Eskimos in Alaska. Conversely, if one runs across a small boat in Alaska, coming to realize what one sees is to a significant extent a matter of acquiring its name, of knowing what to call such an object, and ultimately of being able to project the word "umiak" adequately into all contexts in which umiaks play a role. For a person could not be said to know what an umiak is unless he or she recognizes not only the umiaks on the beach as umiaks, but also the umiaks on the sea as umiaks, how umiaks are used, what they are made of, and so on, indefinitely. Thus, when we master the concept, at the same time we comprehend the nature of the phenomenon. Language and world refer to each other and presuppose each other for their mutual intelligibility. In this account, human learning becomes the process of aligning language and the world.

We can now see more clearly what Cavell wants to achieve by the proposition that ordinary language philosophy is about whatever ordinary language is about. As opposed to science, its aim is not to gather relevant but hitherto unknown facts for explanatory purposes. Nor is it to understand how language functions, though this may of itself, of course, be of great significance. Rather, the situation in which humans find themselves urged to engage in the kind of reflection that Cavell recommends is one in which, despite the presence of all relevant facts, they feel puzzled by what they confront. As in the Socratic dialogues, they experience the question "What is X?" as unsettling, yet their sense is that the answer cannot be entirely foreign to their own self-understanding. Ultimately, some fact about our use of language needs to be recollected and thus returned from repression or forgetfulness:

> We feel we want to ask the question, and yet we feel we already have the answer. (One might say we have all the *elements* of an answer.) Socrates says that in such a situation we need to remind ourselves of something. So does the philosopher who proceeds from ordinary language: we need to remind ourselves of *what we should say when*. (MWM, 20)

The idea that ordinary language philosophy explores the ordinary as forgotten, lost, or repressed comes to figure as a major theme throughout Cavell's writings. Strictly speaking, the ordinary is only knowable retrospectively, as what is distorted or threatened (by philosophy or, empirically, by the way we live our lives). As an equally consequential thought, Cavell later emphasizes that access to the ordinary tends to be difficult and even painful, and that the recovery of the ordinary requires an act of self-transformation. Moreover, traditional philosophers have been particularly prone to disregard the ordinary. It is as if philosophy is intrinsically driven to deny its conditionedness or finitude and "escape those human forms of life which alone provide the coherence of our expression" (MWM, 61). According to Kant, a transcendental illusion arises when reason seeks to obtain knowledge of that which transcends the conditions of possible knowledge, i.e. when the philosopher attempts to escape her own finitude. Similarly, the philosopher of ordinary language attempts to reveal the illusions arising from employing words in the absence of those constraints and responsibilities which provide their intelligible employment, that is, in the "absence of the (any) language game which provides their comprehensible employment" (MWM, 65). In Wittgenstein's formulation, to which Cavell refers, "The results of philosophy are the uncovering of one or another piece of plain nonsense and of bumps that the understanding has got by running its head up against the limits of language" (PI, §119).

These similarities between Cavell and Kant being recorded, it is important at once to notice a fundamental difference between the two thinkers. The categorial status of the statements about what we must mean by asserting that X is F (for example "this is an action") is, as we have seen, not derived from a formal system (in Kant, the logical form of judgments), but from one's own native language. From this it follows that a deduction (or proof) of the objective validity of the complete set of "categorial declaratives" cannot be provided once and for all. Just as importantly, the philosopher of ordinary language relies on his native language *as it is*, i.e. as it happens to be and as it has become; and the source of normativity does not lie in the assertions about use; rather, what is normative is exactly the ordinary use itself (MWM, 21). Consequently, Cavell views transcendental knowledge as historically relative: "It is perfectly true that English might have developed differently than it has and therefore have imposed different categories on the world than it does; and if so, it would have enabled us to assert, describe, question, define, promise, appeal, etc., in ways other than we do"

(MWM, 33). Now this may seem to jeopardize the hardness of the "must" in the philosopher's explications. If an implication *appears* binding to us simply because we have come to speak this way, then that begs the question whether it *really* is binding. In response to this objection, Cavell points out that for any speaker there is only one native language. Given the lack of alternatives, the skeptical appeal to historical contingency is moot. A person who tries to evade this condition by claiming that "anyone may speak as he or she pleases, there is no need always to use normal forms in saying what one says," is right in drawing attention to the flexibility of language, i.e. that on particular occasions, we may change the meaning of words or speak metaphorically, cryptically, paradoxically, and so on. Yet the possibility of speaking strangely is itself provided for in the native language. Outside those parameters, no utterance is extraordinary or weird; outside there can only be unintelligibility and noise.

A further, and to many philosophers a surprising, peculiarity about statements that offer instances of what we say or explications of their implication – that is, categorial declaratives – is that though expressive of a normative relation, they are not correctly represented as prescriptive utterances. Prescriptive utterances (or commands) tell me what I *ought* to do if I want something else, whereas categorial declaratives tell me what I *must* do in order to speak my own language. As opposed to prescriptive utterances, there is no alternative to the "must" of the categorial declaratives: while telling me what I must do in order to perform correctly, they simultaneously describe the performance itself, how it is done. It follows from the normativity of the "must" that mistakes can be made, yet deviations mean that I no longer do what I think I do: I can no longer say what I say "*here* and communicate *this* situation to others, or understand it for [myself]" (MWM, 21). Deviations threaten to make me unintelligible. My words become private; no longer do they make a claim on others nor are they believable. Hence a relationship of complementarity holds between rule and statement. To say how something is done is to say how it must be done in order to be done at all. So although many philosophers tend to think of rules as best expressed by prescriptive utterances, Cavell offers a view which significantly links normativity to the features outlining actual practices themselves. By describing the ordinary, what we say and imply on specific occasions, the philosopher at the same time draws attention to its normativity.

Self-knowledge

As I have already hinted, in another early essay entitled "The Availability of Wittgenstein's Later Philosophy," published in 1962, Cavell explicitly characterizes the knowledge pursued by ordinary language philosophy as self-knowledge. Upon coming to accept that Austin was right in pointing out, against Ryle, that it sometimes makes sense to say "The gift was made voluntarily," and hence that not all instances of fishy actions are *morally* fishy, thus demonstrating Ryle's failure to specify correctly the conditions under which it makes sense to ask whether an action is voluntary or not, I realize what *I* am prepared to say when. It marks me as a speaker that *this* is what *I* would say in *that* real or imagined situation. I thus obtain, or at least aspire to obtain, something that Cavell finds much philosophy to have disregarded as irrelevant or uninteresting: knowledge about myself – about who I am:

> If it is accepted that "a language" (a natural language) is what the native speakers of a language speak, and that speaking a language is a matter of practical mastery, then such questions as "What should we say if . . .?" or "In what circumstances would we call . . .?" asked of someone who has mastered the language (for example, oneself) is a request for the person to say something about himself, describe what he does. So the different methods are methods for acquiring self-knowledge. (MWM, 66)

The claim, then, is not that ordinary language philosophy has anything distinct to say about the self *apart* from the actual practices of procuring self-knowledge. As with Freudian analysis, the emphasis lies with the activity rather than the results. To pursue such an activity, like dream analysis or the use of "free" association in psychoanalysis, is to engage, each one of us, methodically in the pursuit of knowledge of our own selves.

At first blush, this claim seems to raise more problems than it solves. For if what the philosopher of ordinary language recounts are truths about one's own particular self, then Mates's charge that Ryle and Austin, in their debate, fail to transcend their own privacy and reach a position from which to claim universal agreement seems unanswered. As Cavell suggests in "Aesthetic Problems of Modern Philosophy" of 1965, we would then have a practice similar to what Kant calls a judgment of sense. According to Kant's argument in the *Critique of Judgement*, if I find something (for example a

wine) to be empirically pleasant, I may report my subjective sensation to others, but there would be no ground on which I can base
a demand for their agreement: "To strive here with the design of
reproving as incorrect another man's judgement which is different
from our own . . . would be folly."[11] In this region of self-knowledge,
each mind is a potential enigma to the other. We are never in a position to speak *for* another mind; and should our responses overlap,
then that would simply be the result of a contingent correspondence, a crude fact of nature. A demand for agreement would not
appeal to anything shared, and therefore not really be a demand
at all. For such a demand to be possible, something must be in
common, yet on this – for Cavell's purposes – false picture we each
inhabit our own world, closed off from all others. Calling it a skeptical fantasy of self-sufficiency, Cavell at regular intervals returns to
this deluded representation of the self and its relation to others. For
example, in *The Claim of Reason* he explores, as I will return to in the
next two chapters, the wishes and fears that underlie such a picture,
and how its implicit denial of others (and of oneself) is destructive
and ultimately tragic.

But if self-knowledge, understood as knowledge of what I am
prepared to say when, cannot be accounted for in terms of a model
of strict privacy, then is there an alternative? According to a competing (yet, as we shall see, false) model, my practical mastery of
words, though *mine* and hence with some charity a species of self-
knowledge, could be seen as displaying an impersonal knowledge
of a body of theoretical rules and an abstract set of principles. In
Kant's expression, I would then, as in the domain of morality, be
depending on a definite concept of how to proceed. This would
seem analogous to a master of a proficiency, for example an engineer, who, if asked to tell us how he proceeds to construct and set
up a bridge, would instruct us in the rules and principles governing his activity. In so doing he would tell us what it essentially takes
to be an engineer. Obviously, the application of the term "self-
knowledge" would in this case be very strained. Strictly speaking,
that which the engineer imparts would tell a lot less, if anything,
about him, *this* engineer, than about the conditions and content of
his specific expertise. His competence would not be *his* in the same
manner that his awareness of his own character, for example, which
relies on a privileged perspective (though not necessarily his own),
would be his. Yet if transferred to the domain of language, a vision
of mastery based on knowledge of abstract rules or principles,
though it hardly passes for self-knowledge in the ordinary sense,

would seem to offer Cavell an effective means with which to under-
mine Mates's worry about subjectivism. If being a competent
speaker were equivalent to possessing such knowledge, then the
statements of philosophers of ordinary language would indeed, one
could argue, be objectively constrained. Rather than simply expressing the parochial beliefs of the philosopher, such statements, like
physiology or generative linguistics, would refer to facts about
human nature in general. However, if the vision of our life together
on the model of strict privacy implies that we do not count *for
one another*, then the vision according to the impersonalist model is
that *we* do not count for one another: it would not be *I* who count,
or fail to count, for you; instead, mutual intelligibility would be
insured by the linguistic structure.[12] Again, as we shall see in more
detail later, this is yet another way of trying to avoid responsibility
for what we say.

On a more immediate level, though, the problem with the impersonalist model is that it seems incompatible with our real usage of
words. In a chapter of *The Claim of Reason* entitled "Excursus on
Wittgenstein's Vision of Language," Cavell argues that, if true, then
words would be both less flexible and less inflexible than they actually are. Less flexible, because if the correct application of words in
judgments, and hence what can be said in a language, were everywhere determined by algorithmic rule-formation, then the projectibility of words into new contexts would be much more limited
than it is. Of the essence of words is that they always tolerate unexpected and surprising new projections, and this is how it must be.
The world we inhabit continuously requires, as it were, new expressions: for since there are "always new contexts to be met, new needs,
new relationships, new objects, new perceptions to be recorded and
shared" (CR, 180), without the flexibility of words we would not be
able to employ them in order to engage with the world. From saying
"feeding the kitty," "feeding the lion," and "feeding the swans," one
day one of us starts saying "feeding the meter" and "feeding in the
film," and yet such new projections do not prevent communication
and expression. On the contrary, while making perfect sense, they
allow more fine-grained distinctions (for example between putting
material into a machine and adding new material to the construction of it) than more general verbs such as "to put." One might
imagine that using a more specific verb than "to feed" would function equally well and hence make the projections redundant, yet
there are limits as to how differently we are able to view certain
activities and still make sense of our experience. A language per-

fectly intolerant of projection – in which no connection would be seen between, say, giving food to birds and to fishes (such that they would be two entirely different activities, having nothing in common) – would be very primitive. At least from our perspective, it would fail to record relevant relations of similarity. On the other hand, if we imagined it as the language of a culture very different from ours, we would feel strongly tempted to think not only that they *viewed* giving food to birds and to fishes in very different terms, but that these activities, from their perspective, *in fact* were markedly different. Perhaps the cultural significance of the two activities had so little in common that it made no sense *to them* to apply the same designation. But everything cannot simply be different, for then there would be no instances of concepts, and hence no concepts either.

This does not mean, though, that our words possess an unrestricted degree of flexibility. While language in general is tolerant of projection, not any projection will be legitimate and thus make sense. One can "feed peanuts to a goat" and "feed pennies to a meter," yet one cannot feed a child by stuffing coins in its mouth. As Cavell puts it:

> An object or activity or event onto or into which a concept is projected, must *invite* or *allow* that projection; in the way in which, for an object to be (called) an art object, it must allow or invite the experience and behavior which are appropriate or necessary to our concepts of the appreciation or contemplation or absorption . . . of an art object. (CR, 183)

Without an inner constancy and stability, we would never be in a position to know whether a new instance is covered by our concept: our concepts would have no sense. But how do we know *when* a projection is allowed? What makes a context inviting? According to the impersonalist model, in order to know that we would need to possess complete explanations for the correct use of every word. However, as I will return to at the end of this chapter, since we determine something *as* something, and thus make the world intelligible, by means of a vast network of tacit competences that connect us to the form of life into which we are socialized, no explanation (or rule) can control *every* single application of a word:

> You cannot use words to do what we do with them until you are initiate of the forms of life which give those words the point and shape they have in our lives. When I give you directions, I can adduce only

exterior facts about directions, e.g., I can say, "Not that road, the other, the one passing the clapboard houses; and be sure to bear left at the railroad crossing." But I cannot *say* what directions *are* in order to get you to go the way I am pointing, nor *say* what my direction *is*, if that means saying something which is not a further *specification* of my direction, but as it were, cuts below the actual pointing to something which makes my pointing finger point. (CR, 184)

Returning to the relation between ordinary language philosophy and the issue of self-knowledge, we now see that neither strict privacy – in the sense of Kant's judgments of sense – nor impersonal matrices – in the sense of Kant's judgments of reason – can account for the capacity of knowledge about the self, in the specific sense of "what I say when and the implications thereof," to claim general validity. However, in addition to those two types of judgment, Kant also describes reflective judgments of beauty, which on his view is the only genuine form of aesthetic judgment. Without considering the technical terms of Kant's analysis, on Cavell's reading the distinguishing feature of a judgment of beauty is that on the basis of a purely subjective ground, it none the less is possible to be speaking with what Kant calls "a universal voice."[13] For Kant, the subjective ground of such judgments consists in a feeling of pleasure resulting from the free play of the imagination and the understanding when faced with a beautiful form. In so far as the agreement of these two faculties is necessary for cognition to be possible at all, it follows that each agent will be entitled to presuppose that others ought to agree with them in their judgments of beauty. Alternatively, Kant calls the effect of such a necessary interplay between faculties a common sense (*sensus communis*), and argues that the claim to universality bases itself on the assumption of the universality of such a sense. As opposed to determinate judgments of goodness, however, which *postulate* the agreement of everyone on the basis of universally binding reasons, reflective judgments of beauty, for which no subsumption under determinate concepts takes place, only *demand* or *claim* universal validity. If someone disagrees with me about whether an object is beautiful, no proof or argument will settle the matter. In the hope of reaching agreement, though, what I can do is keep on articulating my own response and thereby try to make the other appreciate what I see. The other may continue to hold a different opinion, but doing so does not rule out my claim upon him (or his upon me). It only shows how different we are. Likewise, Cavell insists that when I reflect on *what I would say when*, I do so as a representative speaker; hence I am in a position to claim the assent of others. Thus the task of the ordinary language philosopher is not to discount subjectivity, "but to include it; not to overcome it in agreement, but to master it in exemplary ways" (MWM, 94). In explorations of the ordinary, claims made about my life simultaneously purport to be about yours: I take myself as representative of all human beings, and in so doing I make a claim to community. However, there is always a risk of rejection. Claims to community or commonality, though in most cases they find assent (otherwise communication would not be possible), may turn out to have limited applicability: the most common concept *could* be used differently by others. Depending on the circumstances, this may either be tragic or comic. Of great significance, yet only hinted at here, however, is that the degree of my idiosyncrasy only reveals itself in the representation of my subjectivity as exemplary. Before attempting to master my subjectivity in exemplary ways, not only do I fail to know myself and my position in the world; I also do not know others, or rather the extent of our agreement. Thus my existence is unknown unless *I make myself known*, i.e., express myself; and to possess one's existence, as we will see in more detail later, is ultimately to enact it. In his more recent works Cavell adopts the name "perfectionism" for this concomitant search for the self and the other.

Wittgenstein's Later Philosophy

With the possible exception of Austin, no author has exerted a stronger influence on Cavell's thinking about the ordinary and the status of ordinary language philosophy than the Wittgenstein of the *Philosophical Investigations*. The reading of Wittgenstein is extremely complex, demanding an overview of Cavell's whole *oeuvre* in order to realize its full impact, yet many of his crucial responses are already present in the 1962 essay "The Availability of Wittgenstein's Later Philosophy." Using David Pole's then recently published book *The Later Philosophy of Wittgenstein* as his object of polemic, Cavell plunges straight into a discussion of what scores of philosophers have regarded as the key to the *Investigations*, namely its conception of rules and rule-following.[14]

According to Pole, in order to account for linguistic normativity – i.e., the correctness or incorrectness of particular uses of words – language must be viewed as essentially a rule-governed structure. It is only because agents follow rules that it is possible to distinguish between right and wrong, as opposed to just viewing utterances naturalistically as ways of merely sounding off. Pole accounts for linguistic normativity in several steps. First, in employing language, the validity and rightness of each move within it are assessed by appealing to a set of normative procedures, and, second, for every such move a competent speaker must be able to tell whether a rule is applicable or not. Third, rules are determinate in the sense that where they apply, there can be no question whether a rule has been followed or infringed; their correct interpretation is given with the presence of the rules themselves. Beyond the structure of rules, however, there can be no further appeal. Thus, fourth, if a case appears to which no existing rule applies, one may choose to adopt or invent a new rule, yet its application, while changing the game, is only the result of one's decision to make use of it; there is no right or wrong in accepting it. Echoing the positivist distinction between cognitive and non-cognitive discourse, Pole's account thus drives a wedge between "internal" and "external" questions, where only the former allow rational claims to be made.

In response, Cavell argues that although Pole's "Manichean" conception of rules may seem fit as a description of how a *constructed* language functions, it falls hopelessly short of capturing the way correctness is determined in everyday language. Accordingly, when Wittgenstein in the opening paragraphs of the *Investigations* famously draws attention to the analogy between language and games, he should *not* be taken to suggest that everyday language is best understood as a rule-governed structure. Rather, the notion of language-games is meant to bring into prominence the fact that mastering human speech requires participation in a form of life, involving others, and it does not intimate a vision of speech as presupposing that in every situation a definite set of moves will be open to us. The aim of the analogy, then, is to help us realize that "the absence of such a structure in no way impairs its [everyday language's] functioning" (MWM, 48). While it would be wrong to discard the concept of rules altogether (retrospectively they may play a role, but then as wholly parasitic on what we would say in particular circumstances), philosophically the attention should be shifted from rules to judgments. The basic fact in need of philosophical reflection is that we learn words in certain contexts, and after a while we are expected to make judgments by appropriately projecting those same words into further contexts. As already noted, Cavell's general claim, which entails a dismissal of the necessity-thesis we found operative in "Must We Mean What We Say?", is that no universal can relieve us of the anxiety and responsibility involved in making those projections. No rules or pre-given idealities intervene, as it were, between my judgments and the world to which they are meant to respond.

With reference to Wittgenstein's own discussion of rule-following, several points emerge as consequential. First, rules do not circumscribe every aspect of a meaningful activity or speech act. It belongs to the nature of our linguistic being that there will always be projections of words for which it is not obvious whether or not rules apply. On Pole's view, however, this would imply that rules are "incomplete." However, the sense that they are incomplete ought to vanish, or be seen as idle, upon realizing that the notion of completeness has no application: what matters is that which we are able to say, and how and to what extent we are able to make sense in particular cases. Second, every rule-following activity is learnt and takes place against the background of innumerable other activities. It would be impossible to master just *one* activity. Hence the idea, entailed by the Manichean picture, that every move a speaker makes can be viewed in isolation from this background is incoherent. Normativity ("right" and "wrong") cannot be sustained simply by reference to the concept of a rule, for this would presuppose an atomistic conception of language according to which linguistic activities can be seen in isolation from the background and viewed exclusively in terms of their corresponding rules. Third, no listing of rules can ever determine what taking part in an activity – *playing a game* – amounts to. Indeed, mastery of a game – obeying orders, repeating what other people say, and so forth – ordinarily takes place in the absence of rules, or any reference to them. So linguistic normativity does not involve the strong, quasi-logical (and hence impersonal) conception of material inference and conversational implicature that we seem to encounter in at least parts of "Must We Mean What We Say?". Fourth, what we call a game has no essence. There is no feature that necessarily has to be present for something to be a game; nothing is common to all games. Rather than strict essences, there are at best what Wittgenstein famously calls "family resemblances": "a complicated network of similarities overlapping and criss-crossing: sometimes overall similarities, sometimes similarities in detail" (PI, §66). Thus "being determined by rules" as such has no general application: "Language has no essence" (MWM, 50). Fifth, Cavell suggests that "following a rule," to the extent that such an expression appears applicable here at all, itself *is* a practice. As we have seen, however, the nature of ordinary linguistic practices is such that if you perform them correctly, you simply do them. There is no stage at which their degree of correctness may be assessed: either you make a promise or you don't. Finally, being an initiate of these practices is a matter of participating in a form of life: "That [i.e., forms of life] is always the ultimate appeal for Wittgenstein – not rules, and not decisions." In a celebrated passage, Cavell sums up his vision of language as follows:

> We learn and teach words in certain contexts, and then we are expected, and expect others, to be able to project them into further contexts. Nothing insures that this projection will take place (in particular, not the grasping of universals nor the grasping of books of rules), just as nothing insures that we will make, and understand, the same projections. That on the whole we do is a matter of sharing routes of interest and feeling, modes of response, senses of humour and of significance and of fulfillment, of what is outrageous, of what is similar to what else, what a rebuke, what forgiveness, of when an utterance is an assertion, when an appeal, when an explanation – all the whirl of organism Wittgenstein calls "forms of life." Human speech and activity, sanity and community, rest upon nothing more, but nothing less, than this. It is a vision as simple as it is difficult, and as difficult as it is (and because it is) terrifying. (MWM, 52)

The vision is terrifying in contrast to the view proposed by Pole, according to which rules intervene on our behalf, as it were, and authorize and control the way we talk. According to Cavell's interpretation of Wittgenstein's "forms of life," it does not make sense to ask for the foundation of our practices. In successfully employing language for communicative purposes, we simply rely on a *fact* of agreement in interest, feeling, and response for which there can be no further explanation. To interpret this predicament as indicating *an absence* of foundation, and therefore as an alarming truth about our life with language, rather than simply the condition of intelligibility, is characteristic of the skeptic, who then demands that there *must* be some structure, some presence, or some set of rules, that can relieve him of the anxiety, commitment, and responsibility involved in the exercise and expression of his rationality. As we will see in the next two chapters, much of Cavell's work on skepticism consists precisely in showing up the cost of repudiating our "forms of life" (and thus our humanity and finitude), while simultaneously avoiding a skeptical interpretation, i.e., one according to which our life-forms would be reified and misinterpreted as foundations.

In stressing the fragility of our agreement, Cavell is not denying the importance of social life in coming to master concepts. Without training in the practice of using words, we would not be initiated in the language-games that make speech possible. The claim is, rather, that neither the social nor the numerous practices sustained within it can ever relieve us of our individual stance. *We*, each of us, need to be responsive. As the criticisms of Pole's understanding of rule-following have revealed, rationality cannot be construed as the standing presence of a substance within us, something that by its very nature simply guides us along. Our picture of rationality must leave room for reasonable deviance – for contesting conventions in order to seek a better expression of our own self-understanding and conviction. For sometimes the grammar of an expression just *needs* explaining, and unless we can recognize our own commitments and identity in the account we then attempt to give, it will not appear believable: the essential reference to the self that intelligible speech demands will be lacking. So against Pole's objection that such a struggle to determine and express rationality (that is, do ordinary language philosophy) would be a matter of mere choice, devoid of cognitive value, Cavell maintains that with the acceptance of an expression as expressive of a part of the grammar of (my) language, it also follows a sense of commitment and responsibility. While there is no "right" and "wrong" with regard to such expressions – indeed *they* make right and wrong possible – it would be false to say that nothing binds or constrains them: for Cavell's claim, as we already know, is precisely that *I* must be able to recognize myself in what they express, and that without such an acknowledgment, no elucidation of the ordinary would even get started.[15] Indeed, accepting a categorial declarative (or grammatical proposition) is not essentially different from all other forms of belief-formation: "we no more decide what will express our conviction here than we decide what will express our conviction about anything else – for example, that the road to New Orleans is the left one, that the development section is too long, and so forth" (MWM, 53). However, rather than taking the content of this universal agreement among native speakers for granted, the procedures of ordinary language philosophy invite us to explore the extent of that agreement.

Reference to the community, to intersubjectively shared practices, is indispensable for our understanding of how speakers can have a language in the first place. A language is always inherited, and the ways in which it allows us to make ourselves intelligible to one another are not laid down by single speakers. Where Cavell sharply differs from a number of Wittgensteinians is over whether mere conformity with shared practices is sufficient to constitute a speaker's right to lay claim to linguistic correctness, that is, pose as a representative speaker. Although it appears as something of a leitmotiv in Cavell's writings, his response to Saul Kripke's interpretation of the *Investigations*, printed in *Conditions Handsome and Unhandsome*, is in this respect particularly revealing.[16] According to Kripke's community-based reading, Wittgenstein emerges as a radical skeptic about meaning; and only an appeal to a social consensus, while not refuting the skeptic so much as offering a "skeptical solution," can show how normativity is sustained. While agreeing with Kripke that skepticism should be seen as internal to Wittgenstein's teaching and that the *Investigations* contain no attempt at refuting skepticism, Cavell sharply rejects Kripke's ascription of meaning-skepticism as well as his "skeptical solution." In order to support his interpretation, Kripke crucially relies on the following passage in the *Investigations*:

> This was our paradox: no course of action could be determined by a rule, because every course of action can be made out to accord with the rule. The answer was: if everything can be made out to accord with the rule, then it can also be made out to conflict with it. And so there would be neither accord nor conflict here. (PI, §201)

Any proposed candidate for the meaning of a predicate must be such as to sustain linguistic normativity: from the alleged meaning-constituting property of a word it must be possible to read off the correct use of that word. According to Kripke's reading of paragraph 201, however, nothing about the speaker can be produced that constitutes meaning in such a way as to meet the normativity requirement, and hence the whole notion of meaning falls into jeopardy. Put differently, no fact can be cited which constitutes a speaker meaning *this* rather than *that* – that the speaker means x and not y by "x". So "Wittgenstein's main problem is that it appears that he has shown *all* language, *all* concept formation, to be impossible, indeed unintelligible."[17] Roughly, Kripke's skeptical solution to the paradox consists in accepting that while meaning is never a fact about speakers, normativity is sustained by means of assertibility conditions that refer them to their social life. Knowing what an expression means is to know the conditions in which the expression may find communal assent. Meaning is thus constituted by knowing the circumstances in which a certain "move" in a language-game is permitted. Kripke does not claim that we continually check the assertibility of our own and each other's utterances: predominantly, we rely on practical capacities that have been internalized through training. His point is rather that without the *possibility* of mutual control, we would never know in cases of doubt what the right use of a concept might be. For an individual regarded in social isolation, however, no such possible check on right and wrong uses of expressions would exist; thus in such a case assertibility conditions and therefore also meaning and language would collapse.

Cavell contests all of these claims. Although Kripke is correct in emphasizing the importance of skepticism for Wittgenstein, there is no skeptical paradox to be found in the *Investigations*. For as paragraph 201 continues, Wittgenstein unequivocally points out that the paradox is based on a misunderstanding: it only arises on the false assumption that acting in accord with a rule is to interpret it correctly. The assumption is false because any interpretation is just a new sign which itself stands in need of an interpretation. We could always try to give a rule for the application of a rule, but this would threaten to end in an infinite regress. However, since no interpretation takes place when we correctly project words into new contexts, the lack of any fact of meaning (that is, of the speaker meaning x rather than y by "x") fails to trigger any skeptical consequences. Indeed, Kripke misleadingly turns the absence of fact itself into a fact; yet rather than being a shocking revelation about ourselves as speakers, the absence of a fact of meaning is a requirement on the part of the skeptic. Only on the assumption that the skeptic is right that such a fact is *needed* can its absence appear to be shocking. So no skeptical conclusion *ought* to follow from this imputation of a lack.

Moreover, by emphasizing the skeptical paradox, Kripke launches his investigation from an anti-social, hence skeptical, perspective, and the problem thus becomes one of positioning the individual in the community, rather than showing the costs of repudiating the community. For Cavell, on the contrary, the individual is always already in agreement with someone (otherwise he could not have acquired a language), though not necessarily with us and our practices. However, there is no sense in which human judgments *rest* on communal agreement, as if on a fact: the agreement in judging is itself, as it were, the final fact. While no explicit agreement ever occurred such that I could have been party to it, we agree, due to our shared natural reactions and the way we allow things to count in specific ways, pervasively in judgments and thus in our concepts:

> The idea of agreement here is not that of coming to or arriving at an agreement on a given occasion, but of being in agreement throughout, being in harmony, like pitches or tones, or clocks, or weighing scales, or columns of figures. That a group of human beings *stimmen* in their language *überein* says, so to speak, that they are mutually voiced with respect to it, mutually *attuned* top to bottom. (CR, 32)

Nothing is more fundamental than this agreement, yet nothing – no structure, matrix, or mental dispositions – explains it; rather, it is the basis on which meaning and communication, indeed our representational capacity in general, are made possible. Cavell thus warns against asking, as does Kripke, for ultimate explanations or epistemological accounts of our agreement: all foundationalisms, even those of neo-pragmatism whose appeal to practices is done in the name of anti-foundationalism, must be rejected. Conjointly, as a result of demanding – inappropriately, in his use of the skeptical paradox – the same precision and capacity to determine in advance what counts as an instance of a concept for ordinary concepts as we do for mathematical ones, Kripke betrays an impulse to condemn language for failing to correspond to a given matrix; he thus implicitly sublimes language, thereby repudiating our agreement and driving out responsibility for making sense of ourselves and others. For even though language is essentially shared, humans are separate from the world and others – and nothing except their willingness to continue to let themselves be known to others can ensure the existence of their agreement.

Kripke's (skeptical) repudiation of agreement comes out well in his construal of the public nature of language. For Kripke, what is *normal* in a community *licenses* the correct performance of a given practice. Training, the initiation of newcomers into our practices, thus becomes a question of showing that the pupil's reactions conform to those of the teacher: by matching inclinations, the teacher "judges that the child is applying the procedure he himself is inclined to apply."[18] If the (normal) teacher reaches the limits of what appears justifiable (say if the pupil demands an answer to why, ultimately, the sum of 68 and 57 is 125), then she may confidently, though without "justification," follow her own inclination that her response is the *right* one. As Cavell recasts Kripke's "scene of instruction" by means of a familiar passage from the *Investigations*, "If I have exhausted the justifications I have reached bedrock, and my spade is turned. Then I am *licensed* to say: 'This is simply what I am inclined to do' " (CHU, 70; my emphasis). But, as Cavell quickly points out, in the entry being paraphrased (§217) Wittgenstein does not speak of licensing; what he says is rather that he is "inclined to say: 'This is simply what I do'," and what someone is *inclined* to say is not something she necessarily says. Whereas Kripke hears Wittgenstein identifying normality, and hence normativity, with blind obedience, Cavell senses a certain hesitation, as if the teacher, rather than refusing, like Kripke's authoritarian teacher, to take responsibility for her procedure, wants to present herself as an example, as the representative of the community and not the final arbiter of the nature of all its practices. The good teacher is able to draw the attention of the other – not by threatening to exclude, which only sustains privacy and isolation, but by accommodating herself to the singularity of her pupil. However, there is no fact about the teacher that justifies what she does and says except *herself*, the way her exemplary actions earn her the right to authority: "the fact that [she] can respond to an indefinite range of responses of the other, and that the other, for [her] spade not to be stopped, must respond to [her], in which case [her] justification may be furthered by keeping still" (CHU, 77). Since there is no pregiven normativity by appeal to which their separation can be overcome, the teacher can never relieve herself of the anxiety that their mutual incomprehension might continue. All she can do is be patient, allowing the other the difficult and perhaps even maddening task of finding, if possible, her own way out of her isolation. (Indeed, as Cavell points out, both childhood and madness haunt the *Investigations* from the very beginning: a fact that testifies to its dramatization of teaching and learning "in which my power comes to an end in the face of the other's separateness from me" (CR, 122), and hence also, figuratively, of the endless task of inheriting one's culture.) While at some point excluding the possibility of explanation (the child *comes* to agree), the instruction thus aims at real agreement between separate individuals; it is not satisfied simply with conformity, the impersonal match of inclinations. For agreement to be possible, the individual (qua individual) must involve herself in allowing the other to make sense of her, whereas Kripke leaves out the "I".

Fundamentally, Kripke's conventionalist vision of community accounts neither for our separateness nor for our agreement and accommodation (indeed the possibility of mutual accommodation is on principle ruled out). By assuming that skepticism can only be kept at bay by monitoring each other, by threatening to exclude deviants (the child, the foreigner), and by unquestionably demanding conformity, it does not so much present attunement between individuals as, rather, a crisis of consent:

> I feel sure my sense of Kripke's Wittgenstein's solution to the crisis as more skeptical than the problem it is designed to solve is tied up with my sense that this solution is a particular kind of political solution, one in which the issue of the newcomer for society is whether to accept his or her efforts to imitate us, the thing Emerson calls conformity. The scene thus represents the permanent crisis of a society that conceives of itself as based on consent. (CHU, 76)

Rather than overcoming privacy, Kripke's social conventionalism makes it unexceptional. In the wrong-headed attempt to offer a solution to skepticism, he empties out the individual's responsibility for meaning and replaces it with assertibility conditions. As a result, the agreement he invokes is one between strangers, conventionally united yet indifferent to each other – hence a false view of agreement, a view that denies, rather than affirms, our finitude as participants in a human form of life.

In another essay from the same period, "Declining Decline: Wittgenstein as a Philosopher of Culture" (1988, collected in NYUA), Cavell adds to his assessment of (Kripkean) conventionalism by distinguishing between two senses of Wittgenstein's notion of form of life: one ethnological or horizontal, the other biological or vertical. While the first sense is meant to register features that are culturally and historically variable, such as the difference between, say, "promising and fully intending," or between "coronations and inaugurations," the second recalls features that are universally distributed among humans, regardless of culture, such as the fact that the realization of intention requires action, or that most of us have two arms. Rather than compartmentalizing these two senses, as if they were mutually exclusive categories, Cavell urges us to think of the two dimensions as sliding into one another. By restricting his focus to the ethnological-horizontal aspect, Kripke tends to support a too fluid, conventionalized, and adoptable sense of agreement. He thus fails to record the *depth* of our agreement, the "conventionality of human nature itself" (CR, 111), as opposed, simply, to the conventionality (or tyranny) of human society by which the attempt to establish new conventions would be a matter of arbitrary decision.

Moreover, conventionalism begs the question of skepticism: from the fact of "successful" participation in social life, no conclusion seems to follow concerning the existence, say, of other minds. On the other hand, if the natural appears to us as nothing but a set of bare natural necessities, then the very idea of exploring them in order to find new ways to respond to them would lose its point. We would then be like the builders Wittgenstein imagines in the second paragraph of the *Investigations*: dumb, unimaginative, incapable of achieving an individual existence – in short, taking no interest in our position in the world and with others.

No recovery of interest and passion can ever refute skepticism (the sense that each of us is separate, barred as it were, from the world and others); yet upon realizing the precise way in which our existence is both social and natural, or both mental and physical – how the soul expressively interconnects with the body – the skeptic's vision of confinement may be lifted. This is the background against which Wittgensteinian criteria function: they regulate and keep together the inner and the outer, mind and world. Having in this chapter studied how the pursuit of ordinary language philosophy aims at speaking representatively, bespeaking the world and obtaining self-knowledge, we can no longer postpone a discussion of criteria.

2

Skepticism: Criteria and the External World

The Claim of Reason, Cavell's magnum opus, contains writing produced over a period of two decades – from 1957, while he was still working on his doctoral dissertation, to 1977, when, in addition to *Must We Mean What We Say?*, he had already published extensively on a series of topics, including Thoreau and the ontology of film. Whereas the first three parts, dealing respectively with epistemology, skepticism about the external world, and morality, are written in the dense yet relatively technical language of academic philosophy, the final part, discussing skepticism about other minds, leaps into a more aphoristic and elusive mode. Arguably the most experimental of all his work, the meandering and difficult fourth part is best read as "a limited philosophical journal," a series of fragments in which (as he says of Wittgenstein's *Investigations*) "the way . . . it is written is internal to what it teaches" (CR, 3).

Despite the immense wealth of material being covered, *The Claim of Reason*, like virtually all of Cavell's texts, amounts to a *reading* of someone else's work. Indeed, as he announces on the opening pages of the first chapter, philosophy, rather than a set of given problems to be solved, should be understood as a set of texts to be *read*. Thus the quality of a philosophical text is not primarily to be assessed in terms of its problem-solving capacity; rather, the essential criterion of rank is the quality of other texts it generates. For most philosophers, reading a (philosophical) work either means trying to master it, i.e. producing commentary, or it involves subjecting it to argumentative testing. While philosophers in the Continental tradition are prone to do the former, those in the Anglo-Saxon analytical tradition typically approach a philosophical text by attacking and defending its theses and arguments. Cavell rejects both of these options. None of them allows the text to challenge one's own self-understanding. Engaging with Wittgenstein's *Investigations*, the work which accompanies and sets the stage for most of the discussions in *The Claim of Reason*, Cavell's goal is, rather, to attain a position in which this book may *teach* him (and us) something. To read the *Investigations*, he maintains, means to let oneself be challenged by its voice, or rather by its multiplicity of voices, to the point of a possible conversion. The reader thus records the extent to which she recognizes *herself* – her temptations, her impulses, her insights – *in those voices*. Put differently, for Wittgenstein's words to be addressed *to me*, they also, as we saw in the first chapter, have to speak *for me*, be expressive of yearnings and temptations that I myself have felt. Indeed, as early as in the "The Availability of Wittgenstein's Later Philosophy," of 1962, Cavell distinguishes between two antagonistic voices of the *Investigations*: the "voice of temptation," which is skeptical and metaphysical, and the "voice of correction," which represents the ordinary. Together, the interplay of these voices constitutes a confession. "In confessing you do not explain or justify, but describe how it is with you. And confession, unlike dogma, is not to be believed but tested, and accepted or rejected" (MWM, 71). Being instructed in the matters of ordinary language philosophy is therefore emancipatory; it is to experience a release from some species of mental bondage: hence the partial irrelevance of doctrine. "There is exhortation . . . not to belief, but to self-scrutiny" (MWM, 71). Since some aspects essential to Wittgenstein's teaching cannot be formulated as a set of theoretical propositions, it follows that their communication (by Cavell) will also demand a degree of indirect communication. This point accounts, at least to some extent, for the peculiar style of much of Cavell's later work. It is also intrinsically linked to his response to the threat of skepticism, the main theme of *The Claim of Reason*.

Agreeing with much of the literature on Wittgenstein, Cavell argues that the *Investigations* is everywhere controlled by the attempt to come to terms with skepticism. However, as opposed to most commentators, he denies that Wittgenstein is trying to refute skepticism, or show that it is a pretence; rather, skepticism, if not fully correct on its own terms, contains something like a truth of its own: indeed, it is essential to the way we possess language. As we shall see, though, realizing the truth of skepticism means reinterpreting both what skepticism is and what it threatens.

Criteria and Skepticism

In the opening chapters of *The Claim of Reason*, Cavell seeks to
present this assessment of skepticism by means of an extended and
highly original discussion of what Wittgenstein calls criteria. In the
standard account, the grammatical eliciting of criteria is supposed
to rebut skepticism by establishing the existence of something with
certainty. For example, against the skeptic who doubts that we can
ever know with certainty that other people are in pain, the Wittgensteinian philosopher can point to criteria of pain (for example,
wincing) the presence of which necessarily entails that the other is
in pain. According to Cavell, however, criteria cannot do this, and
neither are they meant to. Rather than proving the skeptic false, a
correct understanding of criteria shows skepticism to be irrefutable.
Since criteria are only human, natural to us in virtue of the way we
agree in language but not metaphysically aligned with anything *in
the nature of things*, skepticism, the repudiation of criteria, is a standing possibility of humans. For Cavell, what this ought to teach us
is that our relation to the world and others in it should not be
viewed primarily (or only) as knowing, where knowing is construed as certainty; rather, the application of criteria is something
for which we ourselves must forever be responsible.

Before prematurely leaping to conclusions, however, the notion
of a criterion needs to be spelled out in a lot more detail. The first
thing Cavell notes is that Wittgenstein's employment of it largely
corresponds to the ordinary rhetorical structure of the word "criterion." According to this structure, criteria are "specifications a given
person or group sets up on the basis of which (by means of, in terms
of which) to judge (assess, settle) whether something has a particular status or value" (CR, 9). Criteria specify and thus define what
it means for a thing to have (or count as having) a given status. If
the specifications by means of which someone confers status are satisfied, then the thing possesses that status. An example of such ordinary or official uses of the word "criterion" would be the admission
policy of a major university. Such a policy is likely to include a
set of criteria – intelligence, sense of responsibility, independence,
etc. – that prospective students will have to satisfy in order to be
enrolled. Another example would be the specifications – serfdom,
vassalage, etc. – according to which a historian identifies a certain
social order as feudal. When Wittgenstein appeals, for instance, to
the application of criteria of reading or thinking, or of someone

being in pain, or of experiencing the meaning of words, it may seem as if he performs exactly the same procedure as in official uses of criteria. Yet even though his manner of eliciting criteria may at first blush seem identical to the official one, Cavell records a series of important disanalogies between the two.

The first disanalogy relates to the inclusion of standards in the process of assessing value or status. Both criteria and standards specify conditions under which something or someone is assigned some special status; but whereas criteria allow one to determine whether an object is of a specific kind, the application of standards tells the *degree* to which that object satisfies those criteria. In official applications of criteria, there is usually a separate stage at which one might assess the extent to which the candidate satisfies criteria. Examining a patient, a medical doctor not only needs to be aware of the criteria for a given disease (as he has learnt them at medical school), he must also be able to judge how seriously the patient is affected, that is, tell the degree to which the criteria are satisfied. Now Wittgensteinian criteria differ from official criteria in that standards play no role. For Wittgenstein, a person does not possess criteria, in an individual case, unless she knows whether or not they apply. There is no separate stage at which one might talk about the degree of satisfaction: an object either *is* (counts as) what the criteria in question specify it to be, or it is (counts as) something else. Thus, judges in a diving competition may disagree sharply over how well a diver enters the water (which is a question of standard), but "not over whether excellence of entry into the water is a criterion of the excellence of a dive" (CR, 12). In this case, doubt about the application of criteria would not merely imply incompetence; it would mean, as I will return to in a moment, that the person in question does not know what the excellence of a dive *is*: she would not count as a judge. This is not to say, though, that we always possess decisive criteria for something's being so.

In "non-standard-cases," someone may be in doubt about the application of criteria without being ruled out as unqualified to make judgments. Cavell offers the example of Schönberg's *Book of the Hanging Garden*. Can this be said to be a tonal work? Our inclination to answer the question by saying "Yes and No" shows that we lack decisive criteria: we simply cannot tell. Yet our uncertainty is precisely a mark of Schönberg's musical revolution, the way he challenged a central category of our musical understanding. Moreover, applying standards would not help: it is neither *less* tonal than, say, an early work of Beethoven, nor *more* tonal than, say, a work of John Cage. We simply do not quite know how to individuate and characterize it in its specificity.

The second disanalogy between the official and the Wittgensteinian idea of a criterion concerns the very point of setting up or establishing criteria, and ultimately the nature of the "objects" at stake. In the official conception, criteria are employed in order to assess or evaluate a candidate with respect to its specific status or ranking. Such a procedure requires that criteria are such that they enable the evaluations to be as rational, accurate, and efficient as possible; thus in the given context criteria must display consistency and coherence, and be as impersonal and non-arbitrary as possible. Moreover, in using official criteria we start out with a known kind of object, and the aim is to judge, by considering the actual evidence or properties at hand, whether it falls under a certain status concept. The objects under consideration in Wittgenstein's appeals to criteria differ crucially from those of official cases in that evaluation and hence consideration of evidence with regard to these objects make no sense. Wittgensteinian criteria are not applied to objects that we already know, and which only need to be classified in accordance with the epistemically most efficient and accurate specifications we happen to dispose of and for different purposes need to use; rather, to remind oneself of such criteria *is* to get to know "what kind of object anything is" (PI, §373). By spelling out criteria, we learn what our concepts mean or imply and hence also the nature of their objects. To know what pain *is* is thus to be able to tell what *counts* for us as pain in particular circumstances. It is to be able to *judge* intelligibly in various circumstances involving instances of pain, and criteria serve as reminders of how those judgments are made. Criteria thus tell us "what we go on" (CR, 29) in producing the kinds of statement we do about a phenomenon. The idea of a criterion gives "a sense of how things fall under our concepts, of how we individuate things and name, settle on nameables, of why we call things as we do, as questions of how we determine what *counts* as instances of our concepts, this thing as a table, that as a chair, this other as a human, that other as a god. To speak is to say what counts" (DK, 204–5).

This has two important consequences for Cavell's project. He can now place his reconstruction of Wittgenstein's notion of criteria squarely within a Kantian tradition "according to which the subject of a judgment is not known prior to the knowledge of the predicates which are taken to hold of it" (CR, 17); thus the limits of human knowledge, rather than coinciding, as realists argue, with the sum of possible true statements of the world, become coextensive with the limits of our concepts in a given historical period. Moreover, he can reiterate Austin's point, previously discussed, that explorations of ordinary language, of "what we say when and the implications thereof," relate us, though open-endedly, to the essences of things, that is, to what (for us) must be the case for something to be of a certain kind. In this account, the point of eliciting criteria, as opposed to evaluating known objects according to their status, is to reorient ourselves "when we are lost with respect to our words and to the world they anticipate" (CR, 34). Such an investigation may be said to involve three different steps:

(1) We find ourselves wanting to know something about a phenomenon, e. g., pain, expecting, knowledge, understanding, being of an opinion. . . . (2) We remind ourselves of the kinds of statements we make about it. (3) We ask ourselves what criteria we have for (what we go on in) saying what we say. (CR, 29)

In a banal yet illustrative example of such a procedure, Cavell considers the concept of hinting. During a difficult game of chess, the teacher gives the student a hint by means of "a gesture of the eyes in a particular circumstance of obscurity" (PP, 153). Afterwards, having made the move the teacher wanted him to make, the student, "almost under his breath," utters the word "Thanks." By reminding ourselves of the statements being made in this particular case of hinting, the example reveals a criterion both of giving and taking a hint: It is thus "part of the grammar . . . of following a gesture that *this* is something we call 'taking a hint'; which is to say that following the gesture is a criterion of taking or understanding the hint" (PP, 153–4). Studying our reactions in a case like this elucidates the nature of hinting.

A third disanalogy between official and Wittgensteinian criteria relates to their source of authority. In official cases, the authority-relation gets established by whoever sets up criteria and grants validity to them. Hence, in the example taken from the university admission process, the source of authority is likely to be the ruling body of the university or of the specific school in question. However, whereas the source of authority for official criteria varies from case to case, Wittgensteinian criteria can be established by reference to *one* source only: the speakers of a language, the human group as such. The appeal to criteria reveals the extent to which we agree *in* judgments – the fine-grained way, as we have seen, in which we are *attuned*. Rather than being dependent on the recalling of a structure of specifications controlling the use of concepts, the appeal to criteria is bound up with recollecting very general facts of nature and culture – of what we take, say, as an expression of anger as opposed to fear, or how we distinguish between a rebuke and an appeal – in short "the whirl of organism Wittgenstein calls 'form of life'" (MWM, 52). For counting implies mattering: an object is what it is (its concept has *this* meaning) in virtue of the way we attribute a certain value to it. Recounting criteria tells us how we respond to the world, its specific ways of mattering to us. And by making explicit how we respond, it expresses our commitments and responsibilities as normal speakers, the kinds of thing, to return to Austin's expression, we are prepared to say when, and the implications thereof. If you declare that *that* is a house or a person in pain, then it follows that you must be prepared to say certain things about it, accept certain questions, act in specific ways, view the phenomenon within a specific temporal context and ordering, and the like. Criteria elaborate the ways in which human beings are able to say what counts, that is, make specific points here and now and thereby be comprehensible to concrete others.

Since my language with all its grammatical nodes and everyday logic was there before me (no single speaker ever invented his own natural language), I cannot help voicing my words as a representative speaker, as one among many to whom I belong in a community of speakers. Thus, in eliciting my criteria not only do I speak for myself; I also speak for others: speaking for oneself is inevitably to speak for others. Conversely, in these matters I must accept that others, in speaking for themselves, speak for me. We act as each others' representatives. However, since nothing, no impersonal structure, can assure us beforehand that our respective voices will be accepted by others as representative (they may or may not), they should be viewed as *claims* to community – claims whereby the degree, quality, and content of our mutual acceptance get explored. Criteria are therefore deeply vulnerable: since sharing an order of criteria depends on our agreement on an order of judgments (our attunement), they allow or even invite repudiation. Indeed, the standing possibility of repudiating criteria, of rejecting our mutuality, is an inevitable function of language itself. As Cavell puts it, "skepticism underlies and joins the concept of a criterion and that of the everyday, since skepticism exactly repudiates the ordinary as constituted by . . . our criteria" (TCR, 335).

In *Stanley Cavell: Philosophy's Recounting of the Ordinary*, Stephen Mulhall offers an interpretation of the nature of Cavell's notion of Wittgensteinian criteria that differs from this in essential respects.[1] Since this interpretation in many ways is highly natural, it seems worthwhile to explain why and how the present reconstruction takes issue with it. According to Mulhall, criteria should be viewed as marks or features that provide "standards governing the application of concepts."[2] The observed presence of these marks or features licenses the proper application of our concepts to phenomena. While functioning as "a set of rules governing [the] use"[3] of a term, criteria thus permit us to subsume objects under concepts. Moreover, each concept, in order to be legitimately applicable, necessarily has a place in a grammatical structure of relations to other concepts. By specifying those relations, criteria determine the range of implications and commitments that each legitimate application of a concept entails. The totality of our criteria thus constitutes a "grammatical framework of language"[4] upon which the condition of linguistic intelligibility rests; and this framework is itself based on the agreement in individual reactions and responses to the world that Cavell, following Wittgenstein, refers to as a form of life. As a critic of Mulhall, Steven Affeldt, puts it, in this account the grammatical framework becomes "a middle term between our contingent agreement in reactions and responses and the highly structured character of our agreement in specific judgments and their implications".[5] While rejecting a view of rules as being impersonal algorithms, the idea of language as a framework of rules implies for Mulhall that our mutual intelligibility in language is supported and made possible by a given structure that constitutes its normativity.

As Affeldt was the first to note, the most fundamental problem with Mulhall's interpretation is that Cavell, as we have seen, dismisses the very idea of "a grammatical framework of language." Indeed, since Cavell's first published essay on Wittgenstein, his position has been that "everyday language does not, in fact or in essence, depend upon . . . a structure and conception of rules" (MWM, 48): no rules could ever account both for the flexibility and precision with which we employ our concepts. Nothing underlies or "governs" our applications of concepts in judgments – no marks or features must be present or observed for my use of a concept to be justified. For Mulhall, criteria must structurally be in place for us to be able to make judgments. Without such a framework, we would lack the grounds of mutual intelligibility in language.

But for Cavell, criteria are simply functions of the judgments we (normal speakers) are prepared to make; there is no level existing independently of our actual or potential judgments by reference to which criteria regulate or justify the intelligibility of those judgments: "no concept is 'bound' by ordinary criteria" (CHU, 90). The point of eliciting criteria is therefore not a matter of uncovering the necessary presuppositions of ordinary speech; rather, it is to respond to a crisis in our agreement: for it is "when we are lost with respect to our words and to the world they anticipate [that we declare] the criteria upon which we are in agreement" (CR, 34). And in doing so, we are able to elaborate on the logic of our judgments, the way we ordinarily agree in judgments and in forms of life. While this may seem like a denial of normativity, in reality it is not. To be a normal speaker means to share a set of commitments and conceptual practices with other speakers; yet normativity, as Cavell sees it, does not rest on an appeal to rules or conventions. What is normative is simply our mastery of language, the infinitely fine-grained capacity to make ourselves intelligible by projecting words into new contexts and remain ready to declare and respect the implications of doing so. Thus, criteria are not somehow constituted by our non-normative agreement in reactions and responses: they do not form a middle-term; rather, by agreeing in judgments we agree in the criteria revealed in those judgments: "The 'agreement' we act upon [Wittgenstein] calls 'agreement in judgments' (§242), and he speaks of our ability to use language as depending upon agreement in 'forms of life' (§241)" (CR, 30). And whereas official criteria serve as bases (marks, features) on the basis of which certain judgments can be made, in Wittgenstein "our ability to establish criteria [depends] upon a prior agreement in judgments" (ibid) – an agreement Cavell speaks of as being "mutually attuned" or "mutually voiced."

When symbolic trust for various reasons is lost, the skeptic typically denies the voice of the everyday or the ordinary – and therefore also our shared criteria. Rather than recalling "what we say and the implications thereof" (our criteria), the skeptic seeks to obtain a certainty in his application of concepts that is based on something seemingly more robust – a structure, a presence, an impersonal metaphysics – that can relieve him of responsibility for his own words, of making himself intelligible in a given context. By placing so much emphasis, in his interpretation of Cavell, on the idea of language as a framework of rules, Mulhall runs the same risk as

Kripke: he sublimes language. While it may seem as if such a move shows language to be public, subliming drives out judgment and hence also attunement; and just as it excludes the speaker's intervention in speech, it also suspends the knower's engagement in knowledge – the acknowledgment which in Cavell's account completes knowledge. In order to further our understanding of the process of skeptical repudiation, we must now turn to Cavell's discussion of epistemology.

The Epistemological Status of Criteria

Criteria are appealed to in the face of skeptical doubt. But what is their epistemological status? The skeptic typically denies that we know something (the existence of the external world, other minds) with certainty. For the recounting of criteria to impress the skeptic, it therefore seems obvious that they must provide the certainty which the skeptic has called into question; otherwise the procedure would seem to be pointless. Thus, according to a prominent interpretation developed by Norman Malcolm and Roger Albritton, the purpose of eliciting criteria is to establish the existence of an object X with certainty.[6] As opposed to symptoms, which contingently mark something off as something (experience has hitherto taught us that the object coincides with the symptom), on their view the presence of criteria of X provide empirical certainty of the occurrence of X. The necessary and sufficient conditions for something's being the case are then satisfied; and hence the existence of the object is beyond dispute.

Applied to the example of pain, the Malcolm–Albritton view entails that, under certain circumstances, a person who satisfies criteria of pain – who winces, groans, wrings his hands, in short exhibits violent pain-behavior – necessarily is in pain: the presence of pain-behavior, itself serving as a criterion of pain, rules out that he is not hurting. However, as Cavell points out, this cannot be true. It is perfectly possible that criteria are present and the man is *not* in pain. For (as Malcolm himself concedes) it cannot be excluded in advance that he may be pretending, rehearsing a part in a play, displaying his hysteria, etc. Drawing on a distinction between the (seeming) *presence* of a criterion and its *satisfaction*, Malcolm argues, however, that the inconsistency involved in both affirming and denying criteria's capacity to yield certainty can be avoided. In cases where it turns out that X is not the case after all, despite the presence (to us) of criteria of X, it simply has to be concluded that the criteria were only *seemingly* satisfied. Yet had they *really* been satisfied, then the non-existence of X could be excluded without further ado. For Malcolm, this enforces the view that criteria only function in certain circumstances. Among the kinds of circumstance we would have to exclude in applying the criteria of pain are those in which someone feigns, rehearses for a play, is engaged in a hoax, etc.

Cavell agrees with Malcolm that there are circumstances in which criteria do *not* find any possible application. Groaning, for example, would not be an *expression* of pain, and therefore not a criterion of it, in circumstances in which someone does it (or seems to be doing it), say, to call her hamsters or sing a song. (In one of his more surreal examples, Cavell imagines a patient in the dentist chair, perspiring, screaming, who, when offered "another syringe of Novacain," tells the dentist, "'It wasn't hurting, I was just calling my hamsters.' . . . And when the door is opened two hamsters trot into the room and climb onto the patient's lap" (CR, 89).) But rather than exemplifying a quasi-logical relation of necessity between painbehavior and the concept of pain, what such examples show is that conceptual projectibility is limited by what we find intelligible. A man who calls his hamsters by groaning would not be exhibiting pain-behavior; indeed, we would not know what to say of him – he would have to be ruled out of "our world of pain" (ibid). Viewing his action as pain-behavior would be unintelligible, a sure sign of non-participation in our lifeform and order of shared judgments. One might here object: but what if someone consistently expressed real pain in ways that for us seem bizarre – say, by laughing or playing the piano? Does the possibility of that call into question the way we speak – the grammar of "pain" that *that* is what *we* call pain?

Cavell does not exclude the possibility that someone might consistently respond in these ways. No fact of nature or logic determines once and for all that *these* are our criteria. Given our difficulty in appreciating this agent's world, the relevant question is rather whether we can still respond to him as a person. Pushed to the limits of practice, no theory of normality can settle this issue on a priori grounds. Apart from our willingness to engage practically with him, no guarantee of intelligibility exists. But this is generally true of our lives: failure to know one another is our responsibility; if viewed as a metaphysical lack, it simply screens our unwillingness to be responsive to the other, to make ourselves known.

While maintaining that circumstances do play a role in the application of criteria (in knowing what *counts* as something, how to value), Cavell differs sharply from Malcolm about what the phrase "in certain circumstances" can do for us. For Malcolm, it implies that criteria can provide certainty about existence – if the surroundings are right. For Cavell, however, it only demonstrates how we make ourselves understood as speakers. In so far as knowing what counts as pain-behavior is a matter of "coming to talk" and thus knowing how to respond adequately in a potentially infinite number of contexts, it follows that when someone calls an instance of groaning "pain-behavior," then that person, in order to speak intelligibly, *must* have taken into account the circumstances in which that groaning *is* pain-behavior. There is in such a situation no room for asking whether the *right* circumstances have occurred and therefore whether the criteria *really* are satisfied: knowing what the criteria of pain are *is* to know what counts as pain. If the criteria are present, then so is pain-behavior, the expression of pain. Hence Malcolm's idea of a seeming presence of a criterion is empty: it has no application.

A related problem with Malcolm's view is that it presupposes that in so far as the criteria are satisfied (the circumstances are right), then the non-existence of pain can be excluded. And yet, as Cavell points out, in cases of acting or feigning, it is precisely pain-behavior, and hence the satisfaction of criteria of pain, that is being simulated. Without the possibility of simulating the satisfaction of criteria, acting or feigning would not exist. This shows that the distinction between the seeming presence of a criterion and its satisfaction begs the question: while rightly drawing attention to context, it fails to provide certainty about *when*, or under which conditions, criteria *in fact* are satisfied. In Malcolm's account, they may or may not be, and we shall never know with certainty; hence the claim that criteria provide certainty about existence must be false. Indeed, criteria are operative in both true and false judgments, and so we are never in a position to know with the absolute and unconditional certainty Malcolm takes criteria to provide that someone *really* is in pain. Criteria give us certainty about identity, not existence:

> Criteria are "criteria for something's being so", not in the sense that
> they tell us of a thing's existence, but of something like its identity,

not of its *being* so, but of its being *so*. Criteria do not determine the certainty of statements, but the application of the concepts employed in statements. (CR, 45)

The insight that criteria are not, as it were, expressions of the order of things, but of the order of human conventions, of what we say and do as mutually intelligible beings, is of tremendous significance for Cavell's thinking about skepticism. First, it implies that skepticism becomes something radically different from the standard (justified or unjustified) attitude or position it ordinarily is made out to be. In Cavell's account of it, skepticism, the repudiation of criteria and thus the rejection of our attunement, is an inevitable function of language itself, a natural consequence of the fact that criteria "are only human, nothing more than natural to us" (CR, 47). The threat of skepticism is therefore neither curable (Kant) nor incurable (Hume); rather, for language to be learned, shared, and possessed, and hence to be employed responsibly by individual speakers, it must be possible to dispossess oneself of the burdens and commitments that intelligible speech exacts. Like the capacities to think and to talk, nothing is more natural. Second, the skeptic who claims that we cannot know with certainty whether the world (and ourselves and others in it) exists cannot be refuted by means of appealing to criteria. Rather than yielding certainty about existence, criteria tell how things count for us – what we take to be this and not that and how this is done. If formulated as a lack or deficiency in our capacity to represent things, this observation might be summarized as what Cavell calls the truth of skepticism: that humans are separate from the world and others in it, and that the criteria by which we align language and world, far from reflecting reality in any absolute sense, simply express our attunement, our human ways of applying concepts in judgments. Hence, "Our relation to the world as a whole, or to others in general, is not one of knowing, where knowing construes itself as being certain" (CR, 45).

At this juncture, Cavell deems it incumbent to start asking why the philosophical skeptic typically insists on interpreting the truth of skepticism (its irrefutability) as a *thesis* about knowledge, that is, a discovery which uncovers an extraordinary and terrible fact about the human predicament, and which ought to be deeply disappointing. If it is correct that knowledge construed as certainty does not adequately capture the way in which we fundamentally relate to the world, then it would seem that the question of knowledge makes no sense at this level. So why envisage our position in the world – our human finitude – as a *failure*? What motivates the skeptic's disowning of our ordinary claims to knowledge?

Cavell and Austin

With the exception of Cavell, philosophers committed to the procedures of ordinary language philosophy have on the whole shown very little sympathy with the skeptic. Predominantly, their approach has consisted in trying to demonstrate that the skeptic is not capable of assigning any real meaning either to his objections about our ordinary knowledge or to the conclusion that we do not know external facts. Thus in his important article "Other Minds" of 1946, John Austin attempts to show that the skeptic, in asking whether a thing *is* so (exists) over and above its being *so* (identity) simply uses words incompetently: the skeptic speaks nonsense and can be shown to be making no claim whatsoever.[7] According to Austin, the types of response that may rationally be given by a claimant to the question "How do you know?" are all directed toward determining what we so far have been calling the identity of things. Essentially, his procedure aims to reveal that the skeptic's intuitions about the meaning (or use) of the words "I know" on which the denial of knowledge depends are wrong. More specifically, on Austin's layout, an ordinary claim to knowledge – for example "There's a bittern at the bottom of the garden" – must be supported by satisfying a set of ordinary conditions for making such a claim:

I must have

(1) been trained in an environment where I could become familiar with bitterns;
(2) had a certain opportunity in the current case;
(3) learned to recognize or tell bitterns;
(4) succeeded in recognizing or telling this as a bittern. (PhP, 79–80)

If these conditions are met, and no relevant question can be raised (hence when the case is not *special*), then the claimant is perfectly entitled to say "I know it's a bittern." She has then shown that she has had opportunities of a certain kind ((1) and (2)), and that she has exerted an amount of specific effort ((3) and (4)). This is enough, Austin insists, and enough is enough: "Enough means enough to show that (within reason, and for present intents and purposes) it 'can't' be anything else, there is no room for an alternative, competing, description of it" (PhP, 84). As Cavell remarks, the conditions Austin specifies in (2) and (4) – those that have to be met in order for the claimant to be justified in telling here and now – are quite similar to official criteria: in both cases, marks, features, or competences are employed in order to know whether the application of a name is warranted. Hence the bird's behavior, its markings, what it eats, and so on are features of the situation that, if observed and adequately linked with the phenomenon, may enable the application of the term "bittern" in the sentence "There's a bittern at the bottom of the garden" to be meaningfully made.

According to Cavell, however, Austin's account suffers from a *naiveté* or dogmatism that distinguishes it from his own progressive delineation of the epistemic status of criteria. The problem is this. We may know that it is correct to call what we see in the garden a bittern, but from this it does not follow that the bittern exists, that it is real. It could, for example, be a stuffed bird, put there by our neighbor to fool us. Austin concedes this point: "[Enough] does not mean . . . enough to show it isn't *stuffed*" (PhP, 84). Ordinarily, however, when there is no reason to think that one might have been deceived, the question of reality does not actually arise. What counts is only whether or not a claimant has correctly identified the object in question. And if it should nevertheless turn out that the bird is stuffed, then that means it has been misrecognized. I thought I perceived a living bittern, whereas what I really had before me was a stuffed imitation of a living bittern. I then, Austin suggests, need to take a second look at *how* I thought I knew, for the ways of making sure it is a *real* bittern are "essentially similar" (PhP, 88) to those I use to make sure it was a bittern – that is, I apply the relevant and correct Austinian criteria in unobjectionable circumstances. And yet in Austin's own account this is impossible: there are no Austinian criteria for something's being real (as opposed to being stuffed, painted, hallucinatory, etc.). More precisely, the criteria are the same regardless of whether the object exists or not, hence existence has no mark or feature of its own.

As a result of his exclusive concentration on scenarios where only the identity of the object is at stake, Austin's set-up, despite its praiseworthy opposition to the idea that claims to knowledge can only be legitimately made if I am prepared to consider each and every possibility that might defeat my claim to be certain, studiously fails to register the worry and spirit that drives traditional epistemology. For the traditional epistemologist, the problem of knowledge has never been to provide correct descriptions and names. Rather, what Descartes, the initiator of the modern tradition of radical questioning of knowledge, dramatizes in his famous dream-argument is whether a person can ever be certain that what she perceives is real, or actually present, and not just a mental construct, a content of her dream. In Cavell's account, the difference between the concerns of traditional epistemology and Austin's reconstruction may be interpreted as a difference between two kinds of object (of knowledge-claims), or, more precisely, between two kinds of "spirit in which an object is under discussion" (CR, 53). Austin's focus is on objects in relation to which *my* position and background is an issue, and where the epistemic goal consists in providing a correct identification. In contesting my claim that I know there is a bittern in the garden, you may refer, say, to my bad eyesight or my previous lack of knowledge of birds. And for me to back my claim is to demonstrate that indeed I have a right to make it with regard to *this* object. Cavell's technical term for such agent-relative epistemic objects is *specific object*. A crucial characteristic of the traditional epistemologist, however, is that for him, specific objects hold no real interest. Rather, his obsession is with objects that no one is in a better position to identify than anyone else. Typically, such objects – generic objects, as Cavell calls them – have included tomatoes, bits of wax, tables, chairs, and so on, all of them in full view and perfect viewing conditions, and the problem has not been to identify them, i.e., apply the correct name to the object and thus tell what they are, but to determine whether we can know they exist and are real:

> When those objects present themselves to the epistemologist, he is not taking one as opposed to another, interested in its features as peculiar to it and nothing else. He would rather, so to speak, have an unrecognizable *something* there if he could, an anything, a thatness. What comes to him is an island, a body surrounded by air, a tiny earth. What is at stake for him in the object is materiality as such, externality altogether. (CR, 53)

Since Austinian (non-grammatical) criteria assign the conditions under which someone may rightly claim to know the specific identity of an object, they can only be applied to specific objects (for example bitterns and goldfinches in the garden), but not to objects for which the question of existence is (or can be) at stake. The problem of existence is, as it were, irrelevant to Austin's claimant, who only cares about the correctness of her descriptions, that is, their ability to identify objects correctly. But other differences between Austinian and Wittgensteinian criteria emerge as equally consequential. First, as opposed to Austin's focus on specific objects, whereby the mastery of criteria requires special training and a specialized environment, and whereby the lack of criteria prevents one from justifiably possessing a specific piece of information (the name, the correct description), Wittgensteinian (grammatical) criteria are shared by every competent speaker; and rather than enabling, on the basis of evidence, the application of the correct predicate to a given object, they are, as we have seen, constitutive of what an object is as such. Thus, in the absence of Wittgensteinian criteria, the Austinian project of identification could not even get started, and there would then be no objects for us to identify. (In order to distinguish a bittern from a goldfinch we need to know, say, what an animal *is*, i.e., be able to tell when and where to treat an entity as a living being, which includes knowing that it is sentient, that it responds in various ways to the surroundings, and so on.) Second, and even more significantly, Austin's account of criteria, which aims to bypass the traditional philosopher's worries about generic objects by refusing to register them as intelligible, fails to thematize our own response to, and responsibility for, criteria as they emerge. Like Austinian criteria, Wittgensteinian criteria yield certainty only about identity: we can be assured that the presence of criteria of pain rules out the nonexistence of *pain-behavior*. But as opposed to Austinian criteria, Wittgensteinian criteria are applied in contexts where the question of existence is at stake; and even though Wittgensteinian criteria do not provide certainty about the actual occurrence of, say, *pain* (the man *might* be feigning or might even be a robot), they are nevertheless used to tell that the other *is* in pain, i.e. that his pain is real. How can that be? What is it that takes up the slack, as the skeptic would see it, between the presence of criteria and the reality of pain, between pain-behavior and the inner life of the other? For Austin, who completely dismisses the skeptic, the notion of such a slack could simply not arise: if the criteria for knowing happen to be satisfied, if we know what something is in the sense of being able to identify it correctly, then there is nothing more to be said, no skeptical voice to be reckoned with: enough is enough.

At this juncture, Cavell introduces the crucial idea that for anything to count for me as a criterion of something X, then *I* must antecedently be prepared to regard or accept it as such and thus use it – not just in general but *here and now*, in this specific context. In the case of pain (to which I will return in chapter 3), the functioning of criteria presupposes my continued willingness to take criteria of pain as expressive of the inner life of the other, and hence my acknowledgment of the other's body as the home of my psychological concepts. "Only *I* could reach that privacy, by accepting it as a home of my concepts of the human soul. When I withdraw that acceptance, the criteria are dead" (CR, 84). This is not just a matter of knowledge as straightforward correspondence between representation and reality on justified grounds; for me to know another's pain, I have to live with and relate to that person as a sentient human being and be aware that she calls upon my response – for comforting and healing. And yet the idea of acknowledging should not be understood as an alternative to knowing, as if unfolding on a non-cognitive basis, requiring a categorially different grammatical account. In Cavell's account, acknowledgment should, rather, be envisaged "as an interpretation of [knowing], as I take the word 'acknowledge,' containing 'knowledge,' itself to suggest" (QO, 8). For knowledge to be possible, it has to be restricted – by my response and responsibility.

Austin's anti-skeptical account fails to allow for the moment of response to the criteria as they emerge. It thus comes to agree with the skeptic's contention that the problem of existence is a problem of searching the other out with certainty, as if the question of existence could be settled on purely intellectual grounds. Both the anti-skeptic and the skeptic rationalize the disappointment we may feel about others, the fact that our knowledge of others is restricted; but whereas the anti-skeptic falsely thinks that mutuality can be continued without my willingness to make myself intelligible to the other, and hence without *my* continued willingness to allow the other to *count* as a sentient being, the skeptic has transformed a separation the extent of which he himself is responsible for into a metaphysical barrier, an abyss. In both cases, the other is effectively put beyond reach and deadened; and rather than accepting the burden and challenge that follow from the requirement of letting oneself be known and allowing others to count, both the skeptic and the anti-skeptic close themselves off and withdraw from their attunement with others.

We should now, at least in general terms, be able to see why the skeptic tends to interpret the apparent irrefutability of his own conclusions about knowledge (human finitude) as expressive of an intellectual riddle. While incapable of accepting his separation from others and the world (the fact that no universals exist which insure the mind's collusion with the world), the skeptic converts the human condition of having to make himself intelligible, of establishing what counts for him in various ways and thus inviting requests for further elaboration of the responsibilities he takes as a speaker, into a problem of *proof* (or its absence):

> In Wittgenstein's view the gap between mind and world is closed, or the distortion between them straightened, in the appreciation and acceptance of particular human forms of life, human "convention". This implies that the *sense* of gap originates in an attempt, or wish, to escape (to remain a "stranger" to, "alienated" from) those shared forms of life, to give up the responsibility of their maintenance. (CR, 109)

Once and for all, the challenge and burden of finitude – to make sense, be intelligible – is supposed to be overcome. Yet by desiring community without the commitments it exacts from each of its members, the skeptic ends up declaring himself unknown. Thus, the idea that skepticism can be contested by providing refutations is fundamentally misguided: it fails to see how skepticism arises naturally from the human condition – that "Nothing is more human than the wish to deny one's humanity, or to assert it at the expense of others" (CR, 109).

The Skeptical Recital

In the second part of *The Claim of Reason*, Cavell offers a detailed assessment of global forms of skepticism about the external world, that is, doubt that ranges over all our knowledge-claims. As he notes, the most famous and consequential expression of such skepticism is that of the opening meditation of Descartes' *Meditations on First Philosophy*.[8] Descartes' steps toward global doubt start with the observation that we often accept false opinions as true, and hence that subjective conviction is a highly unreliable judge in matters of truth. In order to test whether or not we shall ever be in a position to have certain and indubitable knowledge (as this is what our mistakes call into question), he then goes on to investigate a scenario wherein a generic object is presented to the senses in such a way that we would ordinarily think that we are entitled to be certain about its existence. If reasonable doubt can be cast on a "best" case of knowledge of this sort, then it follows that the validity of knowledge as a whole is justifiably without basis.

The final step toward global doubt consists in providing a skeptical hypothesis which, if its falsehood cannot be ruled out, throws reasonable doubt on the knowledge we claim to possess in the best-case scenario. Famously, Descartes considers the possibility that he is dreaming, and since everything he takes himself to experience, including the seemingly evident existence of himself as seated before the fire, is compatible with the hypothesis that it might all be a dream (there are no criteria that allow us to distinguish a dreamt object from a real one), he concludes that no knowledge-claim can ever be justified.

As became clear from Cavell's engagement with Austin, for such an argument to start making sense it is required that the initial claim to knowledge is made about the existence of a generic object. The failure to identify a specific object – say, Austin's bird in the garden – carries an implication about your competence (your eyesight, say, or your knowledge of birds), or about the nature of the epistemic circumstances (the darkness, say, or the distance of the object from you), yet it throws no light whatsoever on knowledge as a whole, the very project of knowledge. Thus, on a formal level a skeptical argument necessarily comprises three components: (a) *the entry of a claim to knowledge about a generic object* (a tomato or a table, but not a goldfinch or a Louis XV escritoire); (b) *a request for basis* (how do you know? – because I see it, or: by means of the senses); (c) *a ground for doubt* (you might be dreaming, or: it might be a decoy, etc.), from which it follows not only that you have no legitimate reason to think that you know the existence of *this* bird or *that* table, but that you have no compelling reason to think that you can ever know anything whatsoever. As Cavell points out, the argument logically rests on a simple principle of closure ($p \rightarrow q$; $\sim q$; $\sim p$): "If I know anything I know *this*. Then it turns out that, as a matter of eternal fact, we do *not* know *this*. As a minor premise, that discovery precipitates the right devastation. To draw the conclusion then requires no proneness to argument, merely the capability of it" (CR, 145).

Epistemologists anxious to demonstrate the failure of such a line of reasoning have predominantly been examining the ground for doubt, and in some cases the request for basis. For Cavell, however, the problem starts with the very notion of knowledge-claims involving generic objects: if such a claim can be entered, then the skeptic's doubts can come to seem both relevant and fatal to our position as knowers, and no Austinian appeal to what we ordinarily say and mean will ever be able to rationally thwart the slide into radical skepticism. Hence, Cavell's strategy is to confront the skeptic with a dilemma: while only generic objects allow skepticism to generalize to all knowledge-claims (and hence to the existence of the world), no real meaning can be attached to claims referring to such objects. Ultimately, claims to knowledge about generic objects, though containing words that are perfectly meaningful, cannot be entered; they remain empty: thus the assertion under attack in skeptical reflection persists in being incoherent or imaginary.

The strategy of trying to frustrate the initial step toward global skepticism might make it seem as though Cavell, like many philosophers of ordinary language, considers the originating question – "How can we know anything about the world?" – as unreal, that is, as failing to express a response to a natural experience. But while denying that problems raised in ordinary practical contexts invite or provoke such reflection, and hence that it is fully natural, he resists the temptation to think of it as wholly unnatural. The intuition that something fundamental is amiss with human knowledge, and therefore that grounds for universal doubt might be made plausible, can at times appear legitimate. But how plausible is the epistemologist's claim that good reasons for raising the question of existence can be offered, when the object – the tomato, chair, or whatever – is there for all the world to see? According to Cavell, humans can indeed undergo experiences that are able to shatter their basic cognitive trust and leave them with a feeling that the real world is unknowable. One may, for example, be mistaken about very intimate knowledge, say, the name of a former lover or a famous person one has admired in the past. But frightening as such intimations of losing one's grip on the world may be, they do not call into question *all* knowledge. No metaphysical implications follow. Their moral is rather that human beings are fallible, that no single belief should always be taken for granted or treated too rigidly, but not that all our beliefs ought to be suspended. Yet Cavell also reports of a more radical sense of being shut off from the world, "one of realizing that my sensations may not be *of* the world I take them to be of at all, or that I can know only how objects appear (to us) to be, never what objects are like in themselves" (CR, 143). It is not as if we all have had such experiences, or that having them inevitably calls for universal doubt; rather, his more subtle claim is that, though not fully natural, the epistemologist's employment of words is not entirely absurd, hence his request for a basis cannot be ignored.

At this point, the anti-skeptical philosopher may object to the denial of unnaturalness by exercising what Cavell here calls "projective imagination," the self-reflective articulation of "what we say when and the implications thereof" in imagined contexts. However, considered as a direct criticism of the epistemologist's context, such an approach carries little or no force. For the skeptic addresses an *actual* situation (though perhaps in imagination), one in which knowledge as such is at stake, whereas the philosopher of ordinary language invites us to *imagine* one. Thus, when the ordinary language philosopher complains about the implausibility or artificiality of the skeptical scenario, she only succeeds in drawing attention to features of situations *as they are imagined by her* (e.g., "ordinarily we do not consider it possible that an object in full view might be a cleverly painted piece of wax"), yet the epistemologist must take into account possibilities beyond those of projective imagination (e.g., "the object could be phoney," "I could be hallucinating"). Hence, projective imagination (such as "you have described the situation incompletely: there is no reason to believe that the table is not real or that you hallucinate" or "you misuse the word 'real'") is irrelevant: it fails to engage with the epistemologist's concerns.

Throughout his analysis Cavell is very cautious not to commit himself to the methodological dogmatism implicit in the attempt to employ observations about how words are ordinarily used as a form of direct criticism of the skeptic's argument. Although the skeptical conclusion dramatically conflicts with what we ordinarily take to be the case, once we have accepted the epistemologist's slightly awkward use of epistemic terms it becomes unanswerable. And although the conclusion carries little or no conviction in our everyday lives, it cannot be dismissed by appealing to what we ordinarily say. Indeed, the epistemologist is right in maintaining that *in his account* there is nothing more to say about the skeptical situation; neither has it been described incompletely, nor is it entirely special or exceptional. On the contrary, it is both fully revealed and describable in ordinary terms; as a result, the ordinary language philosopher's request for a more adequate description seems misplaced. The two language-games – of epistemology and ordinary language philosophy – are, if you like, incompatible:

> When the ordinary language philosopher accuses the traditional philosopher of misusing language or changing the meaning of words or speaking with near criminal unconcern for the ordinary meaning of words; and when the apologist for the tradition replies that nothing is amiss with the language in which traditional ideas are expressed, that no problem of sense and communication is created

by the slight variation from ordinary use, that anyone can simply see
that the words that the traditional philosopher employs are lucid as
they stand; one side is as right and wrong as the other; they are
talking past one another. (CR, 146)

Ultimately, the observation of unnaturalness is itself insufficient to
dismiss the epistemologist. Given the absence of rules or universals
which constrain and insure appropriate projection, naturalness
becomes a function of what masters of language find natural. Thus
the simple assurance that words are not used correctly cannot
bring a genuine resolution of the tension between the unliveability
and the unanswerability of skepticism. Something else, a different
approach, seems called for.

Cavell's suggestion is that rather than taking the lack of full
naturalness to represent a valid criticism of the epistemologist, we
should ask whether the epistemologist's words really mean what
he thinks, wishes, or believes he means. Do they have the point
he takes them to have, or is there a sense in which the way he
has chosen his context prevents him from controlling them? The
first example Cavell draws attention to is the skeptical claim that
because we never see the back half of objects, or their inside, we do
not see the whole object but only that part of it which faces us or
appears to us; hence, generally speaking, we never see objects,
because seeing an object as it is excludes perceiving only a part of
it. Clearly, this conclusion flies in the face of our ordinary use of the
verb "seeing." The projection strikes us as entirely inappropriate.
We seem to feel that there *must* be something utterly wrong with
the skeptic's argument, yet it is not immediately obvious that it is
false to deny that we see *all* of an object. So what exactly is problematic about the skeptic's projection?

As Cavell points out, while the epistemologist objects to the use
of sight as the basis of knowledge or maintains that no object is ever
in full view, ordinarily, when someone claims to see only a part of
an object, the implication is simply that she is prevented from
viewing all of it *in this instance*: the part not seen might be hidden,
concealed, or blocked from view. But are we really entitled to maintain that a generic object might thus be excluded from view? In
order to realize why that cannot be the case, let us look closer
at what the skeptic actually is saying; the skeptical picture then
implies a peculiar (and ultimately perverse) view of our lives with
objects. In the skeptic's account, all objects are like moons: our posi-

tion with regard to them is conceived of as *rooted* or geometrically fixed. The moment we move, however, the sense of there being different parts inevitably loses its hold on us; and with the disappearance of "parts," the skeptical conclusion (that *all* objects are like moons, and hence that we strictly speaking never see objects) fails to get off the ground:

> Apart from the *specific* establishing or re-establishing of some "part" of an object which we do not see by a specific conducting of the philosopher's investigation (a new rooting of our position, a new concentration to fix the great circle) there *is* nothing – no *thing* we do not see: objects are (again?) in "full view." (CR, 202)

The instability of the skeptical conclusion – the fact, as Hume observed, that it evaporates, as it were, upon replacing the imagined context of the philosopher with our concrete life full of objects – suggests that the skeptic, driven perhaps by a Cartesian tendency to want to disconnect the senses from the body, distorts our ordinary relation with objects in the world. For his model to generate a general skeptical conclusion (rather than simply allow the recording of a specific feature of *this* object), it has to repress the internal relation between viewing and acting in favor of a set-up which positions us before objects in a manner analogous to cameras or microscopes. The philosopher has therefore made an invention and not a discovery: his conclusion would not exist but for his own efforts. And while it is true that he needs the invented context to try to make his point, at the end of the day the point cannot be made: since the context excludes the speaker's particular judgment, the making of the point can only be imagined. The philosopher has, in other words, appealed to a model which prevents him from revealing the conditions according to which his words can be made intelligible, that is, be *meant*, and so he fails to make sense. Thus the skeptical investigation is involved in a dilemma: either it employs a model in terms of which our life among objects is radically distorted, thereby preventing a claim about something in *our* world from being made, and, indeed, any claim from being made; or, if the investigation fits its original faithfully, then it fails to produce a conclusion that has ramifications for *all* our knowledge.

A similar dilemma arises at the initial stage of the investigation, that is, with the entry of a claim to knowledge about a generic object: "It must be the investigation of a concrete claim if its procedure is to be coherent; it cannot be the investigation of a concrete claim if its conclusion is to be general" (CR, 220). But why is a claim about a generic object not concrete, that is, well motivated in the context? What is wrong with such claims? Cavell's answer is that they cannot even be properly and intelligibly made. The philosopher operates in a "non-claim context": "no concrete claim is ever entered as part of the traditional investigation" (CR, 217). This characterization rests on the idea, which we have encountered already, that meaning something by an utterance is only possible in so far as the speaker assumes or declares a position from which he speaks. In the case of the philosopher who, in perfect viewing conditions, stares at an object X (a generic object) and says "I know that that is an X," we recognize what his *words* mean, namely "what a good dictionary says they mean" (CR, 207). What is left out, however, is *what he means* in using them there and then: "The point of saying them is lost" (ibid). In the misguided belief that the "because it is true" constitutes a reason or basis for saying anything, the philosopher effectively rejects any condition whatsoever under which a linguistically grammatical stretch of sound would be able to count as *his* assertion. Normally, such conditions would include, for example, that the proposition in question is informative, that the hearer is in a position to understand it, and that it expresses something which is remarkable. Just as there are limits to what can be explicitly learnt, so there are limits to the facts that someone can remark and still make a point. In the absence of a mutual and common agreement that certain features of the world are unremarkable unless special circumstances occur that make them remarkable, language could not function. On the basis of considerations such as these, the sentence "This is a hand," uttered in the presence of hands under optimal conditions, is shown to fail to make itself felt as an assertion. While purporting to record a fact, the saying of it is pointless, as if the concrete subject of the enunciation were replaced by a fact-recording machine, operating with a purely representational language. But such a language is precisely inhuman; it excludes from the outset "our responsibility for *claiming* something to be so" (CR, 216).

Cavell also notes how very odd the notion of reason-giving is in the context imagined by the skeptic. What would be a reason for knowing one's own name, or that one has two arms, or that *this* (object in front of me under ideal circumstances) is a real and existing tomato? Do we know these things because we can remember things and perceive objects? While it certainly would not always be unintelligible or false to say that we remember our name or see our arms, the problem is rather that "in the context in which these 'reasons' are proffered, they are inoperative *as reasons*" (CR, 217). Unless some particular feature of the situation makes it relevant to ask such questions, they fail to add up to a ground for eliciting belief. Instead, they are just as empty as the claims they are supposed to make good.

In so far, then, as the skeptic succeeds in making himself intelligible – to supply real reasons for claiming to know, say, that there is a tomato in front of him in perfect viewing conditions – he must be remarking on his particular epistemic situation, the way he is positioned to make this particular claim to know. But if so, then the possible defeat of that particular claim would have no consequences for human knowledge as such. All it would do is tell us something about the claimant and his position (or lack of) as a knower. Yet, for the skeptic to claim general validity for his conclusion, he must seek to avoid all particular reasons and commitments. What he wishes for is intelligibility without accepting *any* particular conditions in speaking, i.e., without taking any responsibility for meaning what he wants to mean. Rather than being ready to reveal his own grounds of intelligibility – the ways in which he allows things to count for him or have a value – he inevitably appeals to the fantasy of some impersonal structure capable of effortlessly providing sense to his words:

> It is as though we try to get the world to provide answers in a way which is independent of our responsibility for *claiming* something to be so (to get God to tell us what we must do in a way which is independent of our responsibility for choice); and we fix the world so that it can do this. (CR, 216).

For Cavell, the outcome of such a move is not that our words necessarily become unintelligible, it is that *we* become mute, unknowable, incomprehensible: "In the *Investigations* the cost is arrived at in terms (e.g., of not knowing what we are saying, of emptiness in our assertions, of the illusion of meaning something, of claims to impossible privacies) suggestive of madness" (CR, 242). Further, "the cost is the loss, or forgoing, of identity or of selfhood" (ibid). Thus philosophy can be said to be motivated by emptiness, of exempting ourselves from revealing and expressing the criteria we rely on in speech – a wish, in other words, to reject authority over our own minds.

Cavell is well aware that his diagnosis of philosophical skepticism does not amount to a refutation. On the contrary, the skeptic is right that criteria do not confer certainty. It is of the essence of criteria that they are open to repudiation; and if anyone tries to transcend the conditions of intelligible speech and hence her attunement with others, no theoretical argument will be able to prevent that from happening. Rather than refuting the skeptic, Cavell aims at making explicit the existential and psychological price that such a denial has – that it deprives us of a voice in our lives and drives us into a stifling and ultimately maddening privacy in which each of us remains a stranger both to ourselves and others. Thus the problems of philosophy become questions of self-knowledge.

But while the skeptic's message (that we cannot know the world exists) has not been refuted, it does not follow that we ought to think that perhaps there is no (external) world. On this interpretation, the limits of knowledge, our finitude or conditionedness, would simply be taken as failures of it; and every attempt to bespeak the world would be in vain. For Cavell, what skepticism shows is rather that the world's presentness to us cannot be a function of knowing, or only of knowing. Yet if "the human creature's basis in the world as a whole, its relation to the world as such, is not that of knowing, anyway not what we think of as knowing" (CR, 241), then what exactly is its basis? In "The Avoidance of Love" of 1967, Cavell introduces the word "acceptance": "The world is to be *accepted*; as the presentness of other minds is not to be known, but acknowledged" (MWM, 234). In the *Claim of Reason*, however, he denies that acceptance expresses belief in anything: no claims are involved; thus he admits, with Wittgenstein and Heidegger, to "some question as to the mystery of the existence, or the being, of the world" (CR, 241). Echoing Schelling's critique of Hegel's *Science of Logic*, Cavell argues that the existence of the world is beyond demonstration, beyond *logos*.

In part, because Cavell, at least in *The Claim of Reason*, has very little to say on this issue, and also because of its seemingly intrinsic obscurity, it is difficult to know exactly how to respond to his talk of acceptance. And while it returns in his writings on Emerson and Thoreau, as well as in those on romanticism, which I will take up in chapters 5 and 6, for the moment I want to linger not on its resonance with certain poetico-philosophical strands of those authors, but on its capacity to illuminate the logic of skepticism as it has been discussed so far. According to one of Cavell's critics, Barry Stroud, "acceptance" essentially designates an alternative relation to the world around us, or rather, since knowledge fails as a candidate, *the* privileged relation in which we stand to things.[9] Yet, as Stroud points out, if viewed as a metaphysical thesis, purporting to capture a general truth about worldhood as such, "acceptance" simply begs the skeptical question: it invites the quest for grounds. What, he asks, makes "acceptance" less susceptible of scrutiny and assessment by philosophy than knowledge? Why could we not come to "wonder whether our 'acceptance' is properly or securely based"?[10] Indeed, even Cavell himself admits that it "caves in at a doubt" (MWM, 324). So what is the point? Moreover, in so far as this *one* relation to the world lacks cognitive assurance, why is the "truth of skepticism" not skeptical in the Cartesian sense, that is, as straightforwardly denying us reason to think that we are in possession of knowledge of the world as such?

Stroud's objections may seem devastating. Yet they rely on the assumption that Cavell takes the notion of "acceptance" to provide a general solution to skepticism. With reference to the APA (American Philosophical Association) symposium at which Stroud presented his criticisms in 1980, Cavell reports, however, "that by the end of the first two parts of [*The Claim of Reason*] I had convinced myself that there is no such solution, that to think otherwise is skepticism's own self-interpretation" (CHU, 35). What the skeptic seeks is a relation to the world for which the individual is no longer accountable – an absolute presence beyond the vicissitudes of having to establish a connection between what I say and the object before me. So to think there is a solution to skepticism is to give in to it – accept the skeptic's vision of our predicament. More specifically, the interpretation on which Stroud bases his critique misleadingly portrays "acceptance" as a privileged mode of relating to the world as a whole, as if the world is an object, though infinitely big; and thus it naturally provokes the question of knowledge. But for Cavell, in so far as any meaning can be attached to "the world as such," it surely cannot imply that it is an object, and even less so that we need some form of alternative vocabulary, one based on the order of "acceptance" rather than knowledge, in order to bespeak it. All such talk simply invites skepticism.

This returns us to a claim made earlier in this chapter: that the "point of forgoing knowledge is . . . to know" (MWM, 325). Criteria can lead both to and from skepticism: it depends on us. But whereas skepticism about the external world is unsupportable, and thus ultimately remains a theoretical prospect, about other minds no everyday alternative to it exists. It is in affecting a relation between human beings that skepticism betrays its complicity with the tragic. We can no longer defer our discussion of these issues.

3

The Other

Just as Cavell considers how disappointment with criteria and the incapacity to accept human finitude pervades philosophy's quest for certainty about the existence of the external world, so he considers the problem of other minds to be predicated on the wish to strip ourselves of the responsibilities and anxieties that mark our lives in language. In the difficult Part IV of *The Claim of Reason*, he offers an analysis of skepticism about other minds – and in particular the implied relation between the inner and the outer, the mind and its society – which culminates in a reading of Shakespeare's *Othello*. Since it is Cavell's contention that both comedy and tragedy, at least in their Shakespearean forms, study the consequences of skeptical responses to the other (and to oneself), in addition to examining the philosophical discussion of mindfulness and its place in nature and culture, with which I start out, this chapter will end with a discussion of his interpretation of some major plays by Shakespeare.

Skepticism About Other Minds

In chapter 2 we looked at a (Cartesian) skeptical argument that aimed to establish conclusively that the mind-independent existence of the material world is, necessarily, imperfectly known. A similar argument with regard to our knowledge of other minds would start by noting that we claim to know the existence of at least some other minds. We relate, presumably, to other human beings every day – embodied beings endowed with thoughts, fears, wishes, hopes, desires, and so on. But how, or on what grounds, do we really know this? We know, the answer runs, what others are able to show us of themselves. Similarly, others know of us what we are able to show of ourselves. Our access to others is mainly perceptual. But how much can be shown? Well, at least we "see a humanish something of a certain height and age and gender and color and physiognomy, emitting vocables in a certain style" (CR, 443). But this is insufficient, it might be argued, to claim to know *another mind*; for it is compatible with such an experience that the other is a robot, zombie, golem, or any other perfected human-like being without an inner life. Hence it follows that we are not entitled to claim knowledge of other minds. Indeed, for all I know, the human-like others could appear to my senses as they now do and I could be the only human in existence.

So how can the skeptical conclusion be avoided? Typically, philosophers, while conceding that there can be no non-inferential access to other minds, have resisted the skeptical conclusion by appealing to a purported analogy or similarity between oneself and others. In accordance with this intuition – as in the so-called argument from analogy – an inference is made from the premise that I know that my body is sentient to the conclusion that other bodies are as well. Obviously, this inference can only aspire to validity if I also know that the other's body is roughly similar to mine. But do I? As Cavell points out, it seems evident that the other's body is like mine in many respects, and yet the only respect that would make any difference to me in this context would be if, like mine, it were connected with sentience. Indeed, there seems to be no particular reason why I should be entitled to know with certainty that the mind–body association in my case can be legitimately projected onto the other. Hence, the argument is question-begging: it presupposes what it sets out to prove.

Another approach, not explicitly discussed by Cavell but prominent in much recent debate, consists in the so-called inference to the best explanation. According to this suggestion, since adopting the hypothesis that the other has a mind (and a mind–body association) similar to my own offers the best explanations (and predictions) I can come up with of the other's behavior, skepticism about other minds is irrational and should be rejected. At least two objections will have to be met for this argument to be able to go through. First, it is far from self-evident that believing in the existence of other minds provides the best explanation of actions. Indeed, a naturalist skeptic would argue that other types of explanation, such as, for example, the ones acquired in neuroscience, have a better explanatory force, and are more precise and reliable, than intentionalism. Second, even if the appeal to other minds might give us the best *current* explanation, it is questionable whether we will think so in the future. Perhaps all talk of intentional states, and of minds as such, will turn out in 50 or 100 years to be regarded as what Paul Churchland and others have called "folk psychology," that is, a pre-scientific, pre-rational set of beliefs on the same footing as alchemy is today.[1] Since these are empirical, scientific questions, the argument appealing to the rationality of inferring to the best explanation rests its case on the scientific success of the conjecture that minds exist, yet the appeal to scientific success is precisely what opens the door to skepticism.

In order to make some headway with the problem of other minds, Cavell – who for reasons we will soon encounter is deeply skeptical about the very idea of proving the existence of other minds, yet does not feel prepared to accept the skeptical conclusion – turns to Wittgenstein. As he initially notes, many readers of the *Investigations* have tended to think that Wittgenstein's way with skeptics about other minds consists in denying the privacy of the mind. According to their interpretation, privacy essentially entails secrecy, the impossibility of sharing the other's inner life. Denying privacy in the sense of secrecy therefore implies disclaiming one's metaphysical exclusion from the other. As a representative of such a position, Cavell cites John Cook, who finds the idea that sensations are essentially private to be "queer."[2] Yet, while Cook challenges the deep-seated notion that failure to know others must be a result of some metaphysical deficiency, his solution fails to account for our everyday sense of separation. Indeed, the concept of privacy, that the other's mind is inaccessible to me, seems expressive of a far more plausible intuition than the simple endorsement of unrestricted publicness. Cavell therefore turns to another commentator, George Pitcher, who defends the privacy of sensations.[3] From a third-person point of view, sensations are, according to Pitcher, ineffable. Since our language-games contain no reference to sensations, nothing can be said about them, hence the philosophical problem of other minds is solved before it even begins. Finally, Cavell mentions Alan Donagan, who finds Wittgenstein to be distinguishing between direct and indirect representations of sensations.[4] According to Donagan, other people's sensations, though not directly representable, can be represented imaginatively.

An important aspect of Pitcher's and Donagan's discussions is that they both frame their arguments by reference to Wittgenstein's famous parable of the boiling pot:

> Of course, if water boils in a pot, steam comes out of the pot and also pictured steam comes out of the pictured pot. But what if one insisted on saying that there must also be something boiling in the picture of the pot? (PI, §297)

Can anything boil inside a pictured pot? The answer is supposed to reflect the extent to which you are prepared to believe in metaphysical privacy. Thus, depending on their views about this issue, while Pitcher suggests that it makes no sense to say that there is liquid in the pictured pot, Donagan is inclined to say that what the parable offers is an indirect representation (*Vorstellung*) though not a direct image (*Bild*) of anything boiling.

In conformity with his general reluctance to take a stance in metaphysical discussions, Cavell, rather than siding with any of these views, notes that Pitcher and Donagan share one fundamental presupposition: they both find the *question of* whether or not something is boiling in the picture makes sense, hence they both think the parable must allow a coherent resolution. But Wittgenstein's "scene of instruction" seems not to offer anything like that. For by turning to the concurrent entry on pain on which the parable is supposed to comment, it becomes apparent that what Wittgenstein draws attention to is the potential *strangeness* or *emptiness* involved in both affirming and denying that there *must* be something hidden in the pot (or the body). For what the parable, after all, seems to question is precisely the very intelligibility of appeals to (or denials of) the existence of some quasi-entity that accompanies people's behavior:

> "Yes, but there is *something* there all the same accompanying my cry of pain. And it is on account of that that I utter it. And this something is what is important – and frightful." – Only whom are we informing of this? And on what occasion? (PI, §296)

Ordinarily, expressions of pain do not provoke the issue of the existence of the inner as opposed to the outer – or the sensation as opposed to the behavior. If someone shows all the signs of being in pain (the body contorts, he or she grunts or whines, etc.) and the context provides no reason to think otherwise (you see the bruise, say, on the arm, and you just witnessed the accident), then for this person to say that "there is *something* here accompanying my cry of pain" fails to assert anything; it becomes empty. It wouldn't say or tell us anything. And since there would be no point in uttering it, it cannot be fully *meant*: indeed, the very attempt to enter the assertion renders the speaker unintelligible, voiceless, or even mad. Again, as in his analysis of assertions purporting to affirm the existence of generic objects, Cavell's claim is not that the rules of language necessarily prevent such an assertion from being made in this context; rather, his point is that the speaker, given the nature of the context, has failed to offer any reason for his use of words, any position in speaking. In short, the speaker refuses to judge and thus to responsibly project criteria so as to make himself comprehensible.

So the philosopher, in so far as he asks how knowledge of other minds is possible, begins his query in a highly unfamiliar context: he assumes that minds and bodies are radically divided, and that the task of philosophy is to show how they can be connected. Yet ordinarily we speak and act as if no such gulf between the mind and its expressions existed. Pain-behavior (in relevant circumstances) and pain simply go together without further reflection. Pain typically is *manifest* in winces and screams; pain-behavior is *expressive* of pain. It can even be said to be of the nature of living bodies that they are capable of pain: "Only of what behaves like a human being can one say that it *has* pains. For one has to say it of a body, or, if you like of a soul which some body *has*" (PI, §283). It is only when we feel forced to *connect* the behavior and the pain – as if they were two different *things* – that we realize that outward expression does not provide conclusive evidence of the inner. Disappointing as it strikes the philosopher, the "natural connection" does not generate certainty in our judgments – it can fail us.

Thus, the skeptic who envisions the expression as something that stands in the way of knowledge – who is "disappointed" and therefore wants, as Wittgenstein puts it, "to try to use language to get between pain and its expression" (PI, §245) – is not exactly wrong. He does not produce straightforwardly false propositions. Rather, he demonstrates the limits of criteria – that they cannot relieve us of the responsibility we all have as speakers for letting them count, in our uses of words, as our own conditions of intelligibility. For me to employ criteria in contexts involving others requires that I acknowledge the other's body as the home of my concepts of the inner. By responding to the other's expressions of herself, I accept that the other is a live creature, a living being. To quote Wittgenstein, "My attitude towards him is an attitude towards a soul" (PI, p. 178). But criteria do not only fail to guarantee the presence of another *mind* (as opposed to a golem, zombie, and so on), they also do not establish with certainty that pain-behavior, to use that as our example, is accompanied by *pain* (as opposed to any other sensation). For as we have seen, criteria, though capable of determining with certainty whether a given stretch of behavior is expressive of pain rather than pleasure, cannot determine with certainty *what* the other feels.

References to another mind, say of a person's pain, are made up of our *responses* to a call or demand on the part of the other: "[My references to another's pain] are responses to another's expressions of (or inability to express) his or her pain" (CR, 342). The other, in expressing herself, in wincing, crying out, calls out for my response, and only in actually *responding*, in doing or revealing something, thus *acknowledging* the state of my relation to her (and perhaps that I have shut the other out), do I recognize (or know) the other as being *in pain*. This "empathic projection" is very different from merely seeing or registering that such-and-so is the case. Rather than observing something in an objectifying mode, I actively engage with the other to the extent of identifying *with* her. Moreover, the identification with the other singles me out; it exposes me to the specific history of my relation to the other. Cavell's point is not that we always have sympathy, nor that we always respond, nor even that we always ought to do so. There may be occasions on which we need to free ourselves *from* the other (her opinion of us, say, or her anxieties), or when we feel *Schadenfreude*, perhaps, or other responses apart from sympathy. Like Heidegger's *existentiale*, Cavell's central concept of acknowledgment does not describe a given response but is, rather, a category in terms of which such responses are evaluated.[5] Regardless of whether we respond or not, the structure of acknowledgment is in place; the other's demand for recognition, even if unheeded, puts us in a position of responsibility. Although typically denied by philosophy, it forms an intrinsic part of our ordinary lives together. So while "failing to know" characteristically announces itself as an absence of something ("I simply was not aware"), "failing to acknowledge" is "the presence of something, a confusion, an indifference, a callousness, an exhaustion, a coldness" (MWM, 264). However, the bond of sympathy that expressively links me to, and implicates me with, the other's inner life, may be suppressed to such an extent that it breaks, thus threatening to dispossess me of the region in my own mind which my behavioral response to the other is expressing.

The skeptic, then, is unwilling to take responsibility for his own position vis-à-vis the other. While rightly observing that the mere satisfaction of criteria is not enough to constitute certainty in this area of knowledge, the skeptic, by withholding concepts of the inner and by refusing to view the body as expressive, ends up concluding that the inner life of others, both as such and in its specific configurations, is inaccessible, unknowable. The skeptic, in other words, mistakes a failure of acknowledgment for a failure of knowledge. But the problem of the other is not, if anything, one of knowledge. In facing another human being, there is nothing of relevance to the existence of the other that I am a priori prevented from knowing. Rather, such knowing depends on you and me, on our relationship, on whether or not we are capable of maintaining or, if necessary, re-establishing our mutuality. Thus skepticism should be viewed less as an intellectual problem than as an existential challenge or temptation, one which rationalizes a standing threat to our attunement; and as such it needs to be elucidated and explained, in short, acknowledged, rather than refuted.

Thus far we have been examining third-person ascriptions of psychological predicates. According to Cavell, however, the logic of acknowledgment extends to and is equally significant for understanding first-person cases. Just as knowledge of the other's pain finds expression in our behavior, so the recognition of our own pain finds behavioral expression. A refusal to give expression to one's own pain would therefore in the end be tantamount to not knowing it, and, as psychoanalysis amply illustrates, a failure of self-understanding typically presupposes repression. Accordingly, an important aim of psychoanalysis, both in Cavell's and in Freud's view, is to get the patient to acknowledge that which has hitherto remained unacknowledged, in the hope of bringing the ego to a fuller awareness of itself and its own potentials.

From a more orthodox Wittgensteinian point of view, however, Cavell's insistence that knowledge (modified by acknowledgment) applies to the self's relation to itself must seem highly contentious. To quote Wittgenstein, "It can't be said of me at all (except perhaps as a joke) that I *know* I am in pain. What is it supposed to mean – except perhaps that I *am* in pain?" (PI, §246). On the standard reading, the point of Wittgenstein's remark is to call attention to the absurdity involved in conceptualizing the relation to one's mental states on the model of a cognitive relation to inner objects. The inner is not a thing. Moreover, if the notion of an inner *object* can be shown to be void, then the conception of privileged, non-inferential access, which the skeptic holds is available in first- but not third-person cases, loses its credibility. If the inner is beyond reach, then it is not because it is hidden *by* something else, i.e. the body. It is because it remains unacknowledged or unaccounted for. Now, as we have seen, Cavell agrees with Wittgenstein that skeptics (and mind/body dualists) falsely tend to interpret mental states as if they were objects; yet despite what they claim, the sufferer's relation to her own pain is of an expressive nature: pain manifests itself *in* the scream or wince. Cavell objects, however, to the view that utterances such as "I *know* I'm in pain" has no legitimate, or philosophically significant, application whatsoever. While not referring to some quasi-object but rather to the *acknowledgment* (or expression) of a state of consciousness, "I know I'm in pain" might, for example, be perfectly meaningful in response to an analyst who has uncovered my attempts to suppress or deny that truth about myself. Rather than thinking that no criteria are needed for such states, and hence that claims to knowledge logically cannot be entered, such a person has failed to employ the ones she already possesses; hence her problem is not one of knowledge but of acknowledgment, of yielding to what she knows.

Acknowledgment of others may be seen as a problem in various ways. I may conceive of myself as failing or refusing to acknowledge your body as the home of my concepts of the inner. This would typically be the position of the academic skeptic who refuses to apply criteria of mental states to the other on the grounds that criteria by themselves fail to establish a cognitive link between expression and pain. Conversely, the other may refuse to let her inner life be expressed to me. But why would anyone want to overcome expressiveness? After all, expressiveness is our natural condition. Cavell's answer is that expression can be risky and full of anxiety: I may find myself unknown, unable to make myself known, or I may find that what I express is beyond my control. In the first case, my humanity is at stake; in the second, my identity, or rather my own conception of who I am. Such fears give rise to what Cavell calls a fantasy of necessary inexpressiveness:

> A fantasy of necessary inexpressiveness would solve a simultaneous set of metaphysical problems: it would relieve me of the responsibility for making myself known to others – as though if I were expressive that would mean continuously betraying my experiences, incessantly giving myself away; it would suggest that my responsibility for self-knowledge takes care of itself – as though the fact that

others cannot know my (inner) life means that I cannot fail to. It would reassure my fears of being known, though it may not prevent my being under suspicion; it would reassure my fears of not being known, though it may not prevent my being under indictment. – The wish underlying this fantasy covers a wish that underlies skepticism, a wish for the connection between my claims of knowledge and the objects upon which the claims are to fall to occur without my intervention, apart from my agreements. (CR, 351–2)

Thus the fantasy of necessary inexpressiveness is a fantasy about the acquisition of authority. If the references to my pain were not dependent upon my expressions of pain (as Cavell and Wittgenstein argue they are), but only on what is inner or private, available only to myself, then the risks of expression would not occur: there would be no possibility of correction, misrecognition, repudiation, or any other failure of recognition. No one but myself, it seems, would be in a position to know and understand my "inner experiences." While relieving me of the responsibility of making myself known to others, of publicly revealing the criteria I go on in my talk, I would be the sole authority about which concepts correctly apply to myself as a mindful being. The price, though, is that I would remain unknown. Without recognition, without words and deeds and expressions with which we actively insert ourselves in a common human world and respond to others' responses to us, we would have no full existence as distinct human beings. The other may refuse to acknowledge our self-expressions. Alternatively, we may fail to give ourselves expression before the other. Yet without the willingness to implicate ourselves in the lives of our fellow men, to relate to them and thus allow them to relate to us, recognition, and hence the assurance that we exist, would not be possible. Cavell's moral is that we must let ourselves *matter*:

> To let yourself matter is to acknowledge not merely how it is with you, and hence to acknowledge that you want the other to care, at least to care to know. It is equally to acknowledge that your expressions in fact express you, that they are yours, that you are in them. This means allowing yourselves to be comprehended, something you can always deny. Not to deny it is, I would like to say, to acknowledge your body, and the body of your expressions, to be yours, you on earth, all there will ever *be* of you. (CR, 383)

We have seen that the fantasy of necessary inexpressiveness involves the desire for privacy, or rather a private language, a theme featuring prominently in the *Investigations*. In Wittgenstein's thought-experiment in paragraph 243 and onwards, the notion of a private language entails, first, that psychological concepts refer to the presence of metaphysically inner events and entities, and, second, that their meaning is constituted in and through such a naming-relation. A private language can therefore be said to be a language for which a ceremony of private ostensive definition establishes the standard of linguistic correctness. According to most interpreters, Wittgenstein aims to prove the impossibility of such a language, and thus that the fantasy of necessary inexpressiveness can make no sense. By virtue of our public linguistic practices, we are inevitably known to each other, and no "meanings" can exist that are private entities, inaccessible to others. As we saw in the first chapter, however, Cavell objects to this view of publicness. For him, though our language is inevitably shared by the members of our linguistic community, nothing else insures its continued existence except the individual's commitment to sustain commonality by actively revealing, in speech, the conditions of intelligibility that she takes to be authoritative. No proof can ever unburden the individual of this responsibility.

Thus, as opposed to the standard reading of the private language argument, Cavell is interested neither in the provision of such a proof nor in denying that it can be made coherently. His point is rather that a proof of this kind will ineluctably be made in bad faith. By presupposing that the private linguist simply makes a cognitive mistake, one that can be identified and corrected, and that privacy will thus be overcome a priori, it covers up the standing existential option of refusing expression and rejecting the other. Moreover, it fails to come to terms with the human cost of denying, or attempting to deny, the criterial links between the inner and the outer, between the mind and its expressions. On Cavell's view, we should accept that the claims for privacy give expression to a deep-seated fantasy or desire to absolve ourselves from the responsibility for making ourselves known to others. To think that a proof would be sufficient to overcome the anxieties involved in expression would be a skeptical answer: by failing to acknowledge how separate we in fact are, it fails to account for the vicissitudes of having to make ourselves known. And rather than overcoming privacy, it establishes a false sense of unity between body and soul, one which in effect hypostatizes our confinement.

What is the problem of the other if it is not a problem of certainty? In the parable of the boiling pot, Wittgenstein talks about an "image of pain" (PI, §300). But what kind of image? Can more be said about how we encounter other minds? The notion of "image" is based on what Cavell calls "imagination," which "is the capacity for making connections or realizing possibilities" (CR, 353). In facing the other, we do more than simply relate to certain bare facts of no intrinsic significance. The other lets herself be known through a whole register of expressions, ranging from simple bodily movements to the utterance of words and sentences. Moreover, expressions have a significance of their own, one that is connected to something else to which the expression is a response. By means of the imagination, we "see [the other's] blink as a wince, and connect the wince with something in the world that there is to be winced at" (CR, 354). In short, we see something *as* something. Our access to other minds is fundamentally perceptual.

At this juncture, Cavell turns once again to Wittgenstein – this time to his famous discussion, in Part II of the *Investigations*, of aspects and aspect-perception, or what is generally referred to as *seeing-as*. The starting-point of Wittgenstein's analysis consists of the ambiguous pictures, well known from Wolfgang Köhler and *Gestalt* psychology, in which a figure can be read in competing ways. Joseph Jastrow's duck-rabbit, for instance, can be seen as a picture of a duck or a rabbit, depending on the way we receive it or relate to it. We see the figure *in a certain way*. (Occasionally Wittgenstein employs terms such as "mode of appearance" (*Erscheinungsweise*) or "form of appearance" (*Erscheinungsform*) – both borrowed from classical *Gestalt* psychology.) Likewise I may "contemplate a face, and then suddenly notice its likeness to another. I *see* that it has not changed; and yet I see it differently" (PI, p. 193). In its puzzling combination of sameness and difference, the "noticing of an aspect" presents us with a mystery in need of conceptual clarification.

The phenomenon of aspect-perception plays a significant role in Wittgenstein's account of perceptual awareness, not only of other human beings, but of works of art and indeed of our worldly surroundings in general. Moreover, the four volumes of writings on the philosophy of psychology – all of which were published after the appearance of *The Claim of Reason* – testify to the remarkable energy with which Wittgenstein investigated this issue.[6] Considering the huge relevance he ascribes to the concept of aspect-perception, Cavell spends little time on the elaboration of various explanations of this phenomenon. It might therefore be useful to pause for a moment and ask in what sense the noticing of an aspect is a visual experience. For Wittgenstein, three competing theories stand out as candidates – reductionism, Köhler's *Gestalt*-account, and empiricism.

From the perspective of reductionism, explanations of the dawning or noticing of an aspect would predominantly appeal to physiological factors. The aim of such explanations is to account causally for the perceptual shift by referring to law-like propositions, say the known visual effects of particular movements or inflections of the eyeballs. While agreeing that such factors may affect our vision, Wittgenstein dismisses the idea of them being constitutive of the meaning or significance of what we see. If someone were "blind to the *expression* of a face" (PI, p. 210), he writes, we would hardly think that his eyesight is defective. In the more sophisticated account offered by Köhler, the change taking place when we notice a new aspect occurs in what the *Gestalt* psychologists used to call "the organization" of our visual impression. While the impression of shape and color remains the same, a new psychic *Gestalt* has been conferred on the phenomenally given. The problem with this is that the experienced change in one's inner materialization turns out to be inexpressible. No representation based on color and shape of what is seen in the two cases – e.g., say the duck versus the rabbit – captures the difference between them, and if the difference cannot be shown, then it cannot exist. The lesson Wittgenstein draws is that we should avoid thinking of aspects as existing on the same level as color and shape. The capacity to notice an aspect must, rather, reflect our manner of relating to our visual impressions. But how? Empiricism, finally, attempts to accommodate this intuition by distinguishing between direct apprehensions of objects and interpretations (*Deutungen*) of them. Assuming that past experience has caused us to form certain interpretive habits such that specific properties of the object in question tend to generate certain beliefs about what we see, we may project those beliefs onto the object, thus allowing them to appear in this or that way. This, however, is also rejected by Wittgenstein, who argues that while interpretation is an activity (of forming hypotheses and testing whether they match data), seeing, including the noticing of an aspect, is a state. The empiricist distinction between direct and indirect access violates the sense of immediacy involved in noticing an aspect. If we happen to see the duck in the picture of the duck-rabbit, then the immediacy of that image of a duck is undeniable, and no description of it could be more direct than "Now I see a duck."

In view of Wittgenstein's strong criticisms of the appeal to interpretation, it might appear puzzling that Cavell chooses precisely that term to characterize aspect-perception: " 'Seeing something as something' is what Wittgenstein calls 'interpretation' " (CR, 354). According to Stephen Mulhall, in *On Being in the World*, his path-breaking study of Wittgenstein's account of seeing-as, this shows that Cavell fails to offer an adequate account of perception, or at least that the latter's position is deeply at odds with Wittgenstein's.[7] In Mulhall's view, the interpretation-view is too subjectivist: it opens a gap between the thing as it is in itself and the thing as interpreted, and hence lapses into skepticism. But does Cavell really want to suggest that seeing-as is a form of interpretation in the sense suggested by Wittgenstein? Let us follow his discussion a little further. Having presented the reader with the duck-rabbit, he immediately moves on to two neighboring themes in Wittgenstein's examination of aspects: that aspects present a physiognomy and that we are attached to ourselves and others as we are to words. Just as words are expressive, so human bodies are expressive of human souls; our attachments to words are allegorical of our attachments to human beings; thus the body needs to be *read*: "To know another mind is to interpret a physiognomy, and the message of this region of the *Investigations* is that this is not a matter of 'mere knowing'. I have to read the physiognomy, and see the creature according to my reading, and treat it according to my seeing" (CR, 356). What kind of reading or interpretation is at stake here? First of all, as Cavell notes, it is not an occasion of "mere knowing" – for registering a fact that can be translated into a "report." The reading in question exceeds the boundaries of what is strictly conceptual and justifiable. For Wittgenstein, the notion of "technique" comes in at this stage: my ability to read a physiognomy must be related to a continuous scheme of both verbal and non-verbal behavior by means of which I respond to the seen. Cavell, however, chooses to focus on Wittgenstein's concept of *Einstellung* – attitude, as in "My attitude towards him is an attitude towards a soul" (PI, p. 178). An attitude, while not what we ordinarily think of as belief, is not entirely different from knowledge. But whereas conceptually transmittable knowledge can be proven in the sense that some kind of justification for it can be offered, the sort of "knowledge" expressed in a particular attitude tends to be what Wittgenstein calls "imponderable" (PI, p. 228) – or rather, the evidence for it is "imponderable." "Subtleties of glance, of gesture, of tone," he writes, count as imponderable evidence. I would have a hard time specifying *why* I see a glance as full of sorrow – I just do. Unlike dispositions that I can adopt at will, it is "an inflection of myself toward others, an orientation which affects everything and which I may or may not be interested in discovering about myself" (CR, 360). Similarly, Peter Winch, another commentator, interestingly remarks that attitudes "may no doubt be strengthened, weakened or modified by circumstances and to some extent by thought too, but usually, in given circumstances, it is a condition I am in vis-à-vis other human beings without choosing to be so."[8] While such attitudes do not qualify as knowledge in the narrow sense, it is equally important to distinguish them from the non-cognitive attitudes evoked in logical positivism. For Charles Stevenson and others, as we will see in chapter 5, the term "attitude," which they use to characterize our relation to religious, moral, and aesthetic matters, refers to something strictly private; as opposed to Wittgensteinian attitudes, the attitudes being brought to attention in logical positivism exclude from the outset any claim to be binding for other individuals. For Cavell, however, expressions are themselves criteria; they allow us to make claims that have a grammar, and hence they transcend the realm of the merely private.

Given Cavell's stress on the notion of attitude, it seems, contrary to Mulhall's reconstruction, unlikely that his appeal to "interpretation" is meant as an espousal of what I have called the "interpretation-view" of aspect-perception, that is, the conception of aspects as being less immediately presented to us than the object of perception itself. Indeed, "my relation to the other's soul," Cavell argues, "is as immediate as to an object of sight" (CR, 368). Moreover, Cavell's use of the word "read," as in the idea that the human body is there to be read, does not imply that the "signs" – human expressions – are somehow dead and meaningless until an interpretation of them has been conferred. On the contrary, their significance, like letters on a page, strike us as co-presented with the materiality of the signs themselves; thus reading "has something to do with being advised, and hence with seeing" (CR, 363). To read a body as giving expression to a soul is to see behavior-in-context as the bearer of psychological significance: we respond to the other as one who herself is responding to a world of significance. By means of the imagination, we place the other's behavior within a narrative through which the significance of her behavior appears to us. Sometimes this takes thought, hence time; generally, however, it doesn't.

Cavell's exploration of Wittgenstein's model of aspect-perception effects a radical transformation of the skeptical picture (or myth) of our relation to others, and in particular of the human body as such. For while the skeptic views the body as a veil, a blind, that somehow *hides* the mind – indeed the skeptic effectively puts the other beyond reach – what the remarks on "seeing an aspect" help us realize is that the soul can be as present as the body itself; indeed the body *is* a field of psychological significance. In Cavell's words, "not to believe there is such a thing as the human soul is not to know what the human body is, what it is of, heir to" (CR, 400). But does this mean that the other's mind is invariably transparent? Does it prevent the issue of unknownness and hence of skepticism from arising? For Merleau-Ponty, for example, who holds a strikingly similar view of the body to that of Cavell, the skeptic about other minds can be shown to forget or repress the lived body; thus, if the manner in which we encounter each other in the lifeworld is taken heed of, the threat of skepticism, premised as it is on a false ontology, immediately evaporates.[9] For Cavell, however, such a solution to skepticism, in that it rules out the possibility of unknownness, misses the moral of skepticism: that we ourselves, and not some kind of metaphysical abyss separating ego from alter, are responsible for whatever comes between us. Since this responsibility can be forfeited – and in fact often is forfeited – we *are* largely unknown to each other: "The truth here is that we *are* separate, but not necessarily *separated* (*by* something)" (CR, 369). In making the knowledge of others a metaphysical difficulty, the skeptic rationalizes his disappointment about others; thus he denies "how real the practical difficulty is of coming to know another person, and how little we can reveal of ourselves to another's gaze, or bear of it" (CR, 90). In terms of the discussion of aspects and aspect-perception, the relevant point here is that aspects can fail to dawn. The aspect-blind is unable or unwilling to realize the significance of the other's expressions, make a connection with something in the world to which those expressions are responses. While conceiving of this as "a kind of illiteracy" (CR, 369), the failure to become aware of the other's expressions of herself is analogous to the way in which "something absolutely present may be invisible to us" (ibid). Just as the rabbit-aspect is hidden when what we see in the picture of the duck-rabbit is the duck-aspect, so what hides the mind is not the body but our attitude to it. The mind, in being blind to an aspect, hides it. Conversely, the other, as we have seen, may hide her mind by refusing to give it expression:

> If something separates us, comes between us, that can only be a particular aspect or stance of the mind itself, a particular *way* in which we relate, or are related (by birth, by law, by force, in love) to one

another – our positions, our attitudes, with reference to one another.
Call this our history. It is our present. (CR, 369)

If you and I can see one another, we can also be blind to one another.
Either we acknowledge our internal relation to one another or we
deny it. And if we deny it, it is a matter between you and me: I may
fail to grant you full existence, or you me. But can we speak sen-
sibly of a competing way, other than as giving expression to a
human soul, in which persons – or bodies – can be taken? Can we
be soul-blind? Obviously, if there are ways of regarding behavior
which do not amount to a recognition of humanity, we may assume
that our awareness that something is human can fail, or that it can
fluctuate, and that this may make enormous differences in the way
we behave, and justify our behavior, toward others. At this juncture
Cavell brings in two examples – the first of slaveowners trying to
deny the humanity of slaves, the other of antiabortionists calling the
embryo a human life. In both cases the issue is whether or not something – a body, an embryo – admits of being seen as human. The
slaveowner, on the one hand, cannot really *mean* that slaves are not
human. Everything in his relations with his slaves – his converting
them (but not horses) to Christianity, say, or tipping a black driver
instead of patting him – shows that he accepts that they are human
and not simply things on a par with stones or trees. Rather than tes-
tifying to a complete denial of humanity, the slaveowner sees slaves
as *a certain kind* of human being – a kind not deserving of justice.
What he denies, though, is his internal relation to these people; by
viewing himself as completely disconnected from their lives, indifferent to their miseries, "he takes himself to be private with respect
to them, in the end unknowable by them" (CR, 377). The anxiety in
the image of slavery is that humans can treat each other this way;
it is not that the humanity of humans can fade away completely.
The antiabortionist, on the other hand, also fails to be fully intelligible. The claim that the embryo is a human being may seem hollow
or empty in view of the fact that most of us look upon, say,
Herodian infanticide as being far more abhorrent than abortion. The
internal relation between human embryos and human beings
simply fails to strike us as obvious. That is not to say, however, that
the relation appears to be entirely spurious. While siding with the
pro-abortionists on this issue, Cavell finds himself attentive to a
sense of the human embryo as being *a human in embryo*. As a result,
the decision to have an abortion will never be easy, and, ultimately,
must be considered with reference to other facts about society – its
institutions, its capacity to support single mothers, etc.

What these examples demonstrate is that the extent to which we experience something as human depends not on its physical or mental features, but on our relation to it – the quality of our reciprocal stance. Therefore, if a skeptic points out that we lack conclusive reasons to rule out the fact that someone close to us might be a robot, then nothing of any consequence ought to follow for our relationship. Obviously, certain events, such as if I somehow discovered her inside to consist of intricate clockworks, might make me want to disqualify this human-like something from the class of humans. Yet if I were constantly on guard, expecting weird things of this kind to happen, then I would already have restricted my willingness to grant humanity. I would already have shut my eyes to the other.

At this point Cavell starts to unearth a set of asymmetries between skepticism with respect to the external world and skepticism with respect to other minds. For one thing, whereas external-world skepticism cannot be lived except on pain of psychosis, other-minds skepticism is descriptive of a constant possibility inflicting my condition as knower in relation to others. In order to get along in the world, I must forget that the best case of knowledge can fail me. I must accept, as Hume did when he went to play a game of backgammon after having undermined the credibility of his belief in the existence of the world, my life with objects – this tree, that stone – and live with that. With regard to others, however, I must remember the possibility of skepticism: that nothing other than my willingness to respond empathically to the other keeps the other alive to me, and thus that relations between us are restricted. We need therefore to live our skepticism. We have to recognize that "There is no possibility of human relationship that has not been enacted. The worst has befallen, befalls every day" (CR, 432). In short, we must be open to the possibility that my knowledge of others fails me, and that this knowledge, however restricted, might be all we shall ever possess in this area. Cavell does, however, think that we are entitled to talk about best cases of acknowledgment, though always as indexed to specific others in particular conditions. As we will see at the end of this chapter, if the acknowledgment of such specific others should happen to fail – as in Antony's withdrawal from Cleopatra in Shakespeare's *Antony and Cleopatra* – then not only is the other lost but the world itself recedes from the skeptic, or he from it. In these terms, external-world skepticism can be said to be an enactment of precisely the withdrawal of the world that is characteristic of other-minds skepticism.

But yet another asymmetry holds between the two forms of skepticism. In external-world skepticism, if a best case of knowledge fails, then all our knowledge of material objects will be affected: the doubt generalizes to all knowledge-claims. As we saw in chapter 2, while it was possible to uncover generic objects (and thus best cases of knowledge), the problem for the skeptic about the external world consisted in entering a claim to knowledge about such an object. Since a claim could not be entered, it followed that the skeptic was deprived of an assertion on which to focus his attack; hence the radical skeptic, though strictly speaking not refuted, was disarmed before he got started. In the case of other minds, however, the object occurring in the skeptical recital shows up a crucial difference to that of the generic objects in the external-world scenario. If I should happen to project humanness where it is not appropriate (a possibility that our ideas of mutants, automata, zombies, and so forth, give expression to), then that failure does not generalize to all other human-like beings. Only the humanity of this singular being right here in front of me would vanish. Cavell explains this point by referring to the different types of awareness that occur with regard to generic objects and human beings. In the first case, our knowledge receives justification from the fact that we *see* the thing in front of us (the tomato, say, or the chair). Seeing is the way we generally know things, so if sight fails us, we don't generally know things. In the second case, however, we do more than merely *see* the other. The empathic projection by which the existence of fellow human beings is recognized involves me in identifying *with* the creature I see. I *respond* to the other. The specific features of my relation to the other tell something about us, our relationship, yet this need have no implications for my acknowledgment of other people. The invocation of mutants would perhaps show that I can never be certain that I never make a projective error, but it would not be sufficient to establish that I am never right in projecting. Thus skepticism about other minds is restricted to you and me: no conceptual device exists that, analogous to the appeal to a generic object in external-world skepticism, is capable of generating global doubt.

Shakespeare and the Advent of Modernity

Since the completion of "The Avoidance of Love," concerning *King Lear*, in 1966–7, Cavell's sustained relationship to and interest in Shakespearean theater has been nourished by a number of mutually interrelated concerns. As will be traced in the remaining course of this chapter, his central and guiding intuition has been that tragedy (at least in its Shakespearean configuration) displays a skeptical structure. While studying various forms of skeptical doubt, he concluded that tragedy evolves from doubt's death-dealing complicity with denial, disappointment, and revenge. Conversely, skepticism itself – as Cavell aims to establish in the reading of *Othello* which comes at the end of the final part of *The Claim of Reason* – is intrinsically marked by its drive toward the tragic. Incapable of acknowledging that his words only voice the world if he accepts their human terms and conditions, the skeptic tragically finds himself, the world, and others to be withdrawn from each other and devoid of significance. But in addition to the overt thematic relationship forged between Shakespearean drama and skepticism, these literary analyses also occasion a fascinating inscription of skepticism within the culture of modernity.

According to Cavell, Shakespeare (along with Montaigne and Descartes) is perhaps the first major intellectual in Western history to have fully registered and responded to the early modern collapse of epistemic, moral, and political absolutes. Whereas skeptical schools of philosophy surely existed far back in antiquity, the issue posed in the sixteenth and seventeenth centuries is no longer "how to conduct oneself best in an uncertain world; the issue suggested is how to live at all in a groundless world" (DK, 3). By withholding belief upon the realization that every order is conventional and therefore without objective foundation, skepticism seems to be the inevitable response to such an absence. Obviously, the history of this "catastrophe" (DK, 20), which Hans Blumenberg has entitled "modernity's crisis of self-reassurance," would include an enormous panorama of fateful events.[10] Among other things, Cavell draws attention to "the rise of the new science; the consequent and precedent attenuation or displacement of God; the attenuation of the concept of Divine Right; the preparation for the demand for political legitimation by individual consent" (DK, 21). In all of these transformations a premodern vision of an objective, hierarchical order gets abandoned in favor of an anxious attempt at grounding knowledge, values, and norms with reference to human arrangements and consent alone.

Although the repudiation of criteria which takes place in and through skepticism is a ready option for anyone in possession of language, it is only with modernity's relentless critique of all appeals to impersonal, given foundations that skepticism announces itself as an adequate and seemingly natural response to the human condition. When the ordinary becomes disconnected, as it were, from an objectivist vision of a hierarchical order, it may be seen for what it is: a structure dependent on a fragile agreement in judgment which can easily be repudiated. But in Cavell's account, as we already know, with the possibility of skeptical denial there follows a realization of responsibility: the criterial links between oneself, the world, and others, though involving an acceptance of human finitude, can only be sustained on the basis of a commitment to their continuation.

Cavell's first major discussion of Shakespeare appears in his lengthy reading of *King Lear*, "The Avoidance of Love," which was first published in 1969. As indicated by the essay's title, Cavell finds avoidance or denial – i.e., skepticism – to constitute the central preoccupation of the play. Indeed, avoidance makes itself felt just about everywhere: in Gloucester's refusal to recognize Edmund as his legitimate son; in Cornwall's blinding of Gloucester so as not to be seen by him; in Edgar's failure to reveal himself to his father in Act IV; in Lear's unwillingness to be seen by Gloucester; and, most notoriously, in Lear's denial of his love for Cordelia in the fateful abdication scene in Act I. Among feelings that motivate misrecognition, Cavell registers Gloucester's shame (at being recognized as the father of a bastard) and Cornwall's guilt (his incapacity to bear his own cruelty). Moreover, Edgar hides his true identity from his maimed father as the result of his inability to face up to the symmetrical demands of adulthood. What Edgar desires, which casts an ironic light on his Christianity, is to "remain a child" (MWM, 285) and thus to be protected by a powerful father.

Yet the center stage of the analysis is occupied by Lear's troubled attitude toward Cordelia. While desperately needing and wanting Cordelia's love, Lear finds the claim or demand her love makes upon him threatening and fearful. Not only is it impossible to meet (and therefore unbearable, making him feel weak), but the realization that love involves dependence (on her love) strikes him as incompatible with his own cherished autonomy as king. The fact that a father's love for his daughter may seem to be verging on the incestuous, and that his love might therefore be forbidden, only adds to the worry. Overwhelmed by shame and fear of being shamed by the exposure of these feelings, Lear therefore arranges, in the opening scene with the three daughters, for Cordelia to publicly declare her love, thus asking her to make him look like a loved man, but without having to return it in kind. What he wants, then, is a statement that for all the world, yet without his acknowledg-

ment, establishes his belovedness. By offering her a bribe, he hopes
to escape the requirements which love exacts.

But Cordelia, who loves her father, cannot accept this. Rather
than offering, like her sisters, false love in return for Lear's rewards,
she chooses to remain silent. Only by refusing the dissimulated
expression of love that is expected of her, by keeping love secret,
can she continue, despite Lear's ruthlessness, to be responsive to
her own true feelings. Yet it is precisely her silence, threatening to
expose Lear and hence causing his fury, which sets off the tragedy
of *King Lear*. Lear's fatal predicament, in other words, is not that he
wonders whether Cordelia *really* loves him and seeks a proof.
Knowing that already, his problem is rather *to accept what he already
knows* – their mutual love and affection for one another – and to do
so by revealing himself to Cordelia. By failing to expose his dependence (and thus weakness), he rejects the one he loves *and* her
love for him. Like the skeptical epistemologist, who longs for the
world's presence to himself and yet avoids the world he already
knows, Lear, for the sake of possession, dispossesses himself of
what he already possesses. The play thus confirms Cavell's view of
everyday knowledge of others as exposed, rather than confined,
that "There is no possibility of human relationship that has not been
enacted" (CR, 432).

For Lear to acknowledge Cordelia would mean not only to reveal
his shameful feelings vis-à-vis her; it would also require a recognition of how he has distorted their relationship. He must, as Cavell
puts it, reveal "that he is her unjust banishing father" (CR, 429), that
is, confess his guilt through remembrance. Because of his failure to
do so, Cordelia's consequent death becomes an expression of spiritual justice, and therefore of hope: "Cordelia's death means that
every falsehood, every refusal of acknowledgment, will be tracked
down. In the realm of spirit . . . there is absolute justice" (MWM,
309). Despite appearances to the contrary, Cavell's appeal to an
essentially Christian logic of confession of guilt and forgiveness
should not, though, be taken to imply that he accepts the widespread description of *King Lear* as a Christian play. While "testing"
(not opting for) Christianity, one should not regard Cordelia's love,
as many commentators have done, as exemplifying that of Christ's
capacity for transfiguration and redemption; rather, in so far as
Cordelia resembles Christ,

> it is by having become fully human, by knowing her separateness,
> by knowing the deafness of miracles, by accepting the unacceptabil-
> ity of her love, and by nevertheless maintaining her love and the

whole knowledge it brings. One can say that she "redeems nature"
(IV, *vi*, 207), but this means nothing miraculous, only that she shows
nature not to be the cause of evil – there is no cause in nature which
makes these hard hearts, and no cause outside either. The cause is
the heart itself, the having of a heart, in a world made heartless. Lear
is the cause. Murderers, traitors *all*. (MWM, 302)

The notion of denial is also at the center of Cavell's interpretation of *Othello*, which forms the conclusion to *The Claim of Reason*.
Stirred by Iago's evil-minded suggestions, Othello, with a skepticism matching that of the Cartesian epistemologist, seeks an "ocular
proof" of Desdemona's virtue. Something has to be brought before
him, some absolute presence, that beyond all possible doubt can
establish her innocence. While craving to be absolutely certain that
she is not a whore, his doubt drives the tragedy forwards. When
presented, at the end, with evidence (the handkerchief, the sheets)
that fails to establish her innocence, he convicts her in the final
scene, thus causing her death.

The most striking aspect of Cavell's reading is his view that
Othello acts in bad faith. Othello's doubt is only a pretense, a "pro-
fessed doubt"; he neither *really* believes that Desdemona is guilty,
nor that good reasons might exist for thinking so. Both his conspicuous, desperate decision to put faith in Iago *and* his capacity to
elicit Desdemona's desire point to this assessment. But why does
Othello act on Iago's promptings if he knows them to be false?
Indeed, why would anyone want to cast doubt on, hence deny,
something they already know? Cavell's answer is that such a tor-
menting denial reflects Othello's reluctance to accept Desdemona's
independence or otherness: that she is a mortal creature of flesh and
blood, separate from him and yet in need. For if she is, then (since
they are one) so is he. Simply by existing, Desdemona challenges
Othello's idealized self-image, thus forcing him to face his own
sexuality and mortality. In Cavell's words,

> Nothing could be more certain to Othello than that Desdemona
> exists; is flesh and blood; is separate from him; other. This is precisely
> the possibility that tortures him. The content of this torture *is* the pre-
> monition of the existence of another, hence of his own, his own as
> dependent, as partial. (CR, 493)

Incapable of coming to terms with the human condition – its separateness, finitude, and fragility – Othello, like skeptics in general,

converts the condition of humanity into a riddle, an intellectual lack. And yet, as we know so far from the discussion in *The Claim of Reason*, the existence of a human being is not open to proof. Humans exist beyond the range of scientific evidence, beyond ocular proof. Behind such extreme scrupulousness and rationality, however, stands an unbearable fear of and disappointment with one's own bodily incarnation, which in the case of Othello drives him to take revenge.

In Cavell's more recent work, including his short yet important analysis of *Hamlet* (in DK, 179–91), the theme of the acceptance of separation, loss, and otherness, which has surfaced in both *King Lear* and *Othello*, gets explicitly linked to Freud's theory of mourning.[11] In his classic 1915 study of mourning and melancholia, Freud argued that "the work of mourning" should be viewed as a reaction to loss whereby libido is withdrawn from its attachment to the lost object. In a psychic struggle which can often be very painful to the subject, the ego is drawn between, on the one hand, its hyper-cathected memories and expectations of the object and, on the other, the need to detach its interests from those very same representations. When detachment is completed, "the ego becomes free and uninhibited again."[12] While adopting Freud's model of mourning, Cavell extends the scope, as it were, of its application. For Freud, mourning is essentially a response to a singular object-loss. The subject mourns in order to stay alive; ultimately, it is the narcissistic satisfaction derived "from being alive" which drives the work of mourning forward. Although he agrees with Freud's belief in the potentially life-saving power of mourning, for Cavell, the ability to sever one's attachments, to affirm the lost object's independence and transience, becomes a general condition of human existence. It is required for the autonomy of the individual, which forms the goal of a normal psychosexual development, to be possible: for without the acceptance of division and separation, hence mourning, there would be no individual.

In a second step, Cavell links this vision of individuality to Freud's claim that the psychosexual development of children is diphasic, involving not only a first phase of dependence, which culminates in the solution of the Oedipus complex, but also, having passed through a period of latency, a second one, puberty, whereby the individual acquires a much greater independence. In Cavell's terms, becoming a full individual involves both birth and rebirth – both a coming into being of biological existence and a mournful self-authorization of that same existence. What characterizes Hamlet, then, is first and foremost an unwillingness, or incapacity, to achieve a second birth, hence to become a separate individual. Rather than being a play about revenge, *Hamlet* studies the consequences of Hamlet's failure to mourn:

> I see Hamlet's question whether to be or not, as asking first of all not why he stays alive, but first of all how he or anyone lets himself be born as the one he is. As if human birth, the birth of the human, proposes the question of birth. That human existence has two stages – call these birth and the acceptance of birth – is expressed in religion as baptism, in politics as consent, in what you may call psychology as what Freud calls the diphasic character of psychosexual development. . . . To exist is to take your existence upon you, to enact it, as if the basis of human existence is theater, even melodrama. To refuse this burden is to condemn yourself to skepticism – to a denial of the existence, hence of the value, of the world. (DK, 187)

By mapping this set of thoughts onto Shakespeare's play, we see that Hamlet is locked in a double conflict. On the one hand, he is unable to disengage himself from his father's request for revenge, which, as we know, haunts him until the end. The all too willing acceptance of this demand, however, is expressive of a more fundamental urge, namely Hamlet's refusal to accept his father's *dependence* as a sexual being. In the eyes of his son, what the father in effect wants is for Hamlet to revive him sexually after having failed to elicit Gertrude's desire. Rather than rejecting this demand, which, according to Freud, would have been an important step in his own psychosexual maturation, Hamlet tries to revive his father in his own person. On the other hand, what is equally hard for him to accept is the fact of his mother's *independent* sexual being, her apparent abandonment both of her husband and of himself. (Indeed, Cavell considers for a moment the possibility that skepticism as such, and in particular external-world skepticism, might be interpreted as an intellectualization of the sense of loss involved in the infant's separation from the mother's body.[13]) Much of the evidence gathered in order to formulate this view is based on a reading of the play-in-the-play as representing what Freud, in his famous analysis of the Wolf Man, called a primal scene, that is, a fantasy of parental intercourse.[14] For Hamlet, however, what in particular marks this primal fantasy is Gertrude's active, even murderous, role. By considering the possibility that Gertrude, at least in Hamlet's imagination, is the murderer, or an accomplice in the murder, of Hamlet's father, Cavell arrives at the view that Hamlet, while feeling Gertrude's power "as annihilating of his own" (DK, 185), nevertheless is unable to liberate himself from her. He thus remains a dependent being, incapable of accepting the fact of her autonomy. Had he, however, been able to accept his mother's strength and independence, then he would also have been able to consider himself as separate from her, and hence view his own current situation as preventing self-development and autonomy. Like Lear and Othello, Hamlet fails to face up to his own knowledge. He lacks no facts, yet is incapable of acknowledging his knowledge: "Hence the play interprets the taking of one's place in the world as a process of mourning, as if there is a taking up of the world that is humanly a question of giving it up" (DK, 189).

Of course, what drives Hamlet along his tragic path is his desperate wish for revenge. Unable to see the world as beyond himself, he nostalgically wants it to stop, to have it as his own private property, as it were, so that it can be present to him without the need for his response and responsibility. Ultimately, however, this is the same as taking revenge on time and transience – the "It was." At this juncture, Cavell refers to Nietzsche, who in his later works was led to propose a reconception of time.[15] Any recovery from skepticism and nihilism would on this view need to find a position from within which the passing of time, with its threat of either mutability or continuation of the present, can be affirmed, rather than being met with by resentment and the call for revenge. And as Cavell emphasizes in several of his Shakespeare studies, as well as in the analyses of Hollywood drama, to which I turn in the next chapter, such an overcoming of revenge would be known as forgiveness and love. Intimacy requires the acceptance of otherness and distance.

Whereas Cavell's interpretation of *Hamlet* is of crucial interest in that it brings the notion of mourning to the center stage of his own thought, the final piece on Shakespeare to be considered, his reading of *The Winter's Tale*, which was first presented as the last of four Beckman lectures given at Berkeley in 1983, introduces yet another pathbreaking set of reflections. Confirming Cavell's general sense that skepticism tends to take the form of madness or insanity, Leontes, the main protagonist of *The Winter's Tale*, doubts whether his son is his. Such a doubt implies the fear that somebody else, some other man, could be the true father of his child; hence, like Othello, Leontes is jealous: he cannot come to terms with Hermione's, his wife, separateness from himself. Leontes thus experiences female sexuality as a challenge: Hermione is only his if he allows her to be his, that is, if he responds to her demands and elicits her desire; yet that is precisely what his death-bearing jealousy prevents. Rather than acknowledging that intimacy requires the granting of separateness, which would have initiated his recovery from skepticism, Leontes gets caught up in the tragic logic of revenge. While desiring oneness and unity, and thus possession, he drives his wife away.

As we know, criteria cannot be employed to settle the question of existence; all they do is make possible a conceptual space wherein questions of identity, the whatness of a thing, can be resolved. Consequently, when Leontes, in the hope of conclusively establishing fatherhood, starts applying various criteria to his son (such as comparing his son's head to his own, etc.), he finds them to be of no avail; ironically, the further he pushes his doubts, the less he makes sense of himself as a real father. Rather than succeeding in assuring himself of the world's existence and his presence to it, the world withdraws from his grasp. At the end of this process of Cartesian doubt, no one can convince him of anything, because having repudiated the attunement with others in criteria on which language depends, he "loses the ability to count, to speak (consecutively), to account for the order and size and pace of his experiences, to tell anything" (DK, 206). To speak, hence to tell, is to say what counts, but without acknowledgment, nothing counts, not even Leontes's son. Unsurprisingly, "What Leontes is suffering has a cure, namely to acknowledge his child as his, to own it, something every normal parent will do, or seems to do, something it is the first obligation of parents to do" (DK, 203). After the boy's death, recovery in *The Winter's Tale* inevitably takes the form of Leontes's acknowledgment of Hermione, of her life, including her children, beyond his. But such an acknowledgment, which can be viewed as a remarriage, a mournful reaffirmation of their union, presupposes Hermione's forgiveness of Leontes, and therefore also Leontes's acceptance of her forgiveness. Leontes's task is to expose himself to Hermione's claim on him, escape narcissism, allow himself to elicit her desire – *to be for her*. Only through remarriage, the responsive participation in its fragile constituency, can their union acquire the meaning and bindingness they both long for.

Skepticism and Gender

The Winter's Tale, then, displays all the essential features of Shakespearean skepticism: the forgoing of the world for the sake of it; the failure to accept human finitude and conditionedness, and the concomitant call for revenge; the destruction of the desired object; and, finally, the acknowledgment of separateness, the rejoicing in the world's return and one's own return to it. But in addition to moving through this by now fairly familiar terrain, Cavell employs his analysis of *The Winter's Tale* for the purpose of gathering evidence for the view that skepticism's repudiation of language might be inflicted by gender difference. Needless to say, if one considers Cavell's development, this move comes as a surprise. Before the mid-1980s, when the essay on *The Winter's Tale* was first published, Cavell had never, at least not in his writings, problematized his essential understanding of the logic of skepticism as a universalist predicament: since human language is inherently open to the repudiation of itself, it follows that skepticism may arise for all speakers. But in this essay he argues that skepticism may, at least to a large extent, be "a male business" (DK, 16). For part of what his reading of *The Winter's Tale* suggests, he argues, is that Leontes's mad, torturing suspicion that his children may after all not be his is not available to Hermione. Whereas a woman could have doubts, say, about the identity of her child's father, she clearly could not have them about who is the mother of her own child.

Of course, in the absence of more evidence, the ramifications of this argument do not extend very far. For one thing, its conclusion hinges on an extremely restricted representation of skepticism, namely whether your children really are yours; whereas what Cavell aims at is that skepticism *as such* bears a masculine inflection. While unwilling to retract the scope-claim of his hypothesis, but ready to present it as a speculative idea that may guide future research, Cavell concedes, however, that so far little of any general significance has actually been demonstrated. The only conclusion we are entitled to draw from *The Winter's Tale*, he admits, is that "*so far as* skepticism is representable as the doubt whether your children are yours, skepticism is not a feminine business" (DK, 16). For another thing, if one accepts the speculative hypothesis as worthy of further research, then it would seem that wanting to view skepticism, and hence philosophy (in so far as it is concerned with knowledge), as "a male business" potentially represents, to say the least, an act of illegitimate exclusion. As feminist critics and many others have pointed out, the history of Western philosophy abounds with reflections that portray women's intellect as inferior to, or at least different from, that of men, and where the opposition between men and women typically has been accounted for in terms of a naturalization of women's lesser autonomy: whether represented as creatures in thrall to nature, affects, or their role in biological reproduction, women's capacity for exercising intellectual independence has predominantly been viewed as constrained, not by social practices, but simply by their gender.

While fully aware of the possible pitfalls, indeed perversity, involved in the idea that skepticism, and hence philosophy, does not arise for women, Cavell registers several ways of circumventing the exclusion-objection. First, it is far from obvious, except on a rather narrow definition of philosophy's purpose, that the capacity for philosophical reflection rests on a readiness to doubt and deny. Thus, it could be, as Cavell often seems to imply, that a widespread conception of what philosophy, at least in the modern period, is and should be – namely to seek certainty in the face of doubt – needs revision. A related thought would then be that the inclusion of women in philosophy would tend to incur a change in the nature of the practice itself. Second and more significantly, Cavell does not commit himself to a naturalist view of gender. Rather than simply identifying the issue of skepticism versus assurance with *men* and *women* respectively, more precisely what he speaks of are "the masculine and feminine aspects of human character generally" (DK, 16). For Freud, whom Cavell refers to here, since (libidinal) object-choice turns out to be largely independent of biological sex, every biological man or woman, depending on the outcome of his or her complicated history of psychosexual development, may just as well develop feminine as masculine traits. Moreover, in so far as femininity and masculinity in Freud get associated with passivity and activity respectively, Cavell's point can be reformulated as stating that an intrinsic connection seems to hold, on the one hand, between masculine activity and skepticism, and, on the other, between feminine passivity and the overcoming of, or resistance to, skepticism.

The identification of passive femininity as inherently assuring and active masculinity as skeptical reverberates on a number of levels throughout Cavell's more recent work. First, the skeptic typically interprets the ambition of knowledge in terms of exclusive possession. As, for instance, the diagnosis of the so-called private language argument revealed, the skeptic, while anxious to avoid the costs involved in the logic of acknowledgment, interprets his drive to reach the unconditioned as seeking to appropriate and isolate an object so as to become, as Cavell puts it, "undispossessable" (DK, 10). Second, from the analysis of *Othello*, which studies the image of knowledge under the consequences of skepticism, we know that such a wish to possess typically expresses itself violently; it takes the form of jealousy. And, third, when the desire for knowledge gets conjoined with a jealous ambition to exclusively possess an object, then it becomes inevitable that knowledge itself is understood as a kind of domination. While alluding to Heidegger's diagnosis of the violence pertaining to human knowing in the age of technology, Cavell's favorite example is Kant, whose first *Critique* pronounces the acquisition of knowledge to require the employment of a set of invariant, object-neutral mechanisms of synthesis: "In Kant [the] concept of the concept is pictured as that of synthesizing things, putting together appearances, yoking them, to yield objects of knowledge" (DK, 9).

In contrast to the active, masculine picture of knowledge as an essentially aggressive appropriation and privatization of the object, a more passive, feminine approach entails a greater emphasis on receptiveness: on letting the object be as it is in its separateness from the knower, and on allowing oneself to respond to the specific claims made by the other or the object. Indeed, in *The Claim of Reason*, Cavell even speculates that in addition to talking generally, as we have seen, about an attitude toward a soul in terms of the appropriateness of my response, it could be that *each* individual type of thing, or perhaps each singular individual, requires a *specific* form of response:

> But why shouldn't one say that there is a required appropriateness with respect to each breed of thing (object or being); something appropriate for bread, something else for stones, something for large stones that block one's path and something for small smooth stones that can be slung or shied; something for grass, for flowers, for orchards, for forests, for each fish of the sea and each fowl of the air; something for each human contrivance and for each human condition; and, if you like, on up? For each link in the Great Chain of Being there is an appropriate hook of response. . . . Every thing, and every experience of every different thing, is what it is. (CR, 441–2)

As opposed to the object-neutrality and procedurality of masculine knowing, feminine knowing listens, reads, and responds adequately. In his readings of Emerson, Thoreau, and Heidegger, to which I will turn in the last two chapters, Cavell develops the notion of receptivity in a lot of detail. At this stage, however, it should be noted how the distinction between activity and passivity, as it maps on to the gendered character of knowledge, is thought of less as different types of prescription of how knowledge is possible than as different and ineradicable dimensions of human practice in general. Rather than recommending us to shift once and for all, as it were, to a more "feminized" way of dealing with objects and people, Cavell's main concern is to diagnose the temptations that haunt us when we do philosophy. Only on a skeptical interpretation of this predicament could there be a final arbitration in favor of one or the other dimension of the human mind. Another significant issue which comes out of his discussion of masculine versus feminine intimations of knowledge is that while a masculine passion toward the unconditioned, as we have seen, tends to express itself, at least in philosophy, as a drive toward "the given," and hence as doubt, a feminine passion toward the unconditioned expresses itself as love. Whether of a Cordelia or a Hermione, love unquestionably implicates the self in the existence of the other; by acknowledging (confessing) one's shared history as marked by whatever contingencies that have prevented recognition, love, while affirming separateness, simultaneously overcomes it. Alluding to Wittgenstein's "'But, if you are *certain*, isn't it that you are shutting your eyes in the face of doubt?' – They are shut" (PI, p. 224), Cavell, in one of the most beautiful passages in *The Claim of Reason*, links assurance (the shutting of eyes) to love: "To live in the face of doubt, eyes happily shut, would be to fall in love with the world. For if there is a correct blindness, only love has it" (CR, 431).

Theater and Theatricality

With a view to uncovering the conditions of his own work as a Shakespeare scholar, Cavell, in the final part of his essay on *King Lear*, calls into question the status of his own claims. More specifically, he asks how it can be that almost 400 years of Shakespeare scholarship have failed to generate or justify these insights (of denial and revenge); for rather than being obscure products of ingenious methods of research, their self-evidence seems glaring. Referring to Wittgenstein's later philosophy as involving "investigations of obviousness" (MWM, 312), he then suggests that the difficulty, as for Lear, consists not in acquiring knowledge or getting new information, but in taking in the facts, *acknowledging* what is already there on the page (or the stage). Taking this for granted, however, means – since *King Lear*, as we have seen, is all about denial – that the play, literally, as it were, presents us with its own conditions of reception. In other words, just as Lear may fail to acknowledge

Cordelia, so may we, as critics or spectators, fail to acknowledge what happens on the stage.

But this seems to be incompatible with our skeptical impulse to think that characters on a stage are fictional, that they do not exist in reality. For how can we acknowledge a fictional being? At best, it seems, all we can do is watch people play-acting; thus Othello is not *really* strangling Desdemona: what we observe is two actors *pretending* that a murder occurs. Cavell's retort to this objection, which plunges him straight into a grammatical discussion of the ontology of drama, consists in questioning the very ascription of non-factuality. Indeed, the assertion "they are only pretending" is empty when applied to the play itself; it can, however, be said to children, though not in order to help them focus on the play, but to help bring their attention away from it. What we (normal, educated, undrugged adults) see when we watch *Othello* is not someone pretending to strangle Desdemona – that would have been a different play; rather, we witness her actual strangling and subsequent death: it is there before us: "You tell me that woman will rise again, but I know that she will not, that she is dead and has died and will again die, die dead, die with a lie on her lips" (MWM, 328). But if that is true, why do we not run, like the yokel in the joke, on to the stage in order to save Desdemona? The yokel's mistake, Cavell submits, is not to have thought that Desdemona was being strangled; it is to have tried to *go up* to the characters, to *be* in Othello and Desdemona's presence. It is important to see why the spectator is excluded from the characters' presence. It is not because we cannot put ourselves in the presence of entities that are not to be met with in nature – not because these entities, after all, are fictional (if God, the spirit of the age, or the correct tempo of the Great Fugue do not exist, it is not because they are not to be met with in nature). Rather, as the darkened, indoor theater seems to emphasize, we, the spectators, do not exist in their world. Our spaces simply do not coincide: there is no path from the spectator to the character, hence also no distance. When the yokel rushes to the stage, he does not succeed in approaching Othello, for as soon as he reaches the stage, the characters will have vanished. The performance will be interrupted, and the yokel will not have been in the presence of the characters.

The impossibility of ever encountering the characters may seem to put Cavell's initial claim that characters can be acknowledged (and, conversely, fail to be so) in jeopardy. For how can we acknowledge someone in whose presence we can never be? Does not acknowledgment, as the reading of *King Lear* has made plain, presuppose precisely that we can reveal ourselves to the other, i.e., make ourselves present to him or her? Cavell's response consists in differentiating between different forms of acknowledgment. Rather than retracting the claim that characters can be acknowledged, he suggests that there is an essential asymmetry between us and them: although the spectators are in principle excluded from their presence, the characters are in the presence of the spectators. This means that we can see and hear them on their own terms, as it were. We can sense the malicious intent in her warning, or register the suppressed pain in his smile. (Or we can fail to acknowledge some of these features, as Cavell reproaches his fellow critics of *King Lear* for doing.) Given that the performance is successful, what happens on the stage is *alive*; it is expressive of humanity. And we do seem, in some way, to respond to a claim the characters make upon us. In particular, acknowledgment in a theater requires responding to each presented moment of the play's events as the present moment of its characters. To view the characters as people means to respond to them as responding to a world of concrete significance: what takes place on the stage, if fully acknowledged, is an encounter between a certain number of autonomous human beings in which each is exposed to the other, and each is confronted with the necessity of responding or failing to respond to the other as such a being. Although we cannot share the same space, we do share the same time.

However, Cavell maintains, the acknowledgment of characters, though not to be dismissed as an illusion, "cannot be *completed*" (MWM, 332). It cannot be completed – we already know why – because, as opposed to actuality, nothing would count as putting ourselves in the other's presence. Indeed, the condition of the theater may be seen as absolving me from the necessity of self-revelation, "to clean out the pity and terror which stand in the way of acknowledgment outside" (MWM, 333). Yet there is an analogue in the theater to self-revelation in the "real" world. Although the theater prevents us from the possibility of revealing ourselves to the characters as particular persons (nothing I tried to communicate to Cordelia about her significance to me and my life would count as saying anything to her), it allows us to reveal something general about ourselves:

> What I reveal is what I share with everyone else present with me at what is happening: that I am hidden and silent and fixed. In a word, that there is a point at which I am helpless before the acting and the

suffering of others. But I know the true point of my helplessness only if I have acknowledged totally the fact and the true cause of their suffering. Otherwise I am not emptied of help but withholding it. Tragedy arises from the confusion of these states. . . . In another word, what is revealed is my separateness from what is happening to them; that I am I, and here. It is only in this perception of them as separate from me that I make them present. That I make them *other*, and face them. (MWM, 338)

The conditions of theater *literalize*, make plain, the hiddenness, silence, and isolation which mark our everyday existence outside the theater. But by taking account of our theatricalizing, theater presents us with an arena within which this fact may be acknowledged. Thus, the theater, by individuating us through its address, exposes us to our own repressions; it puts our self-possession at stake; it unpacks us. And as such, theater may help us, as human beings or as citizens, to stop choosing silence and hiddenness, that is, to see that theatricality must be defeated. By potentially redeeming us from some species of mental bondage, it has, like psychoanalysis or ordinary language philosophy, a therapeutic function. Hence Cavell's ontology of Shakespearean theater might be regarded as an early version of his theory of redemptive reading.

4

Art and Aesthetics

From the earliest stages of his career, questions of art and aesthetics have been at the forefront of Cavell's philosophical reflections; and any attempt to draw a sharp divide between art and philosophy is bound to misrepresent his work. It is not as if Cavell should be seen as a philosopher merely interested in the arts; rather, the aesthetic dimension, which permeates so many of his writings, forms an intrinsic part of his own contribution to philosophy. Indeed, as the following autobiographical passage from *A Pitch of Philosophy* intimates, perhaps he is most adequately viewed as an artist or writer coming to philosophy as a later subject:

> When a few years ago I was asked to say how as a philosopher I had become interested in film, I replied by saying . . . that the inflection more pertinent to my experience was how a lost young musician had come to recognize his interests as philosophical, one whose education (in narrative, in poetry, in song, in dance) had been more formed by going to movies than by reading books. (POP, 131)

The present chapter will discuss how Cavell's texts on aesthetic themes feed off as well as into the philosophical work pursued in parallel to them.

Cavell's work in aesthetics may be crudely divided into three categories: studies on the nature of aesthetic judgment and modernism; essays and books on the ontology of specific artistic media; and concrete analyses of literature, drama, opera, and film. Corresponding, again roughly, to the early, middle, and late phases of his thinking, these sets of publications span a period of more than 30 years, from the first essays on formal problems of aesthetics, written in the mid-1960s, to the most recent work on cinematic melodrama. Throughout these writings there is a constant interchange of vocabulary and ideas between, on the one hand, problems of language and skepticism and, on the other, reflections on art. As will be traced in the course of this chapter, of particular importance in this respect are the interrelated notions of judgment, voice, modernism, presence, expressiveness, and denial.

Whereas the early work is quite academic, Cavell's interventions gradually become more political, more ethically oriented, and, undoubtedly, more playful. It also takes on a wider variety of types of cultural expression: from the initial focus on "high" art – Beckett, Schönberg, Shakespeare, and so on – it moves on, with great passion and respect, to cartoons, television, and, finally, Hollywood films. Blending criticism, autobiography, and philosophy, the responses to art, more than anything else, seem eminently to have released Cavell's distinctive voice and originality.

Aesthetic Judgment and Modernism

In the essay "Aesthetic Problems of Modern Philosophy," first published in 1965 and later collected in *Must We Mean What We Say?*, Cavell examines the rationality of aesthetic judgment. From chapter 1, we know that one of the most significant claims he makes in the context of this discussion is that aesthetic judgment "models" (MWM, 86) salient features of the judgments made by philosophers of ordinary language when they point to "what we say when and the implications thereof." Investigating the nature of aesthetic judgment may therefore clarify relevant aspects of ordinary language philosophy. While we should keep the heuristic purpose of his inquiry into the nature of aesthetic judgment in mind, the present aim is to focus exclusively on the nature of aesthetic judgment, and then to show how Cavell links the terms and conditions of art criticism to his views about modernism in the arts.

Cavell starts by considering David Hume's view, in "Of the Standard of Taste," that aesthetic judgments are non-cognitive.[1] Rather than making a claim to objective truth, such judgments are expressive of the speaker's taste, that is, of something inherently subjective and immediate. According to Cavell, the problem arising from Hume's empiricist account is that it dissociates the exercise of taste from the effort to account for it, and, as a result, the formation of an aesthetic judgment appears inscrutable and arbitrary. For without knowing *why* the judgment came out as it did, we seem prevented from distinguishing a genuine critic from a pretender, and hence the very idea of reconstructing the rationality of aesthetic judgments loses its point. Hume's reply to this kind of objection is that history will tell: the genuine critic, he argues, is the one who, in the long run, "will be acknowledged by universal sentiment to have a preference above others."[2] Cavell quickly dismisses this appeal to agreement, which in his view makes the critic's worth overly reliant on popularity. A critic's achievement cannot consist simply in conforming with the demands of his culture; rather, of a genuine critic we expect that "he sets the terms in which our tastes, whatever they happen to be, may be protected or overcome" (MWM, 87).

But how is this possible? How can the genuine critic be said to produce judgments that are indeed conclusive and rational? In order to throw more light on this problem, Cavell turns to Kant, who commences his analysis in the *Critique of Judgment* by considering the possibility that aesthetic judgments may carry the same objectivity as the ones we find in science or logic. The problem with this suggestion, however, is that it fails to consider the specific types of reason that can be offered in aesthetic contexts. As opposed to straightforward cognitive judgments ("milk contains calcium," "2 + 2 = 4"), aesthetic judgments cannot claim universal agreement on the basis of impersonal reasons. If someone claims about a work of art that it is "successful" or "beautiful," or, say, about a poem that one of its words alludes to a passage in Shakespeare's *The Tempest*, then although such judgments demand or impute general validity (universal agreement), it would make no sense to hold that the case can be settled, as in science or logic, by appeal to impersonal reasoning. Nobody can be forced to recognize an aesthetic property by virtue of rules, facts, or principles, hence there can be no science of the beautiful. Aesthetic judging, then, cannot take place in the complete absence of subjective response. The critic needs to express her views by reference to her own reactions. However, aesthetic judgments should not be confused with judgments about the merely pleasant ("wine x is better than wine y"). As opposed to judgments of personal preference, aesthetic judgments do make genuine claims to validity, even when we know from experience that people often tend to disagree. For, as Kant maintains, to qualify the attribution of beauty to an object by saying that it is so merely *for me* would be a misapplication of the concept "beautiful"; it would fail to respect the difference between judgments of personal taste and aesthetic judgment. Upon realizing that their empirical preferences differ, people may meaningfully note this and in various ways perhaps make it consequential (for example, by always avoiding wine x when A comes to dinner). But what is thereby observed would simply be certain *facts* about the persons involved. And as mere facts, there is no room for further discussion with a view to rebutting the view of the other. Or, rather, one may discuss matters of personal opinion, but it is perfectly legitimate to break off simply by stating one's preference. Reasons do not really count here; they cannot lay claim to anything. According to Cavell, what distinguishes the grammar of aesthetic judgments from that of judgments of personal taste is that the former allow the formation of *arguable* reasons. A genuine critic is capable of expressing in relevant ways *why* one conclusion is to be preferred over another, and of recognizing and responding to competently entered objections. Therefore, qua rational practices, both logic and science, on the one hand, and art criticism, on the other, rely on engagement in shared patterns of support, rather than agreement in conclusions. Competence in these fields is essentially a matter of knowing how to apply the right reasons. But reason-giving in science or logic differs from that of art criticism: for whereas the former types of reason are designed to guarantee agreement over the conclusion among those who are competent, the latter types of reason do not guarantee such agreement. Obviously, Cavell does not want to deny that aesthetic judgments may elicit agreement. Without the *possibility* of reaching agreement in conclusions about aesthetic matters, art criticism could hardly lay any claim to rationality. His contention is rather that whereas qualified practitioners of science and logic are forced to *rule out* as incompetent those who disagree with any legitimately supported conclusion, in aesthetics, disagreement with a legitimately supported conclusion *does not count* as a criterion of incompetence.

Cavell explains the difference by suggesting that taking art seriously implies taking one's own response to the object-specific dimensions of the artwork into account. No general a priori aesthetic principles can ever unburden the critic of the requirement that qualified judgments about art must be anchored in the critic's own response to the particular features of the concrete object. Thus, "The problem of the critic, as of the artist, is not to discount his subjectivity but to include it; not to overcome it in agreement but to master it in exemplary ways" (MWM, 94). A good art critic is engaged in honestly articulating his or her own experience, and in so doing in tracing the degree of attunement and commonality there might be between herself and others. The art critic, like the philosopher of ordinary language, while establishing the vertical relation to the object, at the same time explores the horizontal depth of our mutual alignment, our agreement in judgments. At times, though, such demands for acceptance will inevitably run out of definite reasons. Then the task of the critic becomes to invite others to share his or her *way of seeing*:

> It is essential to making an aesthetic judgment that at some point we be prepared to say in its support: don't you see, don't you hear, don't you dig? The best critic will know the best points. Because if you do not see *something*, without explanation, then there is nothing further to discuss. (MWM, 93)

In "Music Discomposed," another central essay on aesthetics, Cavell further suggests that "about works of art one may wish to say that they require a continuous seeing of the point" (MWM, 191). In trying to have the other see what I see, I must lead her to feel what I feel, and know what I know *in* sensing the work. Knowing in this area is thus less a matter of getting the facts right than it is of obtaining the right attitude. Although he does not explicitly draw the connection, the underlying theme which Cavell invokes in order to throw light on these matters is Wittgenstein's conception of aspect-perception. Just as acknowledging the other as a mindful being presupposes the capacity to perceive aspects, so relating correctly to a work of art must be understood in terms of taking up a specific attitude to it. Unless one is able to adopt a specific expressive attitude to the seen, manifest in a range of techniques and behavioral patterns, the artwork simply will not speak: there would be nothing to respond to.

Hence, every critic faces the problem of communicating his or her experience, a point that has great ramifications for the teachability of art. Learning to appreciate art emerges as radically different from learning mathematics, where the criterion of understanding consists in being able to correctly apply a set of rules. To use Cavell's favored expression in *The Claim of Reason*, the evidence that comes into question when dealing with works of art tends to remain "imponderable": it cannot be stated directly; hence, "the mark of a good teacher in certain domains [is] to know when to stop prompting, domains in which further knowledge is earned not through further drilling but through proper waiting" (CR, 358–9). Following this line of thought, in *A Pitch of Philosophy*, Cavell, evoking the methods employed by his erstwhile teacher of music, the composer Ernest Bloch, offers an illuminating illustration, worth quoting in full, of the anxieties and difficulties involved in such a process:

[Bloch] would play something simple, at the piano, for instance a Bach four-part chorale, with one note altered by a half step from Bach's rendering; then he would play the Bach unaltered. Perhaps he would turn to us, fix us with a stare, then turn back to the piano and repeat, as if for himself, the two versions. The drama mounted, then broke open with a monologue which I reconstruct along these lines: "You hear that? You hear the difference?" His voice was surprisingly unresonant and sounded pressed with the labor of excitement, an exotic effect increased by his accent, heavily French, but with an air of something else. He went on: "My version is perfectly correct; but the Bach, the Bach is perfect; late sunlight burning the edges of a cloud. Of course I do not say you must hear this. Not at all. But." The head lowered a little, the eyes looked up at us, the tempo slowed ominously: "If you do not hear it, do not say to yourself that you are a musician. There are many honourable trades. Shoe-making for example." (POP, 49–50)

Obviously, such invitations, based as they are on attraction and promise rather than power or authority, may be denied. But as opposed to the automatic expulsion that would take place in the scientific community, the typical risk run by not finding acceptance in the domain of art is separation: in discussing art, we may quickly find ourselves strangers to each other.

For Cavell, an important part of what the onset of modernism in the arts means is that the condition of mutual estrangement has been generalized to become an intrinsic feature of what art calls for and represents. Modernism in the arts signifies a condition whereby art has become *estranged* from itself and its audience, and over the last 100–150 years, indeed since the late Beethoven, the production and reception of art has entered a phase in which all previous conventions have been questioned. With the onset of modernism, tradition, taste, and past achievement no longer function as self-evident sources of authority. This sets modern artists apart from premodern(ist) artists, who generally could rely on undisputed conventions about their art. Cavell is not claiming that their art just *reflected* these agreements. Obviously, no successful premodern artist could proceed simply by copying past masters: in whichever way one understands it, originality has always been a mark of good art. His point is, rather, that premodern artists, as opposed to modern ones, did not have to reinvent or radically rethink the most basic terms and conditions of their art as such. Rather, a prior and tacit agreement existed between the artist and the audience on what constituted, say, a successful painting or piece of music. Thus, by conforming to conventions, the artist was assured of an audience. Conversely, the audience essentially knew what to expect; there was no room for total surprise or estrangement.

For Cavell, the "severe burden" of modernism means that as conventions lose their authority, art explicitly becomes a problem for itself. No longer is there an undisputed agreement as to what art is as such, nor as to what the purpose and meaning of the individual arts might be, that is, what *kind* of object, say, a sculpture is. "What modernist painting proves is that we do not know a priori what painting has to do or be faithful to in order to remain painting" (WV, 106). In this condition, everything concerning art is, as it were, up for grabs. Thus for the artist, "The problem is no longer how to do what you want, but to know what would satisfy you" (MWM, 201). The artist needs to justify and express the terms according to which she proceeds. Art has reached a state of radical autonomy, and it is only by reflecting upon the limits and essence of its own procedures that it can continue to exist: "what a painter or poet or composer has to achieve in his painting or poetry or music is not a landscape or sonnet or fugue, but the idea of his art as such" (WV, 106).

The thesis about art's discovery of autonomy as the defining moment of its own condition of possibility is brimful with implications. One is that art criticism becomes increasingly significant. Indeed, under the conditions of modernism, when knowledge of what constitutes an object as genuine art can no longer be taken for granted, the critical impulse, from having exclusively expressed the audience's need for orientation and assessment, becomes internal even to artistic production itself: the artist must create her work in a mode of radical self-reflection. The numerous programs of high modernism – from Wagner's essays to Breton's surrealist manifestoes and Schönberg's theory of 12-tone technique – readily testify to an awareness that "the artist's survival depends upon his

constantly eluding, and constantly assembling, his critical powers"
(MWM, 208).

A second and related implication is that an authentic artwork
produced under modernist conditions necessarily will be engaged
in exploring the conditions of possibility of its own existence as an
artwork. Modernist art therefore tends to be focused on its own
medium or medium-specificity.[3] Thus, Anthony Caro's sculptures,
to use Cavell's example, are made in search of an understanding
of what sculpture *is*; and rather than presupposing some sort of
knowledge of what makes an object into a sculpture, his work critically explores the conditions of the art of sculpturing. Does a sculpture have to be *worked* (carved, chipped, etc.), or can it be made up
of *ready-made* elements? Does it have to be spatially continuous, or
can it be dispersed and discontinuous? Does it have to have a base,
or can it rest on the ground? These are questions about what it takes
for an object to count as a sculpture. Viewed from the perspective
of ordinary language philosophy, Caro can thus be said to investigate the *grammar* of the concept of sculpture, or rather the criteria
by means of which an object qualifies as a sculpture. Caro displays,
one might say, an interest in the *essence* of his art (cf. Wittgenstein:
"*Essence* is expressed by grammar" (PI, §371)). Likewise, modernist
painting, in its self-reflexivity, has been characterized by an uncom-
promising orientation toward its own essential condition of two-
dimensionality or flatness, as opposed to the representationalism of
premodern illusionist painting. In the absence of acknowledged a
priori criteria for defining a specific art form, art thereby keeps faith
with the tradition by examining those limits and conditions within
which even traditional art, though without full awareness of it
being the case, was conceived. Hence, modernist art does not so
much break with the past as continue the past by questioning it.
Its innovations dialectically and productively relate to its own
traditions.

As a result, work which fails to engage with its own history
as an art form, and which dismisses the concern with medium-
specificity, falls short of the seriousness required to continue its own
art. Cavell here draws attention to pop art, which in its disavowal
of high modernism's quest for autonomy simply fails to qualify as
art. Although highly controversial on its own terms, such a claim is
not meant to question the value or relevance of pop art; all it intends
is to question its dominant self-definition.[4] Another example of a
modern yet not modernist, and hence, in Cavell's account, unsatis-
factory or inauthentic artistic self-interpretation, is to be found in

the serialist composer Ernst Krenek's program of total musical organization. Responding to the crisis in tonality that grew out of chromaticism and culminated in the innovations of Schönberg, Bartok, and Stravinsky, Krenek argues that the traditional conception of composition as a creative act should be replaced by a procedure according to which every aspect of musical transformation should be generated by fixed matrices. Whereas the adoption of rules relies on choice, the outcome, though often unexpected (because unpredicted), is generated on the basis of strict necessity: for, once a set of rules are in place, everything else happens automatically, and no room for individual responsibility exists:

> What in fact Krenek has come to distrust is the composer's capacity to feel any idea as his own. In denying tradition, Krenek is a romantic, but with no respect or hope for the individual's resources; and in the reliance on rules, he is a Classicist, but with no respect or hope for his culture's inventory of conventions. (MWM, 196)

In short, Krenek fails to take seriously the appeal to responsibility that follows from the modernist discovery of the groundlessness of art. For conjoined with the idea that contemporary art is bound to remain constantly in search of its own self-definition is the notion that the individual artist must be accountable for every aspect of her work. An authentic modernist artwork must therefore be *meant* and intended. It is *as meant* by an individual who takes responsibility for everything that happens in it that an artwork today can unashamedly draw our attention to its modernity. Thus artworks are to be seen as human gestures. Their *presentness*, their hereness and nowness, must be absolute: hence modernist artworks, as exemplified by post-Pollock painters such as Olitski, Stella, and Noland, strive toward simultaneity and instantaneousness.[5] Only through unrestricted exposure can the artist achieve sincerity and thus complete self-authorization. It may of course be that the artist finds that her art fails to reach the desired level of seriousness, but, if so, no compromises can be made. Not to be accountable for everything in the work is, under modernist conditions, equivalent to failure. Endemic to modernism is therefore the possibility of fraudulence: since artistic reflection must encompass every aspect of the work, all modernist art is haunted by the possibility that it may just be a waste of time. Nothing, no rules or conventions or expectations, can insure from the outset that the work is genuine. Therefore, only acknowledgment and trust, together with the knowledge that one may be betrayed, can expose us to the full impact of such a work of art.

While emphasizing the notion of intention, Cavell is well aware of the misunderstandings to which it may lead. For one thing, by referring to the artist's intention, he is not implying that the meaning of symbolic expressions is a function of what we intend them to mean. Nor is he claiming that knowing the meaning of a work presupposes access to a purely mental or psychical domain, existing apart from the actual expression. Rather, what an artist intends is nothing more than that which we encounter when we watch, read, or listen to the work itself. This does not imply, though, that the artist necessarily is in full control of every aspect of her expressions: she may retrospectively be surprised by the occurrence of a particular note, brush stroke, or word. Yet surprises of this sort (involving happy accidents, fortunate mistakes, and so on), though they do occur, are usually exceptional. Moreover, if the artist recognizes a mark as hers in the sense that she later can say that though she wasn't explicitly aware of making it at the execution of the work, it definitely reflects what she wanted, or should have wanted, to happen, then she is indeed responsible. Thus, even though one may not have been aware of what happened as intended when it actually did take place, in art it is possible to *become* aware, to retrospectively try the intention on oneself. This is different from a man who unknowingly kills someone by firing a gun. Whereas the latter can *be told* what has happened, the artist can reflectively approach her own work and thereby recognize her own responsibility for it. Unlike games, where intention does not count because what one is responsible for is fixed a priori by the rules of the game, art condemns man to total sincerity. While practitioners need to earn their right to be recognized as artists, once a work has been presented, there is nowhere to hide: the point or position they articulate in expressing themselves defines not only who they are as artists, but proves, in so far as it is theirs, the extent to which they exist as artists at all.

The Ontology of Film

In *The World Viewed* (1971), Cavell sets out to explore the nature of film. As opposed to his two subsequent studies of cinema, *Pursuits of Happiness* (1981) and *Contesting Tears* (1996), which offer analyses of particular cinematographic genres, *The World Viewed* essentially aims at uncovering what Cavell calls the ontology of film, i.e., the specific conditions according to which film is constituted as an artistic medium.

In comparison with the other arts, especially the ones discussed in *Must We Mean What We Say?* (music, literature, painting, and sculpture), film, though historically a *hyper-modern* art, has to a very limited extent been a *modernist* art. With the exception of the films of Bergman, Antonioni, Fellini, Godard, Resnais, and some other experimental work of the 1960s, the cinema has tended, as Cavell puts it, to be "absorbed in its own conventions" (WV, 15). Rather than assuming the burden of seriousness associated with modernist art practices, the history of cinema has largely been characterized by an unquestioned faithfulness to specific audiences, genres, and types. Indeed, it seems far from obvious that film, which traditionally has been produced by an industry oblivious to the problems of modernism and bent on meeting the unreflected expectations of its audiences, should even be thought of as an art form at all. Yet, as the directors mentioned above serve to demonstrate, it does, in at least some of its manifestations, seem to make a legitimate claim to be taken seriously as an art form. This tension needs to be accounted for. One way, then, of formulating the aim of *The World Viewed* would be to say that it seeks to contribute to cinema's own, however belated, self-reflection and self-awareness. This is in line with Cavell's Kantianism: autonomy is the telos of modernism. Moreover, understanding the medium, as we will see, shows how film can be viewed as a metaphor or image of skepticism: film is, as it were, an enactment of the skeptic's self-interpretation.

So what is film? What is its grammar – or, rather, what are its criteria? Cavell starts addressing this question by quoting Erwin Panofsky: "The medium of the movies is physical reality as such."[6] While finding Panofsky's realist intuition promising, Cavell quickly goes on to correct it by pointing out that, if taken literally, this would mean that the cinema, like formal gardens or *tableaux vivants*, simply *is* a physical object, which is absurd. The thrust of Panofsky's remark (as well as similar ones in the writings of other realist theorists such as André Bazin and Siegfried Kracauer[7]) would be better preserved if taken to imply that since our experience of any film is an experience of a projected sequence of photographic images, the basis of the medium of movies must be photographic, and as such films are "*of* reality or nature" (WV, 16). In order to understand the medium of cinema, we must therefore examine the nature of photographic images, and in particular the relation between photographs and that which they depict.

Of great significance to Cavell's realist account of photography is his view that, unlike paintings, photographic images present us "with the things themselves" (WV, 17). Like photographs, paintings can be visual representations of an object, but whereas paintings present us with a "likeness" of what they depict, photographs present us with the things as they are without any kind of intermediary. Thus a painting of a house offers a likeness of a house, while a photograph of a house offers the house itself. Although seemingly straightforward, this reference to "things themselves" is fraught with difficulties. On the one hand, the idea that "photographs present us with things themselves" seems clearly false: a photograph of an earthquake is not an earthquake happening. But, on the other hand, it would be equally false or misleading to point to a photograph of an earthquake and say, "That is not an earthquake." In response to this impasse, Cavell elaborates the connection between the photograph and what it is of by comparing it to recordings of sound. While similar in that both photographs and auditory transcriptions represent something, the two processes show up crucial differences that help to highlight the nature of photography. For if we compare the kind of transcription taking place in photographs to that of recordings of sound, we realize that whereas the latter is capable of *copying* a sound, that is, reproducing it perfectly, a photograph cannot be said to reproduce its object. The auditory transcription is, in other words, an intermediary between us and the object: it presents or copies the *sound* of the object, say a horn or a train, rather than the object itself. Moreover, it is always possible to say that we hear the "sound" of a horn. Its sound can be separated from the object emitting it. In the case of vision, however, the analogy does not work. It would be impossible to say of a visual transcription that it reproduces or copies the sight that the photographer and his camera once faced when taking the shot. The reason for this is that a sight *is* an object; the sight is *that* X (the Empire State Building, Garbo, and so on) which was seen by the photographer. Thus when something is sighted, it is the object itself, and to reproduce, say, the Empire State Building would mean to rebuild the building itself. Although objects can make sounds, they cannot produce sights, or have sights – that is, something that can be reproduced mechanically – which means that a photograph, to be *of* something, must be *of* the object, rather than the sight of it. In visual experience, then, there is no intermediary that can be detached from the object itself and be reproduced: a photograph of the Empire State Building presents us with the Empire State Building.

One might feel that this cannot be true. Obviously, the real Empire State isn't *there*, in my photograph. A possible way of salvaging the idea that photographs reproduce the sight of objects might be to revert to a phenomenalist language and suggest that photographs provide the sense-data of the objects they contain. The problem with this hypothesis, however, is that if the sense-data of photographs were identical with the sense-data of the objects depicted, then we would not be able to tell a photograph of an object apart from the object itself. Anything standing in the way of or being substituted for the object simply will not do. Objects give themselves, not appearances, in photographs. It is the objects we see. And yet, in giving themselves, they leave something crucial behind, namely their existence. What we see in the photograph does not exist in the time and space of its viewing. The perceived identity between the photographic image and what it depicts reflects Cavell's view that criteria do not settle the question of existence: the only difference between genuine and faked or acted emotion, as we remember from *The Claim of Reason*, is one of existence.

Ultimately, we need to combine both the claim that a photographed object *is not* present to the viewer as it once was to the camera (a photograph of the Empire State Building is not the existing Empire State Building) *and* the claim that the photographed object *is* present in the photograph (we can point to the Empire State Building in a photograph of the Empire State Building). By way of underlining this point, Cavell argues that it is always possible to ask of an area depicted in a photograph what lies beyond the frame (this has an intelligible answer), whereas paintings generally do not allow such a question. The two types of frame, then, have different ontological implications. The world of a painting finds "its limits" (WV, 24) at its frame; thus, a painting *is* a world. The world of a photograph, however, has *no* limits – it is an implied and indefinite presence; what comes to an end is not the world but the photograph itself. While painting emphasizes the *identity* of its object (*this* is what X looks like), photography emphasizes the reality of *a portion that has been cropped from an indefinitely larger field*. Rather than extending the senses, as is commonly believed, the camera confines them: "A camera is an opening in a box: that is the best emblem of the fact that a camera holding on an object is holding the rest of the world away" (WV, 24).

We have seen that the object viewed in the photograph does not exist (here and now). Closely related to this is the fact of *our absence from it*. Photography, in its peculiar mode of objectivity, presents us with a reality to which we are not present. The principal reason why photography escapes subjectivity in this way is its *automatism*. The photographic image has not come into being by virtue of human intervention; it is not handmade but mechanically produced through the causal interaction of the light emitted from the physical object and the camera (lens and film). "For the first time," a critic writes, "an image of the world is formed automatically, without the creative intervention of man."[8] Indeed, photography and film, by mechanically assuring our absence from the world, unburden the subject of the task or act of responding to and representing it. Photography thus satisfies an intrinsically modern and skeptical wish to maintain the presentness of the world while escaping the burden of representing it. Like the skeptic in *The Claim of Reason*, when we look at photographs or films, we view the world *as*, or as if it were, an image; what we take to be the world as it is given to us is but an image of it. But the world as image is *ipso facto* not *our* world: it is a world that does not exist – except as past. In short, film is a moving image of skepticism:

> So far as photography satisfied a wish, it satisfied a wish not confined to painters, but the human wish, intensifying in the West since the Reformation, to escape subjectivity and metaphysical isolation – a wish for the power to reach this world, having for so long tried, at last hopelessly, to manifest fidelity to another. (WV, 21)

In Kantian terms, photography figures as the answer to a desire for intellectual intuitions – for being in touch with an absolute reality in the absence of all human constraints. The title of Cavell's book – *The World Viewed* – is in this respect meant to allude to Heidegger's reading of Descartes' model of vision in "The Age of the World View."[9] On Heidegger's reading, the Cartesian subject of modern science and technology is not as such – i.e. as a subject – open to the world; rather, like a camera, it simply transcribes the visually given – the light rays hitting the retina – and transforms it into an image. From a romanticist point of view, however, such a vision of reality – the radically disenchanted world of modernity, the world as *viewed* – presents us with a silent and ultimately unin-habitable and meaningless world: a world lost.

Although Cavell conceives of film as a moving image of skepti-cism, he does not claim that it necessarily reflects a skeptical atti-tude. To the extent that the fact of automatism is acknowledged, the cinema is able to display a drift toward the world as it is apart from the image. After all, the photographic image, although nothing more than an image, is an image of reality, so by revolting against illusion, as certain modernist directors have done, it is capable of letting the world call attention to itself, independently of its enfram-ing, or, as Cavell writes, "to let the world happen, to let its parts draw attention to themselves according to their natural weight" (WV, 25). Directors who have explored this possibility include Dreyer, Flaherty, Vigo, Renoir, and Antonioni.

This is all very different from painting, which, as we remember, represents the world on the basis of "likeness" rather than passive transcription. Of course, the history of painting – the increasing level of abstraction from Manet to the abstract expressionists – seems to belie the view that painting predominantly has been obsessed with likeness. However, as Cavell points out, in their desire to capture their objects – the way things are and *that* they are – advanced painters, while gradually having lost conviction in the traditional techniques of perspectival representation, were forced to forgo likeness and adopt new and more radical techniques. Yet for-going likeness and objective reference does not necessarily imply that painting no longer responds to reality. Although modernist painting and reality do not "assure" each other (the *look* of nature is no longer interesting to most painters), in the works of color-field painters such as Louis, Noland, and Olitski, Cavell detects the attempt to achieve a "higher objectivity." What these painters aim at is nothing less than the uncovering of nature's "conditions, the possibilities of knowing nature at all and of locating ourselves in a world" (WV, 113). In their works, the world is acknowledged as independent and autonomous; in overcoming the skeptical refusal to grant existence and presence to the object (which Cavell has analyzed in *The Claim of Reason*), they "release nature from our private holds" (WV, 114). In doing so, however, they simultaneously allow *our* presence to the world.

Like romanticism in general, painting, by acknowledging the independent existence of the world, is thus able to reintroduce sub-jectivity (and criteria) "as the route back to our conviction in reality" (WV, 22):

Perhaps romanticism can be understood as the natural struggle between the representation and the acknowledgment of our subjectivity (between the acting out and the facing off of ourselves, as psychoanalysts would more or less say). Hence Kant and Hegel; hence Blake secreting the world he believes in; hence Wordsworth competing with the history of poetry by writing out himself, writing himself back into the world. A century later Heidegger is investigating Being by investigating *Dasein* (because it is in *Dasein* that Being shows up best, namely as questionable), and Wittgenstein investigates the world ("the possibilities of phenomena") by investigating what we say, what we are inclined to say, what our pictures of phenomena are, in order to wrest the world from our possessions so that we may possess it again. (WV, 22)

We will return to the issue of romanticism in chapter 6. At the moment I want to call into question the assertion that film, though naturally drawn toward the ordinary and everyday, escapes subjectivity. Is it true that films always represent reality in such a way that we are forced to accept their subjects as having a reality independently of the films in which they appear – a reality from which we as viewers are excluded? In the first place, Cavell's claims seem at best to apply to some films, but not to all. While they may apply to a production such as Andy Warhol's 24-hour-long single take of one side of the Empire State Building, they seem a lot less illuminating of most feature films (not to speak of movies dealing purely with the imaginary or fantastic), in which narrative illusion is generated by a vast amount of technology in addition to that of the bare causal relation between lens and object. While not exactly denying the facts of montage, lighting, camera movement, backgrounds, acting techniques, and so on, Cavell fails to take into account how the director's unfolding and combination of all of these means of her art go to make up the style, atmosphere, and specific quality of a movie – all being "subjective" dimensions of the art of film-making. It is certainly true that with the exception of animated films (or, more recently, computer-animation, which undoubtedly challenges Cavell's causal criterion), the lens inevitably plays a role in the making of a film: in that very weak sense the causal efficacy of objects does serve to underwrite their physical existence. Yet the causal requirement is not sufficient to constitute anything being "a photograph of" something. Whatever caused the parts of Babylon we see in Griffith's *Intolerance*, it cannot have been the "real" Babylon, but rather the studio with all its techniques for creating illusion, and there is no point in asking what parts of Babylon lie beyond these images. What lies there is Los Angeles, hence nothing has been excluded.[10] At times, Cavell responds to objections of this kind by suggesting that what technique shows, in so far as it helps to generate cinematic illusion, is simply "the inescapability of reality" (WV, 191) as a fixed point in all film-making. The problem with this is that it undermines the difference between film and other arts that are capable of employing realist conventions, say, certain types of (landscape or portrait) painting or realist literature. In all forms of artistic realism, a sense of reality remains inescapable, yet the idea that film, due to its causally induced "this is how it was," displays a privileged and thoroughly objective relation to reality would then lose its weight.

While Cavell's defense of realism seems too restrictive to serve as a general, binding definition of the screen's true nature, *The World Viewed* contains numerous other claims, some of them of great power and insight. Of specific relevance to his next two books on the subject is the assessment of film as an inherently democratic medium: in feature films, social role appears arbitrary or incidental. As opposed to the stage, where actors work themselves into a role that allows us to witness a character (King Lear, Nora), the screen presents us with the actor, not as an ordinary empirical human being but, mythically, as a star or a type (Bogart, Garbo): "After Paul Scofield's performance in *King Lear*, we know who King Lear is, we have seen him in flesh. An exemplary screen performance is one in which, at a time, a star is born" (WV, 28). Let us now turn to Cavell's reading of some of these performances.

The Hollywood Comedy of Remarriage

Whereas Cavell's early study of the ontology of film links skepticism to the problem of medium, his two subsequent contributions to film study, *Pursuits of Happiness* and *Contesting Tears* (as well as almost half of the essays contained in *Themes Out of School*), examine skepticism in terms of possibilities of human existence exemplified by actors or stars in two distinct genres of Hollywood drama: "the comedy of remarriage" and the "melodrama of the unknown woman." The shift of attention from general questions of medium to more specific ones of content, or from the ontological ("What is film?") to the existential level ("How is the life of men and women enacted in certain genres of film?"), should not, though, be taken to imply that the studies of Hollywood drama disregard issues of medium. Interspersed with the attempt to offer determinations or definitions of genre based mainly on thematic analyses, Cavell continues to reflect on more general issues of cinematographic ontology, for example, the priority of actors or stars over characters, or the capacities of these dramas to acknowledge the conditions of their own possibility as movies. Moreover, the appeal to the notion of genre does not imply that the nature of its members has been defined on a priori grounds in terms of certain privileged features. Genres are not understood in terms of their intrinsic essence. On the contrary, Cavell's use of the term "genre" seeks to highlight the fact that their members inherit "certain conditions, procedures and subjects and goals of composition" (PH, 28) that they in turn can be said to explore and be responsible for. Just as the human inheritance of language is theorized as an open-ended play of entitlements and responsibilities, so the investigations in *Pursuits of Happiness* and *Contesting Tears* must proceed without talk of a priori characteristics and focus instead on the exemplary claims staked by each one of them. While inheriting the shared conditions that are administered to them, they bear the responsibility thus conferred on them differently. We will return to the Hollywood drama of the unknown woman in the final section of this chapter. For the moment, the aim is to explore Cavell's reading of the Hollywood comedy of remarriage.

The films Cavell takes as defining of remarriage comedy are all from 1930s and 1940s Hollywood: *It Happened One Night* (1934), *The Awful Truth* (1937), *Bringing Up Baby* (1938), *His Girl Friday* (1940), *The Philadelphia Story* (1940), *The Lady Eve* (1941), and *Adam's Rib* (1949). In all these movies the plot involves the bringing back together of a romantic couple, after they have faced the threat of divorce. Thus, as opposed to classical comedies (or so-called New Comedies), the narrative drive concerns not the overcoming of obstacles to a young pair's wish to be together in the first place; rather, as their titles suggest, the emphasis lies with the couple's capacity to withstand the assault of skeptical denial and renew their commitments and care for each other. Remarriage comedies can hence be said to celebrate human beings' capacity to acknowledge and affirm their lives and the ties that bind them by recovering a real interest in those lives.

According to Cavell, the skeptical doubts displayed by such comedies all relate to what he calls the founding myth of the genre, or the myth of marriage, which projects marriage into an incestuous, paradisaical past that gets interrupted by an act of violence. In remarriage comedy, spurned by the irreversible entry of the social, the loss of original intimacy takes the form of betrayal, or at least of its envisioned possibility:

> A running quarrel is forcing apart a pair who recognize themselves as having known one another for ever, that is from the beginning, not just in the past but in a period before there was a past, before history. This naturally presents itself as their having shared childhood together, suggesting that they are brother and sister. They have discovered their sexuality together and find themselves required to enter this realm at roughly the same time that they are required to enter the social realm, as if the sexual and the social are to legitimize one another. This is the beginning of history, of an unending quarrel. The joining of the sexual and the social is called marriage. Something evidently internal to the task of marriage causes trouble in paradise – as if marriage, which was to be a ratification, is itself in need of ratification. So marriage has this disappointment – call this its impotence to domesticate sexuality without discouraging it, or its stupidity in the face of the riddle of intimacy, which repels where it attracts, or in the face of the puzzle of ecstasy, which is violent while it is tender, as if the leopard should lie down with the lamb. (PH, 31–2)

Cavell interprets the disappointment that befalls the incestuous couple as induced by a dawning sense of commonality as being a confining, rather than a liberating, aspect of their lives. Just as the skeptic about other minds who views human finitude as a lack, as an imperfection, and who conjointly seeks to reject the other's independence, so their experience of marriage as limiting leads to a refusal to acknowledge the separate existence of the other. Disappointment produces a need for revenge, yet revenge, by which acknowledgment of the other is actively withdrawn, serves to isolate, rather than liberate. The consequence of refusing to acknowledge the other, of destroying the world of intimacy, is the failure of one's own self to announce itself to the other. While this is the crisis that sparks off a comedy of remarriage, the plot then shows how the couple regains a sense of interest, desire, and involvement in each other's lives, thus overcoming skeptical doubt so as to make a new start. At the end of the day, the willingness to remain intimate may be viewed as an allegory of the human capacity to accept the world and restake one's interest in it, in short to make oneself present to it (and thus it to oneself).

In all Hollywood comedies of remarriage, the process of healing is initially made possible by the man's acceptance of the need to let the woman discern in him those features that may authorize (or make sense of) her as one who desires him. The male counterpart has to do something special in order to redraw her attention to him. Thus, while privileging, though within an atmosphere of equality, the male as the active part, the creation of the new woman takes the form of the woman's education by the man. But in order to avoid his claim being simply the imposition of a demand, rather than the expression of a wish to be claimed by one, the husband must be willing to run the risk of making a fool of himself. He must transcend his inexpressiveness, and thereby, though anxiously and without any pre-given assurance, allow the woman to *read* his physiognomy as worthy of interest and desire.

For the husband to passionately single out his wife to respond to his own self-revelation is tantamount to a request for forgiveness. He confesses his guilt of having denied her, and by implication to having rejected his own dependence on her. If she accepts his confession, that is, if she responds in kind, with appropriate emotion and action, thus showing her unrestricted acknowledgment of him, then the couple achieves what Cavell calls a state of forgiveness, the anatomy of which he explores in his reading of *The Awful Truth*. Cavell's fascinating account of forgiveness resonates with similar ideas in Kierkegaard, Nietzsche, and Heidegger. Moreover, it has broad philosophical implications, bearing on the central issue of human finitude. While, as we have seen in the readings of Shakespeare, the drive to repudiate our attunement in language and thus to deny the other, or rather our relation to the other, can be interpreted as a craving for revenge against the human condition (our separateness), the overcoming or forgoing of revenge results in reconciliation. Following Heidegger's reading of Nietzsche's doctrine of eternal return, Cavell views the achievement of forgiveness as creative and forward-looking.[11] Rather than letting themselves be haunted by the past, the couple accepts each other's freedom and distinctiveness, and they do so in the guise of a renewed innocence and playfulness: they "[clear] the future for a new start, from the same or from a different starting place" (TCR, 193). Comparing the metamorphosis taking place with Nietzsche's celebration of childhood and the "sacred Yes," what the comedies propose is a comic "Yes" to human finitude – the precise opposite, obviously, to the tragic "No." Moreover, the sacred "Yes" epitomizes a reconstructed relation to time, one in which active forgetfulness takes the form of joyful repetition. Echoing Nietzsche's notion of eternal return (as interpreted by Heidegger), Cavell interprets this achievement as a new vision of time. A happy return to the ordinary, rather than being characterized by vain hopes of continual renewal or nostalgic dreams of returning to the past, implies an unconditional willingness to accept the repetitiveness of the diurnal and the daily, and thus a faith in the domesticity of the domestic:

> It is centrally as a title for these three features of diurnal comedy, the comedy of dailiness – its conclusion not in a future, a beyond, an ever after, but in a present continuity of before and after; its transformation of a festival into a festivity; its correction not of error but of experience or of a perspective on experience – that I retain the concept of remarriage as the title for the genre of films in question. The title registers, to my mind, the two most impressive affirmations of the task of human experience, the acceptance of human relatedness, as the acceptance of repetition. Kierkegaard's study called *Repetition*, which is a study of the possibility of marriage; and Nietzsche's Eternal Return, the call for which he puts by saying it is high time, a heightening or ascension of time; this is literally *Hochzeit*, German for marriage, with time itself as the ring. As redemption by suffering does not depend on something that has already happened, so redemption by happiness does not depend on something that is yet to happen; both depend on a faith in something that is always happening, day by day. (PH, 240–1)

Thus the affirmation of marriage through remarriage, while in part an emblem of the knowledge of others, figures as an appreciation of the ordinary as such, the redemption of dailiness. In Cavell's Nietzschean–Kierkegaardian vision of joy, the life of the ordinary – ordinary life – receives its ecstatic affirmation in the bliss of the shared joke. "The moment of laughter and song becoming one another is the voice in which I imagine the conversation of marriage aspired to in these comedies to be conducted" (PH, 263).

The account of marriage as remarriage further serves to throw light on the current relationship between the public and the private (or intimate). For as these films show, modern love can only be authenticated by the individual's personal willingness for repetition. Neither the church, nor the state, nor even children – in short, none of the publicly acknowledged institutions and events set to provide continuity and legitimacy in people's private lives – can remove that responsibility. For good or for bad, such a severing of the private from the need for public authentication, whereby the subject stops identifying herself with socially assigned role-expectations and aspires to shape life in an autonomous fashion, is an intrinsically modern achievement. Classical comedy, by linking the couple's happiness to the public event of marriage, demonstrates a full commitment to the ability of society to sanction and enable a privacy worth having. By contrast, modern romance disconnects the promise of love entirely from the social realm: today, shared intimacy cannot rely on the support of its culture but depends exclusively on the individuals' own capacity for adventure, improvisation, and sociability. Since no ceremony can reward or insure their happiness, these couples' lives thus remain what Cavell likes to call "unsponsored." As suggested in *The World Viewed*, "If all modern love is perverse, because now tangential to the circling of society, then the promise of love depends upon the acceptance of perversity, and that in turn requires the strength to share privacy, to cohabit in one element, unsponsored by society" (WV, 67). Thus movies are "inherently anarchic" because their "unappeasable appetite for stories of love is for stories in which love, to be found, must find its own community, apart from, but with luck still within, society at large; an enclave within it; stories in which society as a whole, and its laws, can no longer provide or deny love" (WV, 214). The redemption provided by the return (or turn) to the ordinary thus becomes a model of what one might call a micropolitics of perversity. Rather than society at large (the state) conferring legitimacy on the private, as in premodern times, it is now the happiness of the private or intimate sphere which authenticates society. Cavell is not suggesting that the ordinary is beyond or exempt from the political; rather, his claim is that since the state must be viewed as answerable to the autonomous individual, the *source* of the political cannot be anything other than the ordinary. That is where the individual carves out her identity – and as such the ordinary becomes eminently political. It is who we are and how we conceive of ourselves and our possibilities as individuals within the space of the ordinary that determine the extent to which society can rightly be called legitimate.

The Hollywood Melodrama of the Unknown Woman

Having laid bare the genre of remarriage comedies, Cavell, during the mid-1980s, starts to uncover a very different cinematic and narrative structure, namely the so-called "Melodrama of the Unknown Woman." This effort culminated with the 1996 publication of

Contesting Tears: The Hollywood Drama of the Unknown Woman, a col-
lection of essays exclusively devoted to the notion of female
unknownness. While working on the assumption that the latter
genre essentially can be derived by the systematic negation of the
comedies, the films chosen to represent melodrama – *Stella Dallas*
(1937), *Now, Voyager* (1942), *Gaslight* (1944), and *Letter from an
Unknown Woman* (1948) – rather than presenting the viewer with the
bliss of a redempted everyday, unfold potentials for disunion, skepticism, and human estrangement only hinted at in the comedies.
Whereas the world of comedy (however threatened and fragile) is
one of mutual recognition and loving acknowledgment, the world
of melodrama, though open to the possibility of attaining greater
integrity, is predominantly one of human isolation and despair. So
if in the comedies marriage figures as a cipher for the achievement
of the ordinary, the melodramas, in their denial of marriage, show
the ordinary at best as something *to be* achieved, that is, as absent
and yet to be made attractive to human desire. As will be clear in
the next chapter, this leads straight to Cavell's recent preoccupation
with Emersonian perfectionism.

Looking more in detail at how the derivation of the genre of
melodrama takes place, the first feature to be noted is that the
woman in melodrama is portrayed as finding herself incapable of
engaging in the kind of conversation that produced the educative
metamorphosis of comedy. She discovers that there is nothing to
learn from the men around her. As opposed to the male hero of the
comedies, the husband in melodrama fails to draw her interest
and elicit her desire. Indeed, since the masculine "taint of villainy"
which in the comedies was located and contained now prevents the
woman of melodrama from experiencing her partner's presence
and thus his recognition of her, she must, in order to achieve a proof
of her (independent) existence, turn away from marriage. Unlike
narratives such as *Anna Karenina* and *Madame Bovary*, however, the
negation of marriage does not involve adultery. Nor do the women
of melodrama necessarily obtain a divorce, although they may do
so. What fascinates Cavell is, rather, how their transcendence of
marriage takes the form of an acknowledgment of their isolation.
In the presence of their mothers and children (who are absent in the
comedies), they find themselves haunting the world; hence their
constant irony, expressive of their sense of absence, or, rather, the
absence of their world from them. Moreover, the irony expressive
of the unknownness of these women implies that their selves have
become questionable, for, from the standpoint of the ironist, every

single description of the self that appears true is false, and vice versa.

All these elements come together in what Cavell calls the underlying myth of the genre of melodrama:

> a woman achieves existence (or fails to), or establishes her right to existence in the form of a metamorphosis (or fails to), apart from or beyond satisfaction by marriage (of a certain kind) and with the presence of her mother and of her children, where something in her language must be as traumatic in her case as the conversation of marriage is for her comedic sisters – perhaps it will be an aria of divorce, from husband, lover, mother, or child. (CT, 88)

Historically, the paradigmatic articulation of this myth is Nora's refusal, at the end of Ibsen's *A Doll's House*, to continue living with a man who, incapable of offering the education and friendship she yearns for, no longer counts for her as a husband.[12] Leaving the oppressive environment that her marriage has become, the play ends with her stepping into the open. The obvious question, then, is how, in their isolation, Nora and the heroines of melodrama find the ability to achieve the self-transformation and integrity they are seeking. How, except on the basis of the friendly and forgiving acknowledgment of the self that takes place in remarriage, is such a process possible? In Cavell's account, the issue these women face is analogous to Descartes' attempt, in the *Meditations on First Philosophy*, to prove the existence of the self.[13] On Cavell's Emersonian reading, Descartes' famous statement, "*I am, I exist*, is necessarily true every time that I pronounce it or conceive it in my mind," rather than being an inference or argument of some kind, is best conceived of as a performance. In accordance with such a view, a prominent interpreter of Descartes in the analytical tradition, Jaakko Hintikka, has claimed that it would amount to a performative contradiction to pronounce or think one's non-existence.[14] Moreover, by assuming, with Descartes, that the mind always thinks, the skeptic, on his view, can be refuted. While agreeing with Hintikka about the performativity of Descartes' proof, Cavell denies that the ego mostly does think, hence the envisaged refutation of the skeptic fails. As we know from chapter 3, Cavell insists on the legitimacy of the skeptic's claim: the life I live is exposed to skepticism. Apart from my continued willingness to declare it and receive recognition, no proof can establish certainty about my own existence. Hintikka's belief that such a lasting proof can be provided amounts to an acceptance of the skeptic's interpretation, namely that the existence of the mind ought to be ascertainable without the acceptance of my responsibility of letting myself be known. On such a cognitivist view, which rehearses a version of the fantasy of necessary inexpressiveness, the problem of my existence is safely detached from the drama of expression and acknowledgment, thus removing the fear that I am not really or fully known by others.

Rather than relying on the dubious claim that the mind always consciously thinks (though it may, as psychoanalysis shows, be said always *un*consciously to think), Cavell holds open the skeptical possibility: that mostly we do not exist but only haunt the world. The burden of the recounting of the self should therefore not be on the side of continual thinking, but on the actual declaration of it. On Cavell's Emersonian view, "I am a being who to exist must say I exist, or must acknowledge my existence – claim it, stake it, enact it" (QO, 109). The self must express itself in such a way as to be able to acknowledge those expressions as its own. But how?

We have seen how Cavell employs Wittgenstein's reflections on the expressiveness of the human body in order to show how the self manifests itself in its embodiment. In *Contesting Tears*, however, he elaborates this idea further in light of Freud's conception of the hysteric's "capacity for conversion," defined as "a psychophysical aptitude for transposing very large sums of excitation into the somatic innervation."[15] Cavell brings several aspects of hysteria to the fore. First, as opposed to the well-known Freudian symptom formations, whereby excitations transpose into consciousness or discharge into practice (as in obsessions or phobias), the capacity for hysterical conversion, though predominantly unconscious, essentially announces itself as a modification of the body: the symptom reveals itself, as Freud puts it, "pantomimically." Second, according to Breuer and Freud's early study of hysteria, "Preliminary Communication" of 1893, hysterical motor symptoms are mainly of a traumatic nature; being "mnemonic symbols," they are, due to the activities of the memory, mimetically connected to some traumatic event of the past. Finally, hysterical conversion, though available as an existential possibility to every psycho-physical being, appears in Freud's case histories (in particular Dora and Anna O.) to be mainly linked with female sexuality. On Cavell's reading, this link is not contingent; rather, it expresses an acknowledgment of how femininity, which is not a biological or natural predicate, but belongs, like masculinity, to a broader human character shared by both men and women, is marked by passivity. Well aware of the dangers with which such an attribution is fraught, Cavell is not suggesting that women somehow are less prepared than men, whether morally or politically, to actively engage with issues that concern them. On the contrary, the passivity involved in "transposing large sums of excitation into the somatic innervation" must be understood in terms of the central Cavellian project of overcoming skepticism, i.e., as finding application in non-psychoanalytic domains, and as such it may demand revolutionary revisions of our conceptions of ourselves and our world, and radical action to enact them. As previously noted, Shakespeare's *The Winter's Tale*, and in particular Leontes's doubt, can be interpreted as a comment on how philosophical skepticism is inflected by gender. Yet whereas the reading of that play focuses on skepticism's masculine determination, the melodramas study how the feminine capacity for hysterical conversion testifies to an ability to allow oneself to be known in the body of one's expressions and thus to counter the skeptic's refusal to match criteria with a real, independent world.

All these claims converge in Cavell's stunning interpretation of Greta Garbo, "the most fascinating, cinematic image on film of the unknown woman" (CT, 106). Most productively viewed as a form of communication, a talent or will to communicate, Garbo's hysterical conversion takes her to the extreme point of "absolute expressiveness" (ibid). Here she achieves what Cavell calls "a somatogram," an absolute unity of body and mind. Her conditions of existence are then literally expressed in every single gesture she makes. One might think that such a complete embodiment of the mind would mean that nothing is hidden, that Garbo's mind can literally be read off from her bodily expression, yet Cavell implies just the opposite: Garbo remains unknown or beyond us – "visibly absent" – because a being capable of such an expressiveness is impossible to acknowledge. Indeed, the proof of Garbo's existence lies in her sublime transcendence of our powers of acknowledgment. She thus makes a claim as to how she would have to be acknowledged – if acknowledgment had been possible. Cavell's point is not simply that the men she is surrounded by in the films fail to recognize her existence. Nor is it that she will remain forever beyond us. Rather, by exceeding our powers of acknowledgment, Garbo forces us to realize that our capacity for acknowledgment has limits, and that we ourselves, though at present incapable of change, are responsible for the maintenance of those limits. However, since Garbo's absence, in addition to the transcendence effected by the bodily expression of her psyche, is mechanically produced (it is an effect of the cinematic image's capacity to present a world from which the viewer is absent), it achieves a separateness that testifies to the radical finitude of the human condition. And as Cavell argues, the only adequate way of responding to finitude – to transience, separation, loss – is through mourning:

> In Garbo's most famous postures in conjunction with a man, she looks away or beyond or through him, as if in an absence (a distance from him, from the present), hence as if to declare that this man, while the occasion of her passion, is surely not its cause. I find . . . that I see her *jouissance* as remembering something, but, let me say, remembering it from the future, within a private theater, not dissociating herself from the present moment, but knowing it forever, in its transience, as finite, from her finitude, or separateness, as from the perspective of her death: as if she were herself transformed into a mnemonic symbol, a monument of memory. . . . What the monument means to me is that a joyful passion for one's life contains the ability to mourn, the acceptance of transience, of the world as beyond one – say one's other. (CT, 106–7)

For Cavell, Garbo's mournful attestation of the human body's claim to total readability, while challenging the beholder's capacity for acknowledgment from a sublime distance, may be seen as raising the question of a specifically feminine expression and language – a "feminine difference of subjectivity" (CT, 3). The women of melodrama "declare their independence" in ways that cannot be accounted for within the logic of masculinist discourse. I deal with this issue in some detail in chapter 3. Even more recently, however, the kindred notion of "passionate utterance" – "one person, risking exposure to rebuff, singles out another, through the expression of an emotion, to respond in kind, that is, with appropriate emotion and action (if mainly of speech), here and now"[16] – has made itself felt in conjunction with Cavell's resurgent interest in opera. Like the women of melodrama, Mélisande in Debussy's *Pelléas and Mélisande* shrinks in horror from a world in which human beings are perceived to have no voice. Here, the ordinary comes to itself as conformity, banality, rigidity, and illusion. The notion of voice becomes increasingly important as Cavell, during the 1980s, starts to speak of the self as essentially on a journey toward the truth of itself – a journey he calls perfectionist. It is to the exploration of this dimension of our moral and political life that I now want to turn.

5

Ethics and Politics

Since the late 1950s, reflections on problems of ethics and politics, though evolving in numerous directions, have continually been at the forefront of Cavell's thought. While initially restricted to developing the implications of Austin's procedures for moral philosophy, he quickly began to align the concerns with criteria and representability with questions of liberalism and the nature of the political. Then, in the 1980s and 1990s, primarily occasioned by his extended reception of Emerson and Thoreau, he introduced and defended perfectionism as a moral and political outlook. Finally, his most recent work displays a conception of friendship and responsibility that may fruitfully be compared with the ethics of responsibility in Emmanuel Levinas. The development of Cavell's views on ethics and politics will be traced in the course of this chapter; suffice it to say at this point that the question of what it means to have or acquire a self, and of how that self can be asserted and find a voice, as well as the responsibilities that this achievement involves, never strays far away from Cavell's interest. As opposed to such current trends as contractarian liberalism, communitarianism, Kantianism, and utilitarianism, for Cavell the community (of speakers) is inherently fragile. Rather than being assured by an impersonal, objective order (of grammar, nature, law, principle, practice, tradition), it rests solely on individuals' willingness and capacity to take an interest in others and themselves, and to position themselves in such a way as to be able to do so. Just as nothing, no fact, guarantees the transmissibility of language, of acquiring the capacity to indefinitely project words into new contexts, i.e. to speak

representatively, other than individuals' abilities to anxiously locate
themselves within the parameters exemplified by statements of
initiation provided by their elders, so ethics and politics are largely
about investigating under what conditions and to what extent we,
as individuals, in speaking for ourselves can speak for others.
Whereas both the skeptic and the anti-skeptic evade the responsibility of making themselves known to others, or of providing themselves with a voice, by appealing to the effects of an impersonal
structure (or its absence), the hero of Cavell's thought in this region
of his work is constantly ready for self-transformation through education and reflection: thus democracy becomes an ongoing task of
repositioning the self in response to others.

Ethics and Moral Argumentation

Part III of *The Claim of Reason*, "Knowledge and the Concept of
Morality," which is a version of Cavell's 1961 doctoral dissertation,
takes Austinian ordinary language philosophy to bear on the issue
of moral argumentation, a dominant issue in the positivistically
steeped postwar American academic scene. A key problem in this
regard, and one according to which skeptics and anti-skeptics were
divided, is whether a method of argumentation can be developed
which is liable to generate rational agreement and conviction about
controversial normative questions (of how we should conduct our
lives, of what is right and wrong, and so on). Several interrelated
questions emerge from the focus on method and "the basis of morality": what is a moral judgment? How can a moral judgment be justified? Are such judgments cognitive or non-cognitive? What is a
moral reason? In confronting these issues, Cavell's guiding interests
revolve around, first, the nature of reason and its role (or claims) in
moral judgment and conduct, and, second, the nature and function
of moral judgment.

A conspicuous feature of the theories (initially developed by
Ross, Prichard, Stevenson, and others) that Cavell refers to is that
they tend to compare morality with knowledge and with (natural)
science in particular. Given the prominence of science as a paradigm
of rational belief-formation, a standard presupposition, whether
explicitly formulated or not, thus arises to the effect that unless
moral argumentation displays a similar or analogous structure to
that of scientific procedure, then morality must be viewed as irrational or at best somehow deficient. On this view, the methods

and procedures of scientific reasoning are taken to have universal validity: reasoning in other areas of human concern simply must conform to that of science in order to count as fully rational. While arguing that both science and morality, each in their own way, commit us to certain modes of argument and justification, Cavell responds to this intuition by maintaining that the alignment falters on a number of significant differences between the two uses of reason.

As noted in the discussion of aesthetic judgment, Cavell takes commitment to scientific rationality to entail the adherence to shared structures of (material as well as logical) inference and patterns of support such that if a set of premises is accepted as relevant and true, then all competent practitioners must agree on a specific conclusion. The goal of scientific practice consists in reaching such an agreement. Moreover, if a person, in default of adducing reasons to question the nature of the inference or evidence, fails to draw the generally accepted conclusion from authorized premises, then he or she must be ruled out as incompetent. Someone who denied, say, the existence of valleys on the moon, and, while failing to adduce further reasons, refused the evidence of telescopes as conclusive, would not count as competent in (current) science. However, we should not think that such a refusal by itself means that the person is irrational; all we could reasonably say is that "That man is no scientist, given the procedures or canons of science which now constitute that institution" (CR, 261). Finally, once someone is committed to and competent in the various practices that lead willy-nilly from accepted premises to a purportedly objective (universal) and true conclusion, that is, a conclusion no competent practitioner in the field can dispute without producing competing reasons, then the identity of the scientific subject making those claims – *who* that person happens to be – is irrelevant: scientific reasoning is impersonal. It takes the position from which claims in question are substantiated to be determined by virtue of shared criteria of competence.

Whereas scientific argumentation requires commitment to impersonal procedures that allow the members of a given research community to settle disputes and reach satisfactory agreement, moral disputes seem to lack such accepted means of resolution. Indeed, for many moral theorists, it is precisely the absence of intersubjectively established ways of resolving moral disagreement that throws the rational status of morality into jeopardy. Put more strongly, if there is nothing intrinsic to moral argumentation, no procedure, that permits a rational agreement to emerge, then what exactly, one might ask, is the point and purpose of such argumentation? Perhaps, as Stevenson and other proponents of emotivism have argued, what people really do when seeking common assent to a moral judgment is to try to obtain an effect on others in getting what they approve of done. If so, however, the result of the investigation would entail a form of moral nihilism. By failing to distinguish between the act of persuasion and the act of convincing, Stevenson does not do justice to morality; in fact, he dismisses it altogether. Despite the wish to clarify the nature of moral argumentation, there is no space in his theory for moral considerations. At no stage is there an appeal to the hearer's commitments and cares; thus in Stevenson's model there is nothing about the speaker's judgment that would constitute a willingness to take the hearer's position into account, in short, no recognition of others as persons. By contrast, theorists who find such non-cognitivist views irresponsible may want to establish claims for the conclusive rationality of morality in such a way that the structure of moral argumentation becomes assimilated to science. A current example of such a strategy is Jürgen Habermas's discourse ethics, which has been explicitly formulated so as to counter moral non-cognitivism.[1] According to Habermas, moral discourse aims at rationally establishing universal norms of action. In this account, what constitutes moral validity is the deliberately achieved agreement among agents who consider themselves free and equal. Notoriously, such a position seems to put unduly narrow restrictions on what counts as moral deliberation. Unless they are capable, like scientific reasoning, of generating determinate agreement under procedural constraints, moral debates contain no claim to rationality.

While holding, against positions such as that of Habermas, that not every moral dispute can be settled such that all competent parties will agree it is the right conclusion, Cavell denies that this entails the irrationality of moral argumentation per se. Rather than thinking that there must in every case be one correct precept or course of action, and that a moral discourse worthy of its name must allow us to establish which one that is, as theorists of morality we must learn to value the productivity of *rational disagreement*. Moral argumentation requires *hope* of agreement, for otherwise argument would be pointless. We would, as it were, not be addressing each other's views. Yet from the need to willingly anticipate a state of agreement, it doesn't follow that a discussion has been pointless unless consensus is arrived at. The purpose of moral dialogue is for participants to uncover, to themselves and others, aspects of their own moral selves. As a way of settling conflict and coming to terms with each other, it provides a discursive space for articulating the position one is taking responsibility for. Whereas science, in questioning a claim to knowledge, compares a claim with the adequacy of one's relevant credentials and statements of facts, moral reasoning, in questioning a claim to moral rightness, determines whether the position one has taken as a person is adequate to the claim being raised. The concern in morality, in other words, is not, as in science, whether on the basis of your evidence and general competence I can agree with what you *propose*, assent or dissent to the meaning of your words, but whether I can respect the claim *as* entered by you. Are *you*, in showing me what you are taking responsibility for, able to demonstrate the claim in question, as entered by you, to be worthy of my respect? In this account, moral argument is rational in so far as it ultimately leads to self-knowledge, to a definition of oneself: who are you as a moral agent entering certain claims and attempting to defend them?

> Questioning a claim to moral rightness (whether of any action or any judgment) takes the form of asking "Why are you doing that?," "What *are* you doing?," "Have you really considered what you're saying?," "Do you know what this means?"; and assessing the claim is, as we might now say, to determine *what* your position is, and to challenge the position itself, to question whether the position you *take* is adequate to the claim you have entered. The point of the assessment is not to determine *whether* it is adequate, where *what* will be adequate is itself *given* by the form of the assessment itself; the point is to determine *what* position you are taking, that is to say, *what position you are taking responsibility for* – and whether it is one I can respect. (CR, 268)

As an example of such an assessment, Cavell offers the following dialogue:[2]

> A: I've decided against offering him the job.
> B: But he's counting on it. You most explicitly promised it to him.
> A: But I've since learned what kind of man he is.
> B: What he did you yourself have done, but you tell yourself that in your case "it was different." It's different in *every* case. And the same. You're muddled, criminally muddled.

Clearly, B challenges A's claim to be rightfully entitled to break promises whenever the promise fails to satisfy certain morally relevant requirements. But rather than assessing whether A's claim is right or wrong as such (qua universally valid precept), what B does is to question whether A really is in a position to responsibly enter such a claim. Since A in her own behavior seems to have demonstrated a disregard for the line of action she now appeals to in order to dismiss the job-seeker, B's conclusion is that there is an inadequacy between the position A has taken and her actual claim (A has shown herself to be a hypocrite); hence B finds A's claim not to deserve respect.

In this example, A and B do not simply disagree about a certain precept; by having A's position elaborated, B comes to learn that their moral universes differ. It may be that continuing the dialogue would reveal aspects of A's position that allowed A, despite disagreement, to regain B's respect; and yet it could also happen that further elaborations (Cavell follows Austin in calling the various excuses, explanations, and justifications that occur in such a dialogue "elaboratives") would testify to a difference between A's and B's moral positions such that they were no longer able to continue their relation as hitherto defined. In each of these possible scenarios, however, the participants would have attained what Cavell takes to be the aim of moral discourse: to disclose aspects of their own selves, and to clarify the nature and sustainability of their relationship, that is, the extent to which they are able to speak for each other and thus be morally authoritative.

Undoubtedly, philosophers who are inclined to think that morality requires the possibility of reaching rational agreement would feel that Cavell's proposal is too weak. If moral dialogue essentially revolves around the voicing of one's position and of getting to know people, then how is one to refute those who seek to repudiate the moral perspective altogether? Cavell's response to this worry takes several forms. First, morality is not designed "to evaluate the behavior and interactions of monsters" (CR, 265). To think that morality can only be valid or rational in so far as it is competent to assess *every* possible action would imply an undue moralization of moral theory. Indeed, such a view, since it asks more of morality than it can deliver, tends to lead to disillusionment and skepticism. On the other hand, it may also carry with it a tendency toward hypocrisy whereby people speak in the name of positions they do not occupy. A central purpose of Cavell's critique of morality is precisely to combat conceptions of morality that appeal to an impersonal procedure the outcome of which is beyond our cares and commitments, and hence what we can be responsible for. Second, it is crucial that people are able to throw morality into question without thereby undermining it altogether. Intellectual figures of an undeniable human greatness, such as Kierkegaard and Nietzsche, questioned morality in the name of "a position whose excellence we cannot deny" (CR, 268); but rather than undermining morality as such, what they showed was "that [morality's] competence as the judge of conduct and character is limited" (ibid). Finally, as opposed to epistemology, morality offers no candidate for a *best case* of knowing and therefore no occasion for skepticism to pose as global. Cavell's argument appeals to the inextricable hermeneutic link between moral argument and expressions of views, precepts, and evaluations of a moral character: "Actions, unlike envelopes and goldfinches, do not come named for assessment, nor, like apples, ripe for grading" (CR, 265). Whether an action constitutes, say, a breaking of a promise depends on how it is described; yet the description is never morally neutral: it always reflects our contested moral views. Likewise, the precept "Promises ought to be kept" only receives a determinate meaning within a specific context of argumentation. If taken to be universally valid, it voices a particular view of morality. Conversely, if it is conceded that it is only valid under certain circumstances, then moral argumentation will be required to specify what those circumstances are. Yet, ultimately, people's intuitions are going to differ on this issue. In short, a best case of moral knowledge or certainty does not arise.

Yet even if one grants the force of such considerations, it seems evident that more work is required to be able to meet the objection about arbitrariness. In order to distance himself from skeptical views to the effect that all moral arguments are of equal value or standing, Cavell therefore submits that differences do indeed exist between respectable and non-respectable arguments: "It is part of the life of the subject that not every opinion has the same weight nor every disagreement the same significance" (CR, 270). The difference in weight and significance is a function of the speaker's authority. But as opposed to features such as height or age, which are given and arbitrary, moral authority needs to be earned, and hence proved. For example, "it makes a difference whether [an argument about the desirability of free love] is conducted by an oversexed, emotionally dependent adult like D. H. Lawrence, or an undersexed, or sublimated, emotionally independent adult like Freud" (ibid). Cavell's point is not that Lawrence and Freud's disagreement, because of their dissimilarities, would necessarily remain unresolved; rather, what interests Cavell is the difference between their positions and how that difference may determine their respective rights to speak for others. Moral argument, again, seeks to establish the adequacy or superiority of a position relative to a given claim; and rather than taking authority for granted, it offers a space for questioning authority, and for allowing justified claims to authority to be distinguished from non-justified ones. To ask for a simple a priori criterion by means of which rightful claims to authority are to be distinguished from irresponsible or unacceptable claims, or to appeal dogmatically to the superiority of specific positions, would drive responsibility out of morality. The necessity of anxiously proving the authority of one's position, i.e., to be answerable for it, would be repressed.

But how do we rationally assess speakers' positions? What makes a reason a moral reason? In order to throw further light on this thorny issue, Cavell discusses three positions: Stevenson's emotivism, the early Rawls's version of rule utilitarianism, and the thesis known as the Autonomy of Morals. While Stevenson's view has already been considered, some aspects of Rawls's work will be addressed in the next section. The remaining part of this section will focus on the widespread view that a factual statement can constitute a reason for an ought-claim only if it appeals to a moral major premise in conjunction with which the judgment can be derived. On this view, morality is autonomous in the sense that nothing counts as a reason for a moral judgment unless it is accompanied by an intrinsically moral premise. Historically, the autonomy of morality has been associated with an early modern sense of the non-derivability of moral judgments from non-moral sources of authority such as God, the church, or kings. Thus, for example, according to many Enlightenment thinkers, including Kant, God's command can only constitute a reason for adopting a moral precept in so far as it is conjoined with an ethical premise stating that "We ought to do what God commands." The autonomy of morals spelled the liberation of moral assessment from dogmatically held belief. While he is sensitive to the historical significance of the autonomy thesis, what mainly interests Cavell, however, is the logical or semantic thesis that an ought-claim can never be derived from or justified by a factual claim.

Consider the traditional philosopher's example "You ought to do X," in which this concluding ought-claim, if rationally advocated, is taken to be necessarily supported by "You promised to do X" (minor premise) and "If you have promised to do anything, you ought to do it" (major premise). Is it really the case that "You ought to do X" needs this kind of backing? According to Cavell, "do X" in the conclusion may, significantly, mean both "keep your promise" and, for example, "return the money." And yet in neither case can "because you promised" (minor premise) serve as a premise from which the conclusion could follow. If a promise really was made, then "You ought to return the money" means the same as "You ought to keep your promise." But then the minor premise becomes redundant, or itself in need of a reason. Conversely, "keep your promise" is a manner of addressing a specific action to which one has committed oneself, in this example to return the money. Thus the relevant reason is one that speaks to that (for example by highlighting the consequences of not returning the money), and not one that addresses the actual promise.

Likewise, the major premise can be shown to suffer from difficulties. On Arthur Prior's view, "If you have promised to do anything, you ought to do it" means the same as "You ought to keep your promises."[3] This is how the major premise is supposed to work: its scope-claim covers all instances of being obligated by a promise. However, as Cavell points out, this assumption rests on the mistake of making "You ought to keep promises" the universal generalization of "You ought to keep this promise," whereas "You ought to keep promises" is a plural that is not a generalization, and as such its use is very special. The question "Why ought I to do anything?" rather than asking for a universal generalization covering all cases of promise-making, asks: "Why ought I to honor the specific claims others make upon me?" And this involves questioning who I am and want to be; it cannot be settled by logical argumentation.

Generally speaking, in ethics the demand for logical validity, in that it disregards the position of the involved parties, is a nonstarter. Ethical arguments are neither deductive nor inductive: indeed, the step to the conclusion is not inferential at all. Rather, "must" or "ought," as in "You ought to keep your promise," are, as Cavell puts it:

> modes of presenting the very reasons you would offer to support them, and without which they would lack meaning altogether; or they specifically set aside reasons. ("I can do no other.") What makes their use rational is their relevance to the person confronted, and the legitimacy your position gives you to confront him or her in the mode you take responsibility for. (CR, 323)

Two sorts of reason allow us to confront the other's position: first, on the "basis of care" a reason points to something the person cares about and thus highlights why she "ought" to do something; second, by drawing on a "ground of commitment," it addresses her actions and their implications, for which she is responsible. In his later work, Cavell transforms this model of moral argumentation into a conception of friendship. The authentic friend confronts the other, not by adducing impersonal reasons, but by speaking from a position she occupies to the other's cares and commitments such that the other may undergo a conversion. However, in order to fully understand the implications of Cavell's notion of friendship, and how it works in tandem with his notion of perfectionism, we need to turn to his discussion of politics.

Liberalism and Perfectionism

Cavell's first explicit discussion of politics occurs in the context of the opening remarks on the nature of Wittgensteinian criteria in the *Claim of Reason*. In voicing my criteria, I inevitably purport to speak for others; I take myself to be a representative speaker. Although I shall not be able to tell a priori who is implicated by me, my words refer me to a community of language-users; and this raises the question of the nature of this community, and in particular the relationship between the individual and his or her community, the political question *par excellence*. This question has been answered in analogous ways in philosophy and politics. While philosophers of language such as Kripke have taken the mutual meaningfulness of words to rest on some sort of agreement or connection between its users, in the liberal tradition of political thought, the political community has likewise been understood as based upon an originating consent among its subjects. Like David Hume, however, Cavell finds it impossible to think of the social contract in historical terms: the compact did not come into being at some specific point of time; and, even if it did, then its origin (of which we seem to have no evidence) is irrelevant to its political significance.[4] Rather than searching in vain "in what records this charter of our liberties is registered,"[5] the contract should instead be viewed as a myth. Calling it a myth, though, is not to detract from its implications; it is to help us understand and explain crucial features of the link between the individual and her society.

But what does the myth explain? According to both Locke and Hume, two of the earliest proponents of the social contract view, it explains why I am obligated to the social order in which I participate – why I should obey the government. Essentially, their claim is that the subsistence of society as it stands is rationally preferable to the state of nature in which my freedom and my rights are either unprotected or non-existent; hence, as long as the government keeps its part of the covenant, I am better off obeying than disobeying. As opposed, however, to the cynicism implied by the classical view of society as based simply on a bargain, where each person once and for all renounces certain freedoms in order to acquire others, thereby consenting to disregard the nature of the government as long as it does not violate the contract, Cavell, while turning to Rousseau's republicanism, argues that the appeal to the advantage of society as it stands is question-begging. The force of the idea of the social contract is not to take the advantage of the current order as a given fact on which to rest the case for obedience; rather, it is to put society, as it stands, in question: then, not only do I consent to obey; I also take myself to be responsible for my society. Participation in a political community implies citizenship, and hence autonomy, not just subjection:

> What I consent to, in consenting to the contract, is not mere obedience, but membership in a polis, which implies two things: First, that I recognize the principle of consent itself; which means that I recognize others to have consented with me, and hence that I consent to political *equality*. Second, that I recognize the society and its government, so constituted, as *mine*; which means that I am answerable not merely to it, but for it. So far, then, as I recognize myself to be exercising my responsibility for it, my obedience to it is obedience to my own laws; citizenship in that case is the same as my autonomy; the polis is the field within which I work out my personal identity and it is the creation of (political) *freedom*. (CR, 23)

Of course, if society were indeed perfect in this sense, then the need to justify one's obedience to it would hardly arise. Then the disadvantage of withdrawing one's consent would clearly be greater than the disadvantages of citizenship. But since societies generally do not display this level of perfection, since men, to quote Rousseau, "are born free but are everywhere in chains,"[6] it makes little sense to try to answer the question "Why ought I to obey?" by appealing to the advantages of citizenship. Mostly, we exercise our will to the particular, to private benefit, hence we do not exercise our general will; and in so far as we fail to put the genuine social contract into effect, the disadvantages of citizenship may seem greater than that of withdrawing one's consent. For Hume, the problem of obedience takes the form of an epistemological puzzle: how can I have recognized this society as mine, as expressive of my consent, if am not aware that I was ever asked? According to Hume, a person's physical presence is enough to conclude that she has consented, though tacitly. The problem, obviously, with this answer is that, rather than taking citizenship to imply a moral *project*, an ongoing responsibility to the community, it sanctions political passivity and cynicism. In Hume's account, there is no room for recognizing society as *mine*. Moreover, by asking the wrong epistemological question – "How can I have consented, since no one ever asked?" – it functions to mystify society: our sociality becomes dependent on a fact, whether of physical presence or prior agreement, rather than on our actual commitment to sustain it. For Cavell, the social contract means that while I take myself to be deeply joined to society, I should also be prepared "to put society at a distance from me, so that it appears as an artifact" (CR, 25). Rather than being secured by simple physical presence, membership in the polis requires my reflective response. On the Rousseauian view he recommends, citizenship implies an obligation to seek a discovery of my own position, i.e. self-knowledge, so as to reveal with whom I am in community, that is, how far we can speak for each other. No prior contract could ever explain the fact of community; rather, the validity of any prior contract can only be explained in terms of the social contract that I now recognize myself to be party to.

As opposed to most current versions of liberalism, which take the self to be fully constituted *outside* the political (or public) realm, politics here, as in the classical republican views of Aristotle or Cicero, appears as an arena (among many) in which the self defines or creates itself: by engaging politically, I shape my (political) identity. It is not the only such arena: religion, friendship, philosophy, art, love, and parenthood also offer possibilities of finding and exercising, as Cavell puts it, one's own voice. However, since the field of the political (according to the stipulation of equality) only exists in so far as I recognize, and am recognized by, others as members of the same community, it follows that this process of self-definition is essentially communal: I cannot work out my political identity on my own; it is only as a member of a community for which those who give their consent are answerable, i.e. who can claim it as their own, that I can know my position in it. Society thus appears as *ours*. Upon entering it, that is, consenting to it, not only does speaking for oneself politically entail speaking for others, it also means consenting to be spoken for by them. Although risky and fraught with possibilities of disappointment, inevitably the political self can only actualize itself, that is, work out its own self-definition, within the framework of communal practices and deliberation:

> To speak for yourself means risking the rebuff – on some occasion, perhaps once for all – of those for whom you claimed to be speaking; and it means risking having to rebuff – on some occasion, perhaps once for all – those who claimed to be speaking for you. (CR, 27)

It follows, contra Locke and Hume, that the disadvantage of withdrawing one's consent would usually be far greater than the imperfections of one's actual political community, for since having a political voice presupposes consent, it would amount to the deprivation of a central arena for working out that aspect of one's autonomy. In the absence of the recognition of a particular community as one's own, there can be no political answerability, and hence no political self or voice: "The alternative to speaking for myself representatively (for *someone* else's consent) is not: speaking for myself privately. The alternative is having nothing to say, being voiceless, not even mute" (CR, 28). Thus Cavell suggests that the classical theorists of the social contract were grammatically wrong when they considered political membership to constitute an "advantage." To have a political self is a condition of the possibility for there being (political) advantages at all; hence, existing politically cannot itself be an advantage, that is, something up for grabs in a bargaining situation. Indeed, mere withdrawal from the community, as in inner or outer exile, would not be sufficient to constitute a withdrawal of consent from it. Since the self on this picture is thought of as fundamentally joined to society, dissent is not the undoing of consent; rather, it initiates a "dispute about its content" (CR, 27), a dispute within political life over whether present arrangements are faithful to our consent. While continuing to identify with the political community as such, dissent amounts to a questioning of the reciprocity between myself and the others, of the extent to which my voice, though still aiming to be representative, in fact *is* speaking for others, and thus also whether others speak for me. Dissent, then, rather than constituting a rejection of political responsibility, amounts to a continuation of the attempt, called for by the myth of the social contract, to make the laws of the polis one's own.

　　Needless to say, perhaps, on this view the greatest danger facing democracy is conformism. Like the epistemological skeptic who refuses to be responsible for meaning what he says and desires only that his words be defined with reference to an impersonal structure, the conformist rejects responsibility for the laws conferred on every citizen by the myth of the social contract. Rather than seeking to define the extent to which he can conceive of himself as author of the social order, the conformist, by failing to estrange himself from prevailing opinion (as well as from himself), lets the community speak for him, yet without interrogating its right to do so. Conformity can thus be viewed as a form of unconsciousness; having repressed or forgotten their responsibility, conformists fail to define their (political) selves – as a result, they fail to have a political existence. Unless the self enacts its existence by expressing and meaning what is expressed – whether in politics or in any other domain where one's autonomy needs to be worked out – it cannot, strictly speaking, be said to exist. Again, the issue for Cavell comes down to the notion of voice. Conformism means being voiceless, having no (expressed) existence. Obviously, a society of conformists, in which the promise of democracy has been forfeited, would be one in which the general will is not exercised: in such a society, every arrangement would be partial, to private benefit.

A conspicuous feature of this vision of democracy is the crucial role it assigns to education, both of oneself and others. Those who representatively exercise their political voice are attempting to discover their position – the substance and range of consent – with respect to the present arrangements of society. In coming to define the limits of what they are answerable for politically, they discover the limits of their political identification, and hence also uncover the limits of their political identity. The self and the self's society mutually offer access to each other. But in seeking to define their own position, they must not only acknowledge that others speak for them, but that they also speak for others; thus, educating oneself politically is inseparable from educating others, that is, the finding and forming of my relations with others. Since whom I speak for is not known a priori but requires a commitment to self-examination and political intercourse, the education of others always risks the rebuff of those for whom I claim to be speaking. Conversely, it also risks having to rebuff those who claim to be speaking for me.

As we have seen with regard to both ethical, aesthetic, and philosophical discourse, such modes of dialogue do not typically take the form of argumentation. On the contrary, "the issue is not to win an argument . . . but to manifest for the other another way" (CHU, 31). The task of speaking, of having a voice, does not coincide simply with uttering one's thoughts publicly in such a way that others may rationally be convinced by one's position; rather, the hero of Cavell's vision of democracy is only able to attain the goal of demonstrating to others the partiality of her society's arrangements by offering herself, the expressions of herself and her position, as representing an alternative self *for* those others. In articulating its own position, the self thus strives to make itself attractive to the other: it calls for the response or responsivity of others. And, as I will show in more detail in a moment, for those others to respond means allowing themselves to be read by this person, thus anticipating a further, hitherto unattained, self by releasing the holds that have prevented genuine self-knowledge. We have already seen how film and Shakespearean drama depict a relationship such as marriage, whereas more recently, as for example in *Conditions Handsome and Unhandsome*, Cavell has become increasingly ready to think of it as friendship or neighboring. This progression in our dialectic brings us to the issue of perfectionism.

Of great centrality to Cavell's work is the claim that modern philosophy, though with some notable exceptions (say Descartes, Heidegger, and Wittgenstein, to mention some of the most salient ones), has repressed or forgotten the self. In his early writings, the attempt to reinstate the self in philosophy took on a variety of different guises. It was felt, for example, in the suggestion made in "The Availability of Wittgenstein's Later Philosophy," that Wittgenstein's *Investigations* can be read as a confession, or in the analysis of responsibility and seriousness in *The Claim of Reason*. Indeed, in so far as the skeptic is one who fantasizes language as a meaning-determining framework that exempts one from the burden of judgment, and hence from having to assume or declare a position from which to judge (or speak), reinstating a notion of selfhood may perhaps be seen as the defining ambition of Cavell's lifelong project of coming to terms with skepticism. Yet in introducing, in his Carus lectures of 1988 (which make up the bulk of *Conditions Handsome and Unhandsome*), what he calls Emersonian perfectionism, he not only hopes to counter the selflessness of philosophy, but to demonstrate that serious reflection on ethics and politics requires an emphasis on the self. This is not to say, however, that Cavell takes ethics and politics to constitute separate realms of thought, distinct from philosophy, so that, by extending his consideration of selfhood to those two realms, he leaves philosophy proper. It is, rather, an expression of his view that philosophy necessarily involves both ethical and political dimensions. By calling, within the contexts of ethical and political thought, for a reconsideration of the notion of perfectionism, he is in effect calling, like Heidegger or Wittgenstein, for a reconsideration of philosophy.

By perfectionism, Cavell does not have in mind a competing theory, say, of morality, that is, a theory set to rival reigning accounts of what constitutes moral life. He is not interested in establishing an alternative to, for example, Kantianism or utilitarianism. Rather, on the most general level he wants to unearth "something like a dimension or tradition of the moral life" (CHU, 2) that has been present to Western thought since Plato and Aristotle, although fatefully excluded by current moral philosophy's one-sided orientation toward impersonal rules or commands. Since perfectionism is thought of more as an outlook than a theory, embodied and developed in a number of more or less canonical texts, ranging from Plato's *Republic* to Friedrich Schlegel's *Athenaeum Fragments* and Nietzsche's *Schopenhauer as Educator* (to mention only three members from the long yet provisional list of sources at the opening of the introduction to *Conditions Handsome and Unhandsome*), it has no strict definition. Like so many of Cavell's philosophical concepts, it is formed in conjunction with readings of various exemplary works. Moreover, as opposed to most current doctrines in moral philosophy, the direction of perfectionism is less to restrain the bad than to release the good. Indeed, from the perspective of Kantianism or utilitarianism, which aim at setting definite limits to the range of morally acceptable judgments, the espousal of Emersonian perfectionism may not even count as taking a stand in moral philosophy at all.

Having warned against the danger of pinning it down too narrowly, perhaps the most useful way of entering the terrain of Emersonian perfectionism is the following. We have already seen that Cavell interprets Rousseau's and Kant's doctrine of autonomy as asking whether the rational will of the citizens is expressed in the laws they give themselves. In this account, what informs social critique is a sense of impartiality, of asking whether our obedience has come into being on the basis of incentives internal or external to the law. While accepting the doctrine of freedom as autonomy, the turn Cavell finds in Emerson consists in viewing my actual partiality as an incentive to side with a further, hitherto unattained, self. Emersonian perfectionism thus conceives of the self as inherently in tension with itself. Torn between conformity and self-reliance – the two poles of Emerson's account of the soul – the perfectionist aim is, by suspending one's commitment to society as it stands and embarking on a journey of the mind, to be true to oneself, to strive toward integrity. And to reach integrity is to hit upon that which really is common – the order of the ordinary or everyday – and which enables the self to genuinely speak for others and overcome isolation.

For Emerson, therefore, the constitution of the public and the private must be thought of as conjoined: the "nation of men" he refers to in "The American Scholar" of 1837 requires a citizenry capable of transfiguring itself from a state of conformity to one of self-reliance. The social order enjoys legitimacy only in so far as it is underwritten by authentic acts of affirmation; hence all men must awaken to what Emerson calls their own genius: "To believe in your own thought, to believe that what is true for you in your private heart is true for all men – that is genius."[7] Liberation, though calling for social change, must start with the restlessness of the individual self. As in Plato, "the good city exists always as a model to the good soul" (CHU, 17). The individual, Emerson thus urges, must become averse to its own conformity; it must feel shame at its own shameful status of being a slave of itself – of being what Emerson calls a "bug," belonging to a "mob."[8] And as the individual starts to feel disgust with its present state of non-existence, with not having proved its own existence by enacting it in exemplary ways, the self experiences a conversion, as if the self were to be born anew. This is the stage at which the subject stands apart from itself, and, as Cavell reads Emerson (as well as Freud's notion of the uncanny, or rather the return of the familiar[9]), experiences the sublime return of its own rejected thoughts: "In every work of genius we recognize our own rejected thoughts. They come back to us with a certain alienated majesty" (QO, 176).

In addition to Emerson, Cavell's perfectionist notion of the self as defined by an ineliminable internal split is indebted to the early Heidegger of *Being and Time*. For Heidegger, the attainment of genuine individuality requires the capacity to transcend the inauthenticity of everyday, conformist existence. In acknowledging the existential groundlessness of its own being, *Dasein*, rather than the anonymous, irresponsibly repetitious "they", becomes the sole author of its own projective concerns. But unlike Heidegger, Cavell refuses to link inauthenticity and everydayness. As opposed to the model developed in *Being and Time*, in which everydayness, or the ordinary, is essentially marked by inauthenticity, and hence according to which authenticity demands departure, the Emersonian (or Wittgensteinian) model calls for a return:

It might help to say: Heidegger finds everyday life a mimetic expression of, exhaustive of the value of, everyday language; whereas Wittgenstein finds moments or crossings in everyday life and the language that imitates it to be broken shadows or frozen slides of the motion of our ordinary words, becoming the language of no one, unspeakable; moments which refuse the value of the experience of ordinary words, their shared memories, disappointed in them. Then we are evidently in touch with these words, but our touch is numbed or burned. (TCR, 344)

In a similar passage, alluding to Plato's myth of the cave, Cavell suggests that "The direction out from illusion is not up, at any rate not up to one fixed morning star; but down, at any rate along each chain of a day's denial" (TCR, 332). Corresponding to the two parts of the self, the attained and the unattained, there is an actual and an eventual everyday, the one a bad iteration of voiceless denial of responsibility, the other a good iteration of "counting by recounting, of calling by recalling" (ibid) – a mournful achievement of the ordinary, though always to be forgone and lost by further denials.

One question that can be raised at this juncture is how the individual can escape conformity in the first place. So far we have been told that the individual must become averse to his own conformity, and that he must be ashamed at his own shameful state of conformism. But if conformity is marked by irresponsibility and a failure to rely on, or find, one's own voice, then it seems difficult to see how the individual can raise himself to a further stage on his own. It seems that some external source of attraction would have to make itself felt. Moreover, this external source or agency would itself have to represent a more authentic form of existence, for otherwise the incentive exerted would simply continue the strictures of conformity. This is the reason why Cavell introduces the notion of friendship. The friend appears as one who incites the individual to strive to attain a further self. Indeed, since the friend represents the hitherto unattained self, to relate to the friend becomes tantamount to enter into a renewed self-relation. In what might be described as kind of "founding myth" of perfectionism, Cavell views this intersubjective transfiguration as a process of education:

Obvious candidate features are its ideas of a mode of conversation, between (older and younger) friends, one of whom is intellectually authoritative because his life is somehow exemplary or representative of a life the other(s) are attracted to, and in the attraction of which the self recognizes itself as enchained, fixated, and feels itself

removed from reality, whereupon the self finds that it can turn
(convert, revolutionize itself) and a process of education is under-
taken, in part through a discussion of education, in which each self
is drawn on a journey of ascent to a further state of that self, where
the higher is determined not by natural talent but by seeking to know
what you are made of and cultivating the thing you are meant to do.
(CHU, 6–7)

Now for anyone to count as a friend in Cavell's sense, he or she
would have to satisfy a number of requirements. Most importantly,
the friend is not there to affirm the individual in his present state.
Consequently, a genuine friend must be ready to provoke. As
Emerson puts it in his Divinity College Address of 1838 (and which
appears as a motto for *The Claim of Reason*), "Truly speaking, it is
not instruction, but provocation, that I can receive from another
soul."[10] Moreover, the friend may appear in different guises. The
main male character in the comedy of remarriage, the female
heroine in Hollywood melodrama, the protagonists in a Shakespeare drama, just to mention some of the figures Cavell use, are all
"friends" who represent another, unattained self for anyone who
seriously engages with them. But perhaps even more striking is
how Cavell considers certain texts to be friends. The writings
of Emerson and Thoreau, Austin and Wittgenstein, Plato and
Nietzsche – all perfectionist authors – manifest a capacity to attract
me toward a further self.

The friend, whether as text, character, marriage partner, or
simply another human being who happens to call my present self
into question, is someone with whom I enter into a complex pattern
of reversals. In order to elucidate the nature of these reversals,
Cavell reverts to the notion of reading developed in *The Claim of
Reason*. The friend is someone who presents his own self as representative of a position that I may be drawn to but have not yet
attained; thus the friend is capable of educating me. By offering his
expressions of himself as exemplary of the attainment of a higher
self, or a higher, more representative level of humanity, the other
presents himself for me as an object of reading. But for me to read
the other, I must simultaneously allow myself to *be read*: reading
requires the readiness to open oneself to the other, to be singled out
and thus read by the other. Just as the recognition of a stretch of
pain-behavior as being *of* real pain presupposes the ability to let
oneself be affected by the other, to open oneself existentially toward
the reality of another human being's pain, so the attainment of a

higher self presupposes the passive mode of allowing oneself to be affected, or read, by the other with whom one has entered into a conversation.

In "Politics as Opposed to What?" of 1981, Cavell extends his notions of reading and being read by couching them in psycho-analytic terms. Echoing Wittgenstein's understanding of philoso-phy as offering therapies aimed at recovering philosophy from itself, reading is in this essay less understood as a process of inter-preting a text than as one of being interpreted by it. Psychoana-lytically speaking, then, while the text may be viewed as the analyst, the reader on this model features as the analysand. More-over, as in Freudian theory, transference is crucially required for the relationship between analyst and analysand to be conducive to the latter's recovery. By being, as Freud puts it, "put in the place of one or other of the patient's parents,"[11] the analyst appears, on the one hand, to the patient as one deserving respect, love, and applause, thus enforcing both collaboration and, since the parents might be seen as representing the patient's super-ego, the possi-bility "for a sort of *after-education* of the neurotic."[12] On the other hand, however, the patient, like the child toward a parent, may also experience negative or hostile attitudes toward the analyst, leading to resistance. Just as reading demands that we (despite our resistance) turn ourselves inside out, allow the text to unpack us, and open ourselves to critical scrutiny, so psychoanalytic therapy is a process of lifting the holds of repressed material through an encounter with the other's reading of oneself. In the essay "Psy-choanalysis and Cinema" of 1985, Cavell specifies the transference in question as being of the nature of countertransference: every act of transference is at the same time one of *responding* to an other's transference to me. Hence, whereas the text reads me, it always does so within a specific moment of my own relation to it. There is no point at which the relation comes into being apart from its constitutive reversals.

The 1972 reading of Thoreau's *Walden* illustrates well how the "epis-temology of conscience" (SW, 88), which Cavell, in the *Claim of Reason*, excavates from Rousseau, functions to underwrite a perfec-tionist conception of political resistance and friendship. Noticing the "intimacy between Rousseau's and Thoreau's understanding of society" (SW, 87), the transcendentalist classic *Walden* appears to Cavell as a form of writing which, by interrogating itself and its own conditions, seeks to question, like a friend, the self-definitions of its readers. Upon writing *Walden*, Thoreau refuses society his voice. Yet by physically withdrawing from his fellow human beings (Thoreau famously writes his tract while living in a small cabin in the woods near Walden pond), Thoreau is not in the business of withdrawing his consent; rather, the complex computations of his words amount to a search for ways to exercise his political voice more responsibly. Ultimately, what is at stake for Thoreau is a transfiguration – both of the self and the community. Thus *Walden* calls for a utopia, a radical transgression of the boundaries of accepted political intelligibility.

Needless to say, such a meditation must find itself faced with a sense of crisis. Indeed, Cavell's *The Senses of Walden* is itself permeated by a feeling of alarm. Written in a particularly turbulent phase of recent American history (including civil unrest and geopolitical warfare), it envisions Thoreau's writing as responding to a deep-seated sense of disappointment. Whereas the crisis it addresses may be said to occur on both personal and cosmological levels, perhaps its most immediate concern is of a political nature, namely the promise of America:

> Everyone is saying, and anyone can hear, that this is the new world; that we are the new men; that the earth is to be born again; that the past is to be cast off like a skin; that we must learn from children to see again; that every day is the first day of the world; that America is Eden. So how can a word get through whose burden is that we do not understand a word of all this? Or rather, that the way in which we understand it is insane, and we are trying to buy and bully our way into heaven; that we have failed; that the present is a task and discovery, not a period of America's privileged history; that we are not free, not whole, and not new, and we know this and are on a downward path of despair because of it; and that for the child to grow he requires family and familiarity, but for a grownup to grow he requires strangeness and transformation, i.e., birth? (SW, 59–60)

America is yet to be discovered – indeed it exists in a state of deferral, i.e., as a promise. But in order to articulate that promise, the self – Thoreau's self – must bring itself in a position to do so. From a state of melancholia – of inauthentic, mindless repetition, indeed of nihilism – which he takes to be characteristic of his fellow men, Thoreau therefore turns to language: by attempting "to make the word good" (SW, 30), he recreates himself, thus turning himself into a writer who aims to redeem every word of his own language. Indeed, while searching for "a literary redemption of language" (SW, 92), Thoreau may be said to engage in a recounting of criteria in the sense already outlined. Each word he employs must be rediscovered such that the world (of things, of others, of oneself) it tracks becomes visible in its concrete and essential reality. Hence by practicing a form of writing in search of its ultimate conditions or criteria, Thoreau (like Emerson) "underwrites" the methods and procedures of ordinary language philosophy as represented by Austin and Wittgenstein: both the American transcendentalists and their latter-day counterparts engage in an ongoing quest to recount the specific conditions of language. But whereas Austin and Wittgenstein, as we have seen, are persistently oriented toward "what we say when and the implications thereof," transcendentalism offers, as it were, a more concrete way of recounting what ordinary language is *about* – that is, the world of the ordinary. The crisis, then, both in its personal and cosmological dimensions, affects the very constitution of meaning and signification. Thoreau's fellow men speak, yet they have no voice; their language is devoid of affect and interest, there is no subject *meaning* what is said. In short, then, Thoreau teaches us to accept the burden of language, and indeed of finitude: that no impersonal structure, and no God for that matter, can ever replace our responsibility for aligning word and world. Saying what there is entails acknowledging an independent, separate world, one in which interest is taken, for only thus can we be responsive to the shared criteria that govern the world-directed use of words.

According to Cavell, Thoreau's prophetic call for a transfiguration of himself and his fellow men constitutes an act of political friendship: by withdrawing from political organization as it stands in order to reconsider its terms and conditions, he in effect associates with it. For Thoreau, as a self-established stranger, the task is to imaginatively explore the extent of our commonality, and ultimately to provoke his readers to take a renewed interest in their own experience. Given the apparent heroism of such a strategic withdrawal, Emersonian perfectionism may, as Cavell points out, in many of its formulations seem reminiscent of the sort of aristocratic rebuke of culture that we find in Nietzsche. (Nietzsche, as is well known, was an ardent reader of Emerson.) If it is true, however, that a certain desire for aristocracy and a disgust with the leveling effects of public life are features that unite Thoreau and Emerson with Nietzsche, then how can Cavell's employment of their work be made compatible with an affirmative stance toward democracy and equality? Indeed, how democratic is Cavell's perfectionism?

In John Rawls's account, whose criticisms of this doctrine Cavell takes very seriously, perfectionism is understood to be elitist, authoritarian, and aristocratic.[13] While holding perfectionism to be a teleological theory, i.e., a theory that identifies the good in terms of certain ends to be achieved, Rawls distinguishes between a moderate and an extreme version, both of which are at odds with his own, or any, democratic principles of justice. In its moderate version, the doctrine is one among others and "[directs] society to arrange institutions and to define the duties and obligations of individuals so as to maximize the achievement of human excellence, in art, in science, and culture."[14] The problem, though, with Rawls's understanding of moderate perfectionism is that in its exclusive emphasis on maximization it entirely forgets to ask about the conditions for something to count as culture. It takes for granted that high culture as it is now institutionalized deserves to be maximized. For Emerson and Nietzsche, however, the question is not how we can get more of the same, it is how culture can be found and consecrated: "There is, before finding [what Emerson calls 'the conversion of the world'], nothing to be maximized" (CHU, 49). Indeed, for most, if not all, of the authors Cavell enlists as proponents of perfectionism, existing culture is confronted, not with a desire for maximization, but with a sense of disdain or even disgust. Despite this aversion, however, they are not urging an abolition of democracy but rather, on the contrary, a transfiguration of culture, though one that must start with the individual. So on a truly democratic conception of perfectionism, whereas the capacity for self-criticism is universally distributed, a good culture is one forever to be arrived at. While excluding a fixed notion of perfectibility, Cavell's perfectionism thus respects each and every individual's right and capacity to work out a position in which his or her voice can come into being. On the other hand, as soon as a society starts taking its cultural standing for granted and only asks for its maximization, the responsibility on the part of each of its members to work out a conception of culture gets forfeited. Hence, what Rawls's moderate version of perfectionism really recommends is conformism; and this hardly constitutes a satisfactory basis for a living democracy.

In Rawls's extreme version of perfectionism, the maximization of excellence is the sole principle of institutions. This might easily suggest that society ought to be divided into two separate classes – the elite and its servants. Whereas the elite is intrinsically valuable and significant, its servants only live for the good of the elite and are deemed valuable in accordance with their success in providing for their masters. Obviously, Cavell rejects such a view. Moreover, like the moderate version, it fails, in its emphasis on maximization, to account for the moment of transfiguration; hence it definitely does not coincide with Emersonian perfectionism.

Ultimately, Emersonian perfectionism does not result in any particular moral or political demands. Rather, in its complex existential configurations, it figures as "the condition of democratic morality" (CHU, 125). As such, it is a dimension of representative democracy that cannot be delegated.

An Ethics of Infinite Responsibility?

In a paper presented at a conference on skepticism and interpretation in Amsterdam in the summer of 2000, "What is the Scandal of Skepticism? Moments in Schopenhauer and Levinas," Cavell started to explore some of the fascinating affinities that exist between his own work and that of Emmanuel Levinas.[15] Levinas's thought, culminating in *Totality and Infinity* (1961) and *Otherwise than Being, or Beyond Essence* (1974), has exerted a tremendous influence on contemporary approaches to ethics and theology, as well as to problems of subjectivity and experience; and it would certainly be impossible to do full justice to the complexities involved in trying to compare the two thinkers within the scope of this book.[16] Nevertheless, for students of his work, the fact that Cavell himself explicitly acknowledges the importance of Levinas for his own philosophical self-understanding is itself highly significant, and ought to cast further light on the ethical implications of his reflections on skepticism, in particular with regard to other minds. While acknowledging this necessary caveat, the rest of this chapter will be devoted to a discussion of the paper he presented in Amsterdam in 2000.

The concept Cavell focuses on in order to get his conversation with Levinas's thought going is that of responsibility. For Levinas, responsibility, issuing from a demand placed upon me by the other, constitutes the basic and determinative fact of subjectivity. In a face-to-face encounter with the other, the freedom of the subject is subordinate to, or indeed conditional upon, his or her "subjection" to the other. Both an *hôte* (host and guest) and an *otage* (hostage), the subject is infinitely responsible to and for the other, and bonded to her. Ethics is thus a first philosophy: it identifies and lays bare the transcendental conditions not only of the subject's relation to herself and the world, but of an ethical answerability set to counteract all forms of moral skepticism. Ultimately, for Levinas, the face of the other, which in its destitute alterity and exposedness reduces the ego to an absolute passivity, attests to what he calls "the glory of the infinite," a Good beyond being, and hence in the final instance the beyond of God.

As we have seen, for Cavell, the question of responsibility, which permeates so much of his work, gains its specific momentum within the context of skepticism. By subliming language and thus replacing or repudiating the ordinary (represented as the shared criteria speakers employ in order to make themselves and their experience intelligible), the skeptic effectively drives out the responsibility to make himself known to others, as well as others to himself. In the case of skepticism about the external world, the position of the skeptic, as we saw in chapter 2, is highly unstable, and as the analysis in *The Claim of Reason* shows, it is far from clear that the skeptic, though capable of constructing a best case for knowledge (one that generalizes), ever manages to enter a definite claim on which to focus his attack. To live one's skepticism with respect to the external world would be tantamount to psychosis: what the skeptic opens our eyes to is that *this* is the best, that our everyday life with objects, though not immune to the possibility of failure, is all we shall ever have. With regard to skepticism about other minds, however, the situation, as we remember, is quite different. Here the skeptic's incapacity to uncover a best case for knowledge engenders the sense that our failure to know others is indexed to particular others (to *my* relation to *you*), and that only a case-by-case assessment can reveal the full extent to which we are mutually unintelligible to one another. But in both forms of skepticism, the skeptic can be said to attempt to rationalize our disappointment with knowledge: rather than accepting or acknowledging the existence of the world and himself and others in it, and hence also the criteria by means of which those existents can intelligibly be addressed, the skeptic interprets our separateness (from the world and others) as an intellectual deficiency or lack. Regardless of whether skepticism is consequently responded to with an appeal to an impersonal structure or presence that is meant to overcome isolation or simply affirmed as a metaphysical truth, the responsibility (before the world and others in it) that comes with the possession of an ordinary language gets lost along the way. Thus, the "scandal of skepticism" is neither, as Kant claimed, that no proof has so far been given that is able to rebut the skeptic; nor is it, as Heidegger suggests, that such proofs are attempted over and over again. Rather, the scandal lies with the skeptic himself: by hypostatizing my indif-

ference and disinterest, or my fears of being known, by offering a
metaphysical account of my separateness, *I* am the scandal.

In "What is the Scandal of Skepticism?" Cavell again points to
Kripke's reading of Wittgenstein as a revealing example of a philosophical repudiation of the ordinary. For Kripke, as we have seen,
the "skeptical solution" to skepticism about linguistic meaning
consists in bringing the community of speakers to account for our
mutual accommodation or accord in language. But this deprives us
of our responsibility to make ourselves intelligible to another, and
initiation into linguistic practices becomes a matter of monitoring
rather than allowing the other, while relating to our attentive invitations to follow our example, to go on for himself. We are attuned,
though not as a given fact of our lives in and with language, but
rather as a function of our separate outcalls of phenomena, of our
singular attempts to make ourselves known and our experience
intelligible. Whereas postmodernism (in tandem with global capi-
talism), in all its celebration of the world as simulacra and appearance, might be said to represent an endorsement of skepticism qua
indifference, a modernist rejoinder consists in reminding us of the
seriousness that ought to follow from our being condemned to linguistic as well as bodily expressiveness. While Schopenhauer (and
later Freud and Wittgenstein) can be credited for having uncovered
the infinite responsibility to the world and others that comes
with human embodiment and finitude, Levinas translates such an
emphasis on responsibility into an ethics of alterity. Focusing upon
the relation to the other, Cavell identifies a number of shared concerns. First, in both thinkers' accounts, the other places us in a position of infinite answerability: for Cavell, in so far as our relations,
in the absence of a best case for knowledge, are restricted, there
is nothing about other minds that satisfies us for all purposes,
and hence we need to recognize ourselves as denying others; for
Levinas, in so far as the face of the other resists our desire for
cognitive possession and control, the ego is located within the
imperative call of the other. In one passage highly reminiscent of
characteristic claims in Levinas, Cavell thus writes that "I (have to)
respond to [the other's life], or refuse to respond. It calls upon me;
it calls me out. I have to acknowledge it. I am as fated to that as I
am to my body; it is as natural to me" (CR, 84). And in another
passage, amazingly redolent, both in tone and implication, of
Levinas's famous claim that his whole message as a philosopher is
contained in the politeness of someone's "*après vous*," he says of
knowing others:

Just *this* – say expecting someone to tea; or returning a favor; waving goodbye; reluctantly or happily laying in groceries for a friend with a cold; feeling rebuked, and feeling it would be humiliating to admit the feeling; pretending not to understand that the other has taken my expression, with a certain justice, as meaning more than I sincerely wished it to mean; hiding inside a marriage; hiding outside a marriage – just such things are perhaps the most that knowing others comes to, or has come to for me. (CR, 439)

Second, both Cavell and Levinas conceive of the coming-to-be of responsibility for and to the other as presupposing a trauma of awakening whereby our primary narcissism is shattered. In Cavell, this may occur, or be represented, in an indefinite number of ways: as the desire for remarriage, as Kleinian reparation after an initial phase of pre-oedipal aggression, as Freudian hysterical conversion, as Shakespearean tragic insight, as Thoreauian "thinking beside oneself in a sane sense," and essentially as acknowledgment of the other. In Levinas, on the other hand, the opening toward the other is thought of in terms of the infinite irruption of immanence in Descartes' first proof of God's existence in the third of his *Meditations*, or, say, as the reverberation of a sublime call for a Good beyond being that transcends the horizon of cognitive meaning.

While strikingly similar in their twofold emphasis on infinite responsibility and passivity, one crucial difference between the two philosophers' understanding of the ethical demand ought to be highlighted. As opposed to Levinas's divinization of the relationship with alterity, for Cavell, the other is fundamentally a finite other.[17] In acknowledging the other as a mindful and thus potentially suffering human being, I recognize our separation, even mourn it, thereby allowing the other to appear as endlessly other, yet there is no moment at which it would be appropriate to employ a religious vocabulary. This refusal to accept the grammar of religion as binding displays a long, and yet highly fragmented, history in Cavell's work. It makes itself felt in his early essay on Kierkegaard, in which he argues that the Danish thinker, like later Wittgenstein, is engaged in an exploration of the a priori possibility of applying certain concepts, in this case Christian ones, but that, unlike the spiritual fervor associated with aesthetic and philosophical modernism, the categories thereby articulated no longer express positions that seem alive to us today.[18] Likewise, in *Disowning Knowledge*, he claims that detailed dependence on God, of the type we find in Descartes's philosophy, "is no longer natural to the human spiritual repertory" (DK, 198), and that "Respectable further theologizing of the world has, I gather, ceased" (DK, 36n). In *The Claim of Reason*, this Nietzschean sense of modernity as entailing the death of God is conjoined with more explicit criticisms of religion. In particular, Cavell, in an equally Nietzschean vein, charges the Christian interpretation of human nature for requiring the "mortification" (CR, 471) of the human body, as if only "the denial of the human *is* the human" (CR, 493). But probably the most weighty reason why religion no longer represents a worthy competitor to philosophy or modernist art practices consists in its displacement of authority from individuals to a source beyond possible critical assessment by autonomous individuals. While alluding to Heidegger's sustained distinction between philosophy and religion, Cavell writes that "philosophy cannot acknowledge religion as letting – the way religion works to let – truth happen, say by authority or revelation" (NYUA, 3). Faithful in this respect to Kant's critical (modernist-liberal) turn, ultimately the only valid source of authority lies with the reflexivity of the individual. To disregard in principle the demand for a free exercise of critical reflection would be tantamount to denying the ontological freedom and equality of individuals that Cavell takes to be definitive of modernity.

This final motivation to resist a religious language seems to chime in with Cavell's and Levinas's disagreement about the problem of freedom. For Cavell, like Kant, freedom is essentially a matter of self-determination, of being bounded exclusively by laws that the individual has rationally imposed upon itself. Unlike Kant, though, who views self-determination as involving only the solitary individual, Cavell's Emersonian perfectionism recognizes the need to include in its account the acknowledgment of a relationship through which my present state of heteronomy may be made manifest: in marriage or friendship, the acknowledgment of the other entails the discovery of my own denial, and hence of the possibility of a more authentic positioning of myself, a regaining of voice, in that and other relationships. In Levinas's account, however, the relation between freedom and the other gets thought of in rather different terms, ones that diverge not only in the choice of bias, but also, it seems, in intent. While agreeing with Cavell that the exercise of freedom is best understood from the perspective of a response to the attractions of an exemplary other such that its exercise always requires the by now well-known reversals of reading and being-read, Levinas offers a metaphysical account whereby freedom comes on the stage only *after* the event of susceptibility to the other:

> For the condition for, or the unconditionality of, the self does not begin in the auto-affection of a sovereign ego that would be, after the event, "compassionate" for another. Quite the contrary: the uniqueness of the responsible ego is possible only *in* being obsessed by another, in the trauma suffered prior to any auto-identification, in an unrepresentable *before*.[19]

Indeed, for Levinas's antihumanist humanism, the human person, free and for itself, has lost its primacy. In its place, the ego appears in and through the infinite responsibility for the suffering and vulnerable other. For Cavell, on the other hand, the human being is free even in its complete state of conformity and indifference to the other: although responsible for its own being, a person (the skeptic) may not exercise, or live up to, his freedom; as a comfortable replacement for the burden of responsibility he may simply yield to the temptation to sublime language; and yet there is no escape from freedom except on the pains of one's own unknownness and unintelligibility.

Cavell's interest in Levinas's ethics of alterity brings a number of his crucial concerns to the fore. In particular, it enforces a recognition of the tension between his unmitigated modernism, on the one hand, and the pressure toward introducing a religious, or non-modernist, language, on the other. There is no denying that even though one strand of his work, the one I have stressed so far, staunchly resists the appeal to sources of authority for which the individual in principle cannot be held accountable, there is another, especially in his essays on romanticism, that seems to allow for something like religious motives to resonate. Among these, the call for a redemption of the ordinary might be the most pronounced. The next and final chapter will be addressing this issue.

6

Between Philosophy and Literature: Deconstruction and Romanticism

Cavell's extended engagement with contemporary literary theory, and deconstruction in particular, has throughout been marked by a fundamental ambivalence. While expressing admiration for, as well as a sense of affinity with, the works of Stanley Fish, Paul de Man, and, especially, Jacques Derrida, he none the less has registered profound differences between their approach and that of his own. Surely, on the one hand, a number of similarities seem to exist: a desire to allow philosophical writing to be open to its literary dimensions; an attempt to conduct a philosophical critique of philosophy (or metaphysics), and in particular of all forms of foundationalism; a distrust of the canons and procedures of current academic philosophy; and a strong emphasis on problems of language, as well as the morality and politics of speech. But while, on the other hand, the philosophical programs of ordinary language philosophy and deconstruction may, in many respects, appear to be collusive, they significantly oppose each other with regard to the question of the ordinary. For Cavell, the ordinary voice comes to its own on the return from the metaphysical; for Derrida, however, the ordinary is simply an effect of the metaphysical, and so no critique of metaphysics can proceed with reference to what we say when and the implications thereof. Thus in Cavell's account, by depriving itself of our ordinary links with the world and each other, deconstruction appears essentially fated to skepticism.[1]

Deconstruction and the Ordinary

Cavell's first major discussion of deconstruction (and postmodern textual theory) comes in his lengthy assessment of Stanley Fish and Paul de Man, "Politics as Opposed to What?", of 1982. As is appropriate for an encounter with theorists of textuality who prefer to develop their positions through readings of other people's work, Cavell's critical entrance into the logic of their arguments takes place by means of challenging their respective appropriations of Austin. We already know that Austin's legacy occupies a central position in Cavell's own writings, and although Austin's robust investigation of the ordinary fails to reach the depths of Wittgenstein's more fragile acceptance of the "truth of skepticism," its importance and relevance is taken as beyond doubt. In particular, Cavell points to its drive to overcome self-mystification by investigating the public conditions of an individual's discourse, and, hence, against charges of conservatism, to its political dimension. Philosophy, in Austin's account, has the power to change an individual's self-interpretation. Despite having no privileged discourse in which to exercise its reflection, ordinary language philosophy is able to challenge our present interests and orientations: it is inherently involved in what one might call a "politics of interpretation" (the title of the 1981 conference in Chicago at which "Politics as Opposed to What?" was initially presented).

Cavell's comments on Fish's now classic book *Is There a Text in This Class?* start with the large issue of Austin's theory of performative utterances. Briefly, for Austin in *How to Do Things with Words* and elsewhere, such speech acts are categorially distinct from statements in that, rather than simply being true or false, their utterance constitutes an action: "if a person makes an utterance of this sort we should say that he is *doing* something rather than merely *saying* something" (PhP, 235). So, for example, when someone in the right circumstances and with the appropriate authority says "I name this ship the *Queen Elizabeth*," then not only has something been said, but an action (of christening) has been performed. Words, for Austin, are capable of serving other purposes than those of simply stating truths or falsehoods; they also allow us, within the constraints of conventional procedures, to perform innumerable types of action (apologizing, excusing, promising, marrying, etc.).

Following Fish, Cavell warns against taking Austin's doctrine of performatives to have provided a full-blown theory of language. In view of the nature and complexity of ordinary language, it would be misleading, as some theorists of literature have done, to use it in order to help oneself to definitions, say, of literature or fiction. That is not to say, though, that a theorist such as Fish is uninterested in the philosophy of ordinary language. On the contrary, Fish finds Austin's work, and especially his theory of performative utterances, to be of the utmost relevance to his own thinking about language. According to Fish, however, Austin's account suffers from an inconsistency. On the one hand, it asserts a distinction between so-called ordinary and literary discourse. On the other hand, by claiming that ordinary language is permeated by "values, intentions, and purposes which is often assumed to be the exclusive property of literature,"[2] it ends up blurring or even canceling the difference between those two forms of language. For Fish, this means that ordinary discourse, like literature, is essentially non-cognitive: rather than being (as in the classic representationalist picture) responsible to facts or reality, it should be thought of in terms of performative utterances functioning in accordance with intersubjective constraints: "When we communicate, it is because we are parties to a set of discourse agreements which are in effect decisions as to what can be stipulated as a fact."[3] Clearly, Fish's objection must be placed within the larger context of his project of showing that no facts of the matter or truth conditions determine textual meaning; rather, meaning is a contingent effect of historical appropriation: a text means whatever the interpretive community makes of it. Against the claims of "objectivists" or "foundationalists," the idea of there being a categorial difference between interpretation (trying to assess what a text *really* means) and application (using a text to some purpose) therefore rests on a mistake.

In his response, Cavell is quick to point out that Fish's use of the term "ordinary" differs from Austin's. By initially opposing ordinary discourse to the order of the non-cognitive and then afterwards, in order to resolve the alleged contradiction, placing it within that order, Fish ironically assimilates Austin's notion of the ordinary to the arch-positivist notion of emotive or non-cognitive meaning – as distinct from cognitive discourse. As we have seen, for positivist thinkers such as Ayer and Stevenson, the fundamental difference between science, on the one hand, and aesthetics, ethics, and religion, on the other, is that while the first type of (descriptive) discourse is answerable to an objective world, the second (normative) one can lay no claims to objective truth. However, Austin's distinction between constative and performative utterances, rather than reiterating a central doctrine of positivism, radically calls into question the opposition between cognitive and non-cognitive discourse. First, Austin comes to reject any hard and fast boundary between performative and fact-stating discourse:

> If . . . we loosen up our ideas of truth and falsity we shall see that statements, when assessed in relation to the facts, are not so very different after all from pieces of advice, warnings, verdicts, and so on. We see then that stating something is performing an act just as much as is giving an order or giving a warning; and we see, on the other hand, that, when we give an order or a warning or a piece of advice, there is a question about how this is related to fact which is not perhaps so very different from the kind of question that arises when we discuss how a statement is related to fact. (PhP, 251)

Second, the ordinary is not *opposed* to any other discourse, whether scientific, religious, ethical, or literary, and its ongoing quarrel with metaphysics (or philosophy), while a central component of Austin's thought, does not imply that the ordinary and the metaphysical are two separate modes or realms of discourse. Indeed, Austin's "claim, largely implicit, is that the philosophical is not a special mode of discourse at all; it has no interests of its own (as, say, science or religion or sports or trades have), or it ought not to have" (TOS, 37). Third, Fish, by eventually opposing ordinary and fact-stating discourse, falsely makes it sound as if performatives do not enjoy any measure of rationality. However, on Cavell's reading the most compelling sense in which Austin's doctrine of performative utterance represents an attack on positivism consists in its insistence on "the performative utterance as *retaining* an adequation to reality (to certain factual conditions) equal to that of verifiable statements" (PP, 50). What Austin substitutes for the concept of truth is not some order of the non-cognitive but "felicity." According to Austin, the felicity/infelicity distinction designates the various ways in which performatives may or may not be in conformity with their constitutive conventions. For example, the "appointment" of someone who already is a consul to be a consul, or the "divorce" of one's spouse simply by saying "I divorce you," amount to failures to let the purported act come off arising from the non-observance of its rules. Whereas Fish takes such utterances to lack any possible adequation to a cognitive order, Cavell sees their specific form of adequation (or, in these cases, lack thereof), which in these two examples accounts for their infelicity, as residing in their normativity. And rather than being assimilable to Austinian performatives, what the positivists used to refer to as emotive (non-cognitive) meaning is better thought of in terms of Austin's notion of per-locutionary acts. According to Austin, perlocutionary acts are distinguished from illocutionary (or performative) acts by virtue of a difference in *force*: whereas the former involve doing something *by* saying something, the latter involve doing something *in* saying something.

Both Cavell and Fish hold ordinary discourse to be made possible by virtue of a sense of agreement underlying communication. Yet Cavell reproaches Fish for interpreting these agreements as based on decisions, thus making language seem more conventional than it actually is. In, for example, Austin's theory of excuses, it would be implausible to describe the differences between "doing something mistakenly, accidentally, heedlessly, carelessly, inadvertently, automatically, thoughtlessly, inconsiderately, and so on" (TOS, 40) as attributable to agreements that are expressible as decisions. Indeed, as we know from *The Claim of Reason*, skepticism typically reacts to itself by conceiving of language as essentially conventional. If the space of all intelligible linguistic moves and reactions were constructed in advance by a set of decisions, then the call for a responsible application of words would lose its pertinence.

In his discussion of Paul de Man, Cavell again returns to Austin's notion of performativity, and in particular the constative–performative distinction. For de Man, who wishes to employ Austin's thought for the purpose of defending a deconstructionist distinction between grammar and rhetoric, or between referentiality and non-referentiality, whereas constative utterances refer to something in the world, performative utterances have "effects" or "forces." De Man's failure, however, to acknowledge that both constatives and performatives are responsible to facts, that is, are binding on rational agents in various ways all of which are irreducible to producing effects on others, reiterates the latent positivism of Fish's initial distinction between cognitive and non-cognitive modes of discourse. Ironically, Austin gets taken to defend a distinction the thrust of which his whole philosophy, both implicitly and explicitly, rebels against.

Of course, in *Allegories of Reading*, the work Cavell comments upon, de Man ultimately attempts to deconstruct the opposition between constatives and performatives, claiming there is an "aporia" between the two.[4] Indeed, for de Man, a number of crucial distinctions in philosophy and literary theory, including grammar and rhetoric, original and quoted, natural and conventional, referential and non-referential, generate what he calls undecidability: by being determined by local or conventional criteria, the decisions made on their basis, while neither objective nor rational, reflect only self-serving community agreements, and ultimately these distinctions can be shown to collapse. In undoing such distinctions, de Man generally points out how what initially seems the derived term in a pair ends up inflecting its opposite. For example, the pair "original/quoted" collapses upon taking into consideration the fact that all words are learned and thus cited. Hence no words are original, nor are any quoted (since that would presuppose the existence of the original). Likewise, nothing in the grammar of a speech act (for example "I'll see you at home") determines whether it rhetorically should be taken as a prediction, an agreement, or a promise, to name just some of the possibilities.

While admitting to hear in the deconstructionist use of the term "undecidable" "a soft literary pretension to hard philosophy" (QO, 131), Cavell's critique of de Man is predominantly indirect and restrained, setting off by way of a parallel argument:

> Someone says that the difference between knives and forks is that you cut with a knife and spear with a fork; a second objects that you can also cut with a fork and spear with a knife; whereupon a third concludes that there is an aporia between knives and forks. (TOS, 42)

By offering the argument as a "scene of instruction," Cavell abstains from giving any comments. Its moral is, however, evident. To hold that the distinction between knives and forks is aporetic just because they can be used interchangeably, reveals less about the unruliness of cutlery than about its adaptability to various demands. Even though you *can* spear with a knife and cut with a fork, such behavior, far from undoing the distinction between the two, mainly reveals something about you – say your interests and desires, or perhaps your (neurotic?) wish to absolve yourself of the commitments that stem from taking a piece of cutlery in one or the other way.

In another and more elaborate example, Cavell draws attention to de Man's well-known analysis of a gag about Archie Bunker, a character in the television series *All in the Family*.[5] Asked by his wife Edith whether he wants his bowling shoes laced over or under, Archie replies "What's the difference?" Edith then goes on to patiently explain the difference, though in return she only receives his scorn. According to de Man, Archie's response might be taken in two mutually exclusive ways. While his wife understands it as a request for information, "What's the difference?" can also be meant as denying that there is any difference, or as expressing contempt for any attempt to explain the difference. Archie's irritation at being told the difference shows that he intends his question this way. Obviously, the humor in the scene arises from their incapacity to resolve their misunderstanding: the more Edith tries to explain, the more angry Archie gets, which in turn provokes her to add detail to the very explanation that he does not want. De Man brings his discussion to a close by writing that "the same grammatical pattern engenders two meanings that are mutually exclusive: the literal meaning asks for the concept (difference) whose existence is denied by the figurative meaning."[6] Rhetoric, then, deconstructs grammar, leaving the meaning of Archie's utterance undecidable.

In de Man's view, the gag demonstrates the essential uncontrollability and non-transparency of language. No speaker can ever be in command of the effects that rhetoric and figurality have on her speech, hence communication continually involves the risk of misunderstanding. Cavell, however, while accepting de Man's premise that no grammatical pattern by itself will ever be sufficient to unequivocally determine the effects of its rhetorical realization, resists the skeptical generalization to the effect that language as such is untamable or even perverse. Such a move would be analogous to "saying that it is perverse or aberrant of the normally functioning human hand that it can grasp, and make a fist, and play arpeggios, and shade the eyes, and be held up to bless or to swear" (TOS, 43). The fact that people negotiate rhetorical questions contradicts the deconstructionist view that, because no criterion is at hand for settling their status, these utterances demonstrate the unnaturalness, or forced character, of language. Like Cavellian skeptics in general, de Man observes that criteria come to an end, that no final set of criteria exist for distinguishing, to stay with this example, assertions from questions in rhetorical questions; and yet to conclude that such issues are undecidable is to accept the skeptic's inference that since criteria do not yield certainty there is nothing to be known; hence a decision has been made that the skeptical conclusion is correct. In other words, by emphasizing undecidability, the deconstructionist paradoxically allows that knowing questions from assertions in rhetorical questions is a matter of (arbitrary) decision.

Moreover, in interpreting the gag's "What's the difference?" Cavell contends that, like "Who cares?" or "Who's to say?" Archie's question is "a hedge against assertion" (TOS, 44); yet it also, like a rhetorical question ("Isn't the weather glorious?") asks for a response, though it is not evident that Archie really wants one. Hence, whatever Archie wants from his wife fails to be unequivocally revealed by his question; indeed, it is not even clear that he knows it himself. It could be that Archie knows the difference between the two ways of lacing shoes, and, if so, that he refuses to care and is angry at being told what he already knows. But it could also be that he does not know the difference, in which case his anger might be occasioned by an unwillingness to be told by a woman what to do. Thus, speaking involves risks: there is always a possibility that what we say does not come across, that not enough or too much has been said, and so forth. We always need to strive in order to make ourselves known. Yet, ultimately, what we mean by what we say is our responsibility: whether ambiguous or not, what we say is *our* words. And not only do words have a semantic meaning, they also define us as speakers by revealing the position we inhabit in our life with them. Hence the ambivalence in what Archie says "is a fact about some Archie, not about the inevitable relation between grammar and rhetoric. The moral of the example [is] that there is no inevitable relation between them" (TOS, 45). No external structure or constraint can remove the responsibilities we have for what we mean: "Grammar cannot, or ought not, of itself dictate what you mean, what it is up to you to say" (TOS, 45).

Thus the performative meaning of Archie's question becomes a function of what Cavell elsewhere calls "the conversation of marriage." Rather than being undecidable, it gets decided in and through the repetitive, everyday, and unending negotiations that constitute Archie and Edith's attempts to read one another and come to terms with each other.

In addition to the issue of rhetoric and performativity, another important difference between Cavell and de Man hinges on the problem of quotation. As already mentioned, in the deconstructionist account the distinction between quoted words and their originals is seen as undermined by the fact of inheritance: since linguistic behavior is learned, all words are imitated or quoted; and yet, since there are no original words to which quoted words can be contrasted, no words are ever quoted. In the spirit of Nietzsche's anti-metaphysical attack on the distinction between appearance and reality, the claim, put differently, is that something can be an imitation only where an original exists to which it can be contrasted: but without originals, the very point of counting something as derived disappears. For this argument to make full sense, it necessarily has to be viewed in conjunction with the defining aim of detecting and undercutting each and every appeal to the original. Indeed, for both de Man and Derrida, the yearning for the original is expressive of an illicit metaphysical desire to stabilize meaning by reference to some sort of self-presenting presence (conspicuously, in Derrida, that of the human voice). But if, as these theorists argue, all institution of meaning presupposes a general text, that is, the repetition, roughly, of essentially arbitrary signs whose meaning is accounted for with reference to the differential nature of signification, then the appeal to pure presence becomes a myth. Within the history of Western metaphysics, a whole series of different names have been given to the conception of founding center: origin, end, *arché*, *telos*, *eidos*, *ousia*, consciousness, God, man. For de Man and Derrida, all of these permutations of the notion of a self-present being must be recognized for what they are: not reality but unattainable objects of desire produced within a perpetual process of substitution whereby absence is masked with an illusion of presence.

While sharing de Man's and Derrida's sense that language is there before we are, that it is inherited and learned, Cavell considers the determination to undo the opposition between "original" and "quote," though not in itself misguided or false, as evidence of a desire to deflect attention from the crucial yet risky act of appropriating words. In Wittgenstein's "scenes of instruction," which repeatedly invoke the figure of the child, the inheritance of language becomes a continual task, rather than a singular event (or set of events). There is no stage at which language can be said to have been fully inherited – once and for all. In *The Claim of Reason*, Cavell refers to the willingness to continue the process of appropriation as a second inheritance of language, as opposed to the child's first. Moreover, in *The Senses of Walden* this distinction gets reinterpreted on the basis of Thoreau's distinction between what he calls the mother tongue and the father tongue. Depending on the readiness and capacity to originally declare one's commonness in language, and thus to escape the imitative declaration of uniqueness characteristic of skepticism's conformity, a person can be said to achieve the "reserved and select expression" of the father tongue. But this means that the distinction between quoting and saying, rather than being rejected, should be underlined, though in a more complex and devious manner than what happens in the (traditional, metaphysical) position under attack by deconstruction. For one thing, it becomes necessary to distinguish the quotation or imitation taking place in (Emersonian) conformity (in which a father tongue has not been achieved) from that of an original declaration of commonness (which marks the achievement of a father tongue). This shift, one might argue, toward an authentic quotation, marks the upward movement of perfectionism, out of the Platonic cave. For another thing, since the father tongue can be seen as representing the "maturity and experience" of the mother, it follows that the father tongue is "both later and at the same time more original than the mother tongue. Accordingly there is a locale in which quotation becomes more original than its original" (QO, 133). Rather than enacting a deconstruction of the opposition between original and quoted words, this line of thought calls for a further distinction as between whether "quotation" and "original" are being employed in the mother or in the father tongue. So in Cavell's account of it, deconstruction, like skepticism in general, "names our wish . . . to strip ourselves of the responsibility we have in meaning (or in failing to mean) one thing, or one way, rather than another" (QO, 135). It can thus be viewed as a way of theatricalizing oneself, of depriving oneself of one's voice.

In the context of Cavell's engagement with deconstruction, the most extensive reflection on the issue of the voice occurs in "Counter-Philosophy and the Pawn of Voice," the detailed discussion of Derrida which occupies the second section of *A Pitch of Philosophy*. It should not come as a surprise that the voice comes to have a central role in the dispute between Cavell and Derrida. As we have seen, for Cavell, the orientation toward the voice, "our unastonishing yet astonishing ability to say what we say, I for you, you for you" (POP, 59), has throughout been of central importance. Indeed, if he were to give, he says, "a one-clause sense" of why he wrote *The Claim of Reason*, then it would be "to help bring the human voice back into philosophy" (POP, 58): that is, to suspend traditional philosophy's skeptical suppression of the voice. For Derrida, however, in stark contrast to Cavell, the voice represents all that is wrong with philosophy. Thus, in *Speech and Phenomena*, his first principal work in philosophy, Derrida argues that for Husserl, whose writings he takes to be representative of Western logocentrism (or "phonocentrism"), the voice establishes the unity and origin of both sense and presence.[7] A prime example of unmediated self-presence, the voice, while existing "before" language, allows a pure consciousness to assign meanings to the words it requires to express its essentially extralinguistic thoughts: in establishing the ultimate form of ideality, it thus escapes the vagaries of temporality and intersubjectivity. Roughly, in Derrida's account, a closer consideration of the language in which phenomenology produces the results of its reductions shows that the distinction between pure expressivity, on the one hand, and communication and indication, on the other, collapses. At the end of the day, Husserl is unable to protect the purity of the (metaphysical) voice from linguistic contamination: there is no original presence, only representation; no pure present moment, only a contamination of past and future, self-division and difference.

Cavell is quick to point out that "The voice Derrida finds over-praised, or over-counted, is not exactly the voice on which Austin and the later Wittgenstein pin their hopes" (POP, 59). No philosopher of ordinary language would promote the kind of metaphysical determination of the voice that Derrida finds in Husserl, or, for that matter, in the tradition of Western metaphysics. Yet Cavell does not terminate his discussion of Derrida by simply noticing their dissimilar use of this key notion. He also suggests further lines of inquiry along which deconstruction and ordinary language philosophy both concur and differ. And as in the discussions of Fish and de Man, he again chooses to focus on Austin, whose conception of speech acts and performativity, in particular, has been of great interest to Derrida.

Crucially, both Austin and Derrida see themselves as anti-metaphysical thinkers. They both attempt to "dismantle" (Austin) or "deconstruct" (Derrida) key assumptions and preoccupations within the history of Western philosophy. But whereas Austin views metaphysics as based on a denial of the ordinary, and hence the ordinary as an alternative to metaphysics, Derrida considers the ordinary to be permeated by logocentrism: consequently, the deconstructive philosopher, while seeking to unravel and undo metaphysical oppositions, has no choice but to accept speaking metaphysically. To quote Cavell, "[Derrida] may think [metaphysics] intellectually moribund, and to lead to a certain political and cultural corruption of Western culture as such. But this takes metaphysics to have institutional and linguistic bases which cannot vanish at the touch of the ordinary; on the contrary, it is bound to swamp the ordinary, to take it under its own protection, or interpretation" (PP, 75). Thus deconstruction has from the outset no recourse to the ordinary; indeed, Derrida's critique of metaphysics,

Cavell argues, amounts to a flight from the ordinary. In order to substantiate this fundamental thesis, Cavell adduces a number of differences (which I will now get to) between his and Derrida's understanding of Austin.

Upon deconstructing a text (say of Rousseau, Plato, Kant, or any other figure of classical Western philosophy), Derrida typically proceeds by attending to what he calls its "margins" – the often neglected yet revealing aspects of texts, such as footnotes, appendices, metaphors, or exclusion of cases, or other such seemingly minor textual devices. Yet for Derrida, paying attention to these marginal dimensions of a text is not something that should be done out of deference to a special procedure (i.e., that of deconstruction); doing so just *is* to read. It may therefore appear slightly ironic, though potentially very effective as criticism, that Cavell, in a series of remarks, accuses Derrida of not having properly read Austin.

First, in order to counter Derrida's claim, in "Signature Event Context,"[8] that Austin fails to conduct a critique of a metaphysics of presence, Cavell refers to Austin's dismantling, in *Sense and Sensibilia*, of the empiricist tradition's view of presence, that is, the thesis "that we can know only what is present to our senses, and that this presence is the foundation of empirical knowledge" (PP, 71–2). For just as Derrida critically considers how Husserl, in his reading, tries to ground meaning and knowledge by reference to the self-presence of the *ego cogito* (as expressed by the voice), so Austin mercilessly exposes the failures of A. J. Ayer, in *The Foundations of Empirical Knowledge*, to establish his doctrine of sense-data as the non-inferential foundation of synthetic knowledge-claims.[9] And just as Derrida views Husserl as representative of the whole tradition of Western metaphysics, so Austin, by choosing Ayer "as chief stalking-horse," seeks to put the whole tradition of empiricism to an end. Despite Derrida's failure to recognize Austin's ambition, both thinkers are in the business not of criticizing specific doctrines or views, but of deconstructing/dismantling the very context within which those doctrines or views arise. Cavell illustrates his point further by drawing attention to the similarity between Austin's crusade against the "descriptive fallacy" and Derrida's attack on logocentrism: in both cases, a rejection takes place of the primacy of knowledge in accounting for our relation to the world. Both thinkers resist what Derrida refers to as a "limitation of sense to knowledge, of logos to objectivity, of language to reason."[10] But whereas Austin replaces the old empiricist bifurcation between verifiable statements and judgments (of religion, of aesthetics, of ethics) lacking adequation to reality with his theory of performativity, in which adequation is accounted for by means of an appeal to felicity conditions, Derrida, like Fish and de Man, though ready to reject traditional metaphysical theoreticism, fails to appreciate the thrust of Austin's position. Rather than, as Derrida argues, substituting for truth the non-cognitive value of force, Austin excavates an alternative form of adequation that is just as binding as truth. By disregarding the "hardness" of Austinian felicity conditions, Derrida ends up destroying Austin's counter to positivism; and, like positivism, he thereby suppresses Austin's fundamental concern, namely the ordinary.

In addition to the omission of *Sense and Sensibilia*, which prevents Derrida from recognizing Austin's criticisms of a metaphysics of presence, Cavell charges him with failing to take into consideration Austin's theory of parasitic or imitative speech and excuses. While this may sound like a pedantic demand for completion, Cavell's complaint goes to the heart of Derrida's critique of Austin in "Signature Event Context." For in this essay, upon discussing his account of infelicitous performatives, Derrida argues that although Austin recognizes the possibility that *any* performative utterance may fail, he only views such failure as a contingent possibility, and one that should therefore be excluded, whereas for Derrida it is a constitutive condition of any utterance that it never is fully "happy." In particular, Austin excludes from his analysis so-called "nonserious" usages of language – play-acting, fiction, quoting – on the grounds that they are parasitic. For Derrida, however, the significance of non-serious speech acts lies in their capacity to illuminate the nature of ordinary performative utterances. Non-serious speech acts are performed in the absence of the intention of the speaking subject; and they may be said to involve a kind of citation. In Derrida's terminology, they function in accordance with a logic of iterability, that is, a repeatability of the performative within multiple, essentially uncontrollable contexts. The problem with Austin's exclusion of non-serious speech acts, Derrida argues, is that these are features they share with ordinary performatives: the favorite Austinian examples of promising, marrying, baptizing, etc. all involve highly ritualized operations; and far from being dependent on speakers' intention, their felicity is mainly a function of context and citation. In short, ordinary performatives are just as "hollow" and contaminated by the logic of iterability as the parasitic ones; hence the distinction between them falters.

As already mentioned, in response to these objections, Cavell's first move is to question Derrida's knowledge of Austin's work, and in particular his familiarity with the two essays "A Plea for Excuses" and "Pretending," in both of which Austin, rather than excluding the non-serious, offers extended accounts of precisely the kinds of speech act that Derrida accuses him of brushing off as insignificant. Of greater importance, however, is his discussion of Austin's reference, in the opening lecture of *How To Do Things With Words*, to Euripides' tragedy *Hippolytus*, and in particular to Hippolytus's line "My tongue swore to, but my heart did not," the implications of which are neglected, strangely, by Derrida.[11] The quotation appears in the context of Austin's reply to the objection that his theory fails to take into account the seriousness required for a performative to function: then it seems that marrying, for example, cannot be a matter of simply saying some words on the right occasion; it would lack, we are tempted to suggest, some sort of inner commitment, or, as Austin puts it, "the performance of some internal spiritual act, of which the words are to be the report" (PP, 236). According to Austin, what leads people to postulate the need for such a metaphysical supplement is the logocentrism involved in taking all utterances to be statements. On this assumption, the performative consists in *describing* the performance of inward and spiritual acts, rather than in doing something. The line from *Hippolytus* demonstrates how this craving for metaphysical depth and solemnity may even screen immorality. By providing Hippolytus with the chance of using the fact that he did not mean (or intend) what he said, it allows him to excuse his words from the status of a promise. Thus Austin concludes that "Accuracy and morality are on the side of the plain saying that *our word is our bond*."[12]

Austin's comments on Euripides' tragedy unequivocally testify, against Derrida's reading, to Austin's rejection of intentionalism. Hippolytus enacts Austin's suspicion that metaphysics can be used "to get out of the moral of the ordinary, out of our ordinary moral obligations" (PP, 75). Yet such a "metaphysical dodge" fails to exempt him. Regardless of whether he disclaims it or not, a promise has been made (in so far as all the requisite circumstances have been in effect), and Hippolytus will be expected to bear responsibility for having done so. Thus if Derrida had paid attention to the quote from *Hippolytus*, it would not have been possible for him to attribute to Austin the view that "one of these essential elements [for an utterance counting as a performative] – and not one among others – remains, classically, consciousness, the conscious presence of the intention of the speaking subject in the totality of his speech act."[13] As we have seen, for Derrida, the absence of such an "organizing center"[14] means that the context, though uncontrollable in its capacity for generating semantic play and rupture, becomes the main factor in accounting for the performance of the performative. For Cavell, however, although the context surely should not be forgotten in philosophy, the absence of an originating, isolated *ego cogito* (in the metaphysical sense) does not imply the rejection altogether of some notion of intention or responsibility. By taking a metaphysical conception of intention to be the only alternative to the powerlessness implied by contextualism, Derrida shows himself to be ridden by the skeptic's desire to escape the finitude (and burden) of the ordinary. Against the skeptical either/or of Derrida's ultimate rejection of all intention, Cavell defends a non-metaphysical notion of accountability:

> For Austin as for Wittgenstein intention is anything but something inner making up for the absence of something outer; it lines the outer. Intention can guide the variation of signal flags through a sequence of positions, but it cannot – that is, *that* intention cannot – guide the establishing of the flags, and what counts as their positions, and what the positions signify, and so on. In the absence of this institution no such intention is formulable. It may help to say: a context *is* what allows such a thing as an intention to do so much and to be so little. (POP, 111)

Tracing intentions reveal what consequences a person takes responsibility for, and hence may serve as an explanation of conduct. Yet no one (except perhaps the modernist artist confronted with the exigencies of her work) can set up the institutions that make responsible behavior possible. Promising has its "logic" regardless of my intentions. In completely ritualized performances, such as in games, intention does not even count, because in games, all possible consequences are limited a priori by the rules of the game. In morality, however, as we have seen, a human being can be fully responsible for all the moves she takes within the parameters of intelligible behavior. Consequently, Hippolytus's line does not count as an excuse. As Cavell puts it, "the price of having spoken, or remarked, taken something as remarkable . . . is to have spoken forever, to have entered the arena of the inexcusable, to have taken on the responsibility for speaking further, the unending responsibility of responsiveness, of answerability, to make yourself intelligible" (PP, 65). In refusing to distinguish between serious and non-serious performatives, in arguing that all performatives essentially are "hollow," irresponsible rituals, Derrida forgoes this crucial dimension of speech. His account, then, though capable, perhaps, of escaping the pitfalls of a metaphysics of presence, does not avoid the emptiness which Austin and Wittgenstein take to characterize traditional (skeptical) philosophy. For Derrida, "absolute responsibility for an essential predicate cannot be tethered to a mortal" (PP, 64): the performance, say of a promise, thus becomes an empty act, comparable to the emptiness involved in the epistemologist's assertion that he knows that *that* table (in front of him under perfect epistemic conditions) really exists.

Indeed, as Cavell suggests, even Austin backs off from the burdensome implications of everyday speech. For whereas Austin is ready to interpret Hippolytus's "My tongue swore to, but my heart did not" as an excuse (for not sticking to his word), a more plausible reading would view him as unwilling to reveal what he knows about Phaedra's forbidden passion for him. However, it is exactly because he stands by his word, even though his heart had not sworn to it, that the tragedy generalizes, drawing his father, Theseus, Phaedra, and himself, to their deaths. While emphasizing the moral that *our word is our bond*, Austin thus fails "to appreciate the case in which that motto is more a curse than a sensible maxim" (POP, 101). Does this mean that Austin fears the case in which seriousness is abused? To be sure, no marks or tokens exist by which to distinguish sincerity and seriousness; in that, Derrida is right. The threat of skepticism cannot be blocked by the invocation of criteria. And yet, in so far as a promise has been made, the breaching of it is not excusable the way the performance of actions is. If I forfeit my bond, then since I do not dispose of the institution of promising, "what I forfeit is language itself" (POP, 104). And forfeiting language means that I become unintelligible, "that the words I would give in my utterance would become ungraspable, not receivable, not currency" (POP, 104). By accepting Hippolytus's line as an excuse, Austin fails to realize that unless I mean what I say, unless, that is, I apply criteria in the absence of any impersonal finality capable of blocking skepticism, then I do not fully exist; I remain unknown. Once again, Austin's anti-skepticism sides him with the skeptic.

Romanticism

As Cavell presents them, both deconstruction and romanticism aim to call the distinction between philosophy and literature into question. While he is not necessarily calling for the assimilation of the one to the other, in both traditions the two modes of writing have persistently been forced to acknowledge how they mutually condition and reinforce each other. But whereas deconstruction, in all the authors under consideration, is marked by an evasion of the ordinary, and hence can be viewed as succumbing to a skeptical impulse, romanticism, while deeply sensitive to the issue of skepticism, offers ways to recover the self and the ordinary human voice. Romanticism – whether in Emerson, Thoreau, Wordsworth, Coleridge, or Heidegger – holds up the promise of redemption, of liberating the claims of the everyday from the inhuman denials of the skeptic. It is therefore of vital importance to our understanding of Cavell's recent thinking about the potentially death-dealing threat of skepticism that romanticism gets taken into account.

Even though both *The Senses of Walden* (1972) and the earliest essays on Emerson ("Thinking of Emerson" and "An Emerson Mood") may be viewed as permeated by a romantic sensibility, the first texts that explicitly deal with the theme of romanticism are the lectures printed in *This New Yet Unapproachable America* (1987) and *In Quest of the Ordinary* (1988). Before entering the discussions contained in those volumes, however, I want to turn for a moment to the issue, featured in an essay on Friedrich Schlegel and Wittgenstein, "The *Investigations'* Everyday Aesthetics of Itself,"[15] of the literary versus the philosophical. Very roughly, the Jena romantics, and the Schlegel brothers in particular, pleaded for, on the one hand, a poetry that would contain its own theory, and, on the other, a philosophizing that would aim for a poetic expression.[16] Intellectually as well as emotionally, the Jena romantics experienced the split envisaged by Kant between freedom and nature, transcendental subjectivity and nature under laws, as alienating, and ultimately as distorting of both subject and object. For these writers, therefore, the call for a unification of philosophy and literature was intended as an effort to create a form of discourse that would be able to anticipate the subject's overcoming of his self-imposed estrangement from nature. In such a discourse, the subject would find his own freedom expressed and articulated; the ideal and the real would thus be brought together in a unity. For poetry, this translated into the notion of *poiesis* as the imaginative articulation of freedom or spontaneity. For philosophy, however, it signified a participation in the expressive efforts of spontaneity, and hence a refusal of all doctrines in favor of irony, the paradoxical movement of self-reflection which the romantics practiced in the form of the aphorism.[17]

In "The *Investigations'* Everyday Aesthetics of Itself," Cavell interprets Wittgenstein's aspiration of perspicuous representation as a way of inheriting the romanticist concern with the aphoristic, hence literary, quality of philosophy.[18] In Cavell's account, perspicuous representation, like geometrical proof, is the achievement of transparency, of "completeness, pleasure, and the sense of breaking something off . . . words that epitomize, separate a thought, with finish and permanence, from the general range of experience" (TCR, 385). Although the *Investigations* obviously contain a huge variety of rhetorical forms other than the aphoristic, an example of such a representation would be "The human body is the best picture of the human soul" (PI, p. 178), the qualities of which, Cavell suggests, attest to Wittgenstein's romantic sensibility.

Cavell's position is more complex than it may seem at first glance. He certainly does not opt for the downright anti-intellectualist stance which Habermas, in *The Philosophical Discourse of Modernity*, calls a "leveling of the genre distinction between philosophy and literature."[19] In taking issue with Habermas, Cavell insists that from the attribution of beauty to some of the most rigorous passages in the *Investigations* it should not be inferred that the distinction between philosophy and literature is meant to be leveled, but rather "that the genres occur simultaneously, and perhaps work to deepen their differences, even to bring them to a crisis" (TCR, 373). Cavell here draws a parallel with a set of works by the late Heidegger, "which characteristically philosophizes off of the reading of certain poetry, thus 'containing' it, but not by competing with it, anyway not by composing something like poetry of its own" (TCR, 374). Moreover, in the context of addressing the nature of an Emersonian essay, he employs Philippe Lacoue-Labarthe and Jean-Luc Nancy's notion of literature becoming its own theory:[20] while announcing and providing its own conditions of comprehension, Emerson's writing, even though it actualizes itself in the form of the essay, achieves the self-containedness and autonomy that Cavell associates with the aphoristic or fragmentary. Thus every Emersonian sentence is as complete as one of Schlegel's or Wittgenstein's aphorisms.

Even if it is granted that the romanticist interpretation of Wittgenstein's notion of perspicuous representation does not involve a naive collapse of the grammatical (and institutional) distinction between philosophical and literary discourse but only a persistent problematization of their mutual boundaries, its consequences for Cavell's understanding of the ordinary remain to be explored. One difficulty would seem to consist in the comparison with geometry: for if perspicuous representation, as Cavell maintains, in fact satisfies the criteria of completeness, closure, and breaking off – analogous to the proof that the inner angles of a triangle equal 180 degrees – then he seems to require the same kind of impersonally or algorithmically achieved certainty for the successful recounting of criteria that he otherwise dismisses as engendering skepticism and voicelessness. It is thus important not to read the idea of perspicuity being comparable or analogous to the work of proofs as entailing that the writing of ordinary language philosophy should be aligned with the formal rigor of the mathematical. Philosophical investigations of the ordinary demand neither formal argumentation nor systematization: the perspicuity, while outside the realm of technical or formally a priori demonstration, requires a return to the ordinary – not as something new, but as the undiscovered "essence, the ground of everything empirical" (TCR, 378). From being lost, the movement toward perspicuity is an ecstatic achievement of finding oneself, a shock of freedom whereby privacy is overcome:

> To count, as I do here, on a willingness to maintain a continuity between near and far, is to count on a certain way of following the continuities implied between the pleasures I claimed for certain literary gestures in the *Investigations* and the portrait of human pathos I sketched from it. The way of following requires a willingness to recognize in oneself the moments of strangeness, sickness, disappointment, self-destructiveness, perversity, suffocation, torment, lostness that are articulated in the language of the *Investigations,* and to recognize in its philosophizing that its pleasures (they will have to reach to instances of the ecstatic) will lie in the specific forms and moments of self-recovery it proposes – of familiarity (hence uncanniness, since the words of recovery were already familiar, too familiar), of soundness, of finitude, of the usefulness of friction, of acknowledgment, of peace. (TCR, 383)

The reference here to "familiarity," "friction," and "peace" leads to another, yet closely related, problematic consequence of the romantic investment in the notion of perspicuous representation, namely its potential failure, despite Cavell's assurances to the contrary, to take modernism (in the arts, philosophy, and politics) seriously. For it seems that Cavell cannot have it both ways: he cannot conceive of the skeptical impulse as intrinsic to language and at the same time be tempted by Wittgenstein's injunction "that the philosophical problems should *completely* disappear" (PI, §133). Declaring, as, say, Wittgenstein's or Emerson's texts do, one's conditions in speech can only achieve completeness on pain of forgoing the essential incompleteness of modernist forms of self-reflection: that the realization and hence completion of each enunciation remains a task that is *specific* to each one of them. Philosophy always has to start, as it were, from scratch, or rather from "where we find ourselves": it cannot rely on any pre-given structure of intelligibility. Thus, the recurrent metaphorics of a pre-industrial rural counterworld – of proximity, of simple and immediate presence, associating proximity with the values of home, peace, and listening – enforce the suspicion that Cavell's vocabulary at times harbors a latent essentialism at odds not only with his modernism, but also with his own stress on skepticism as intrinsic to the very possession of language.

While Cavell's rhetoric occasionally conflicts with his more predominant sense that the ordinary, like America in Emerson, is to be achieved or discovered – that the ideal culture is one where "we are all teachers and all students" (TCR, 352) – and hence that peace should not be confused with dogmatism, he significantly refuses the endlessness of deferral typical of Derrida and other proponents of deconstruction.

> It is the practice [involving unguardedness and openness, the commitment to go on in a certain way] that constitutes diurnalization, a way or weave of life to challenge the way or weave that exhausts the form of life of talkers. This is how I understand Wittgenstein's claim to give philosophy peace. (TCR, 351)

Philosophy is fated to respond to someone else's words; its most important virtue is therefore responsiveness; but no response "will be total" (ibid): rather, "[philosophy] will be tireless, awake when the others have all fallen asleep" (ibid). As culture's own guardian, constantly questioning the inheritance of language, philosophy equally needs to resist the temptation to be parochial *and* the drive toward transcendence. Both would arrest its straining of language against itself – the movement toward self-recovery and authentic authorization of one's own linguistic practices.

Cavell's attempt to inherit the Jena romantics' stress on the aphoristic requires very careful reconstruction so as not to be misunderstood. More promising, perhaps, are his reflections on Kant and more recent forms of romanticism in *In Quest of the Ordinary*. I have already alluded to the centrality of Kant's thought for the Schlegel brothers. On Cavell's reading, though, the challenge of Kant's complex way with skepticism continues to haunt writers and thinkers such as Coleridge, Wordsworth, and Heidegger. Like the Jena romantics, their crucial notion, which gets formed with reference to Kant's *Critique of Pure Reason*, is that of a life and death of the world, dependent on thought's own configuration. Roughly, the account of Kant that would fit this idea is the following. For Kant, the fundamental aim of a critique of pure reason, and hence of philosophy, is to settle the claims of dogmatic rationalism and skeptical empiricism, the former proclaiming objective knowledge of things as they are in themselves, the latter denying the very possibility of knowledge. The settlement consists in demonstrating that experience necessarily is of appearances, that is, of experiential intake that conforms to, or is a function of, specific transcendental endowments of the human being. On Kant's view, then, the conditions of human knowledge are at the same time limitations of it. Human beings, due to the transcendental laws governing experience, can in principle obtain objective knowledge of nature as it appears under laws; on the other hand, although reason by its very nature is driven to transcend its own limits, it must renounce all claims to know the ground of appearance, the thing-in-itself.

As Cavell points out, the romantic response to the Kantian conception of conditions as limits consists, as is the case in most of post-Kantian idealism (Fichte, Schelling, Hegel), in questioning the very achievement reached thereby. While happy to admit the existence of terms or conditions according to which humans can place themselves as knowers and doers among the things of the world, the romantics rebel against taking Kant's limitation of knowledge of appearances as amounting to an overcoming of skepticism. To them, as it should be to us (Cavell argues), this is, on the contrary, a prolonging, and indeed a radicalization, of the skeptic's denial that human knowledge is of things as they are in themselves: "You don't – do you – have to be a romantic to feel sometimes about that settlement: Thanks for nothing" (IQO, 31).

The portrait of Kant as a skeptic, or at least of his anti-skepticism as a species of skepticism, resonates with Cavell's own understanding of skepticism. Typically, the skeptic's quest for certainty involves a jealous desire to overcome the separateness of the world from himself. Like Othello, whose death-dealing relation to Desdemona may be viewed as an allegory of material-object skepticism, the (Kantian) skeptic craves absolute possession: unless the world offers an inalienable bonding to himself, the subject can be in no position to lay claim to knowledge. And yet, for knowledge to be possible, it is necessary to accept the separateness of the world, its sheer externality (and yet closeness), without which there would not *be* the world to which the skeptic wishes to be bonded at all. Thus, on the romantics' reading, Kant's epistemology provides a skeptical solution to skepticism: rather than accepting the fragility of our own position as knowers in the world, our separateness, it hypostatizes the death of the world – by our own hands. Indeed, as opposed to Kant's construction of conditions as limits that place the world (or our experience of it) within our own impositioned categories, we should refuse to adopt the metaphysical distinction between appearances and things in themselves altogether. To think of something as appearing is to conceive of it as appearing this way rather than that way, or under some conditions rather than others. But employing such a characterization means to turn conditions into facts about ourselves – facts that might be otherwise; and yet that *this* is (what we call) a chair, a smile, or a warning, is not a fact, as it is a fact about me that I tend to prefer certain chairs over others, or fail to take notice of people's warnings about my smoking; and for this reason it is not contingent, and hence not a feature of our lives that should be thought of as limiting (constituting one perspective to the exclusion of another).

While keeping in mind the refusal to endorse a *metaphysical* (and skeptical) account of the distinction between appearances and things in themselves, Cavell nevertheless makes the, from a Kantian point of view somewhat bizarre, claim that "*Walden* provides a transcendental deduction of the category of the thing-in-itself" (SW, 106n). In order to understand this assertion, it is imperative that it is read in conjunction with the contention that Kant's impoverished conception of experience, based as it is on the synthesizing role of the twelve concepts of the understanding, leaves no room for the poetic dwelling, or receptive intimacy with existence, associated with Emerson, Thoreau, Heidegger, and the romantics. More specifically, it harks back to the so-called truth of skepticism – "that the human creature's basis in the world as a whole, its relation to the world as such, is not that of knowing, anyway not what we think of as knowing" (CR, 241) – which implies that something does indeed escape what we understand as knowledge, and hence also what we can know as a thing. While denying, against the skeptic (and with Kant), that the "truth of skepticism" implies a *failure* of knowledge, Cavell submits the following claim:

The idea of the thing-in-itself is the idea of a relation in which we stand to the world as a whole; call it a relation of the world's externality (not each object's externality to every other – that is the idea of space; but the externality of all objects to us). When I said that Kant ought to have provided a deduction of the thing-in-itself, I meant that he had left unarticulated an essential feature (category) of objectivity itself, viz., that of *a world apart from me in which* objects are met. The externality of the world is articulated by Thoreau as its nextness to me. (SW, 107n)

As it stands, this formulation is beset with difficulties. For one thing, what does it mean to say that we stand in *a* (that is, a single) relation to the world as a whole? Doesn't this reintroduce the interpretation, discarded in *The Claim of Reason*, of the world itself as being an object, albeit an indescribably big one? For another, if we are said to stand in *a relation* to such a super-object, is not the skeptic thereby invited to ask how this relation is epistemically grounded, and thus to return us to the problem of knowledge (its basis or justification)? Certainly, all attempts to provide a set of straightforward descriptions of such a presumed precognitive relation would seem to be question-begging from the perspective of the skeptic. (The same difficulty arises if Wittgenstein's appeals, in *On Certainty*, to an indubitable framework of knowledge are construed as wanting to rely on a set of unquestionable *propositions*: then the problem of justification inevitably returns, and hence also the skeptic.) At times, though, Cavell seems very aware of this challenge. For example, in "Thinking of Emerson," of 1979, he invokes, explicitly against Kant's one-sided cognitivism and with a nod toward Heidegger (who, he argues, inherits Emerson's stress on receptivity or passivity – again in opposition to Kantian spontaneity), the notion of moods as the best way of capturing our being-in-the-world: "sense-experience is to objects what moods are to the world" (SW, 125). And in "An Emerson Mood," of 1981, Emerson's idea of closeness or intimacy becomes crucial – "that our relation to the world's existence is somehow *closer* than the ideas of believing and knowing are made to convey" (SW, 145) – implying that silence, not words, best expresses that relation. But perhaps the most useful discussion of romanticism's attempt to retrieve from Kant the thing-in-itself occurs in the second and third Beckman lectures, of 1983, where Cavell takes up the issue of animism.

As Cavell recognizes, hardly any concept has been more discredited in post-Enlightenment philosophy than animism, the ascription of mental predicates to inanimate objects and natural phenomena. As Max Weber put the point in an image that has become commonplace, with the rise to cultural prominence of modern science, nature has been left "disenchanted": there seems no longer to be any room for an intelligible or authoritative conception of nature other than one that emphasizes lawlike relations between intrinsically meaningless events. In spite of the "nervous laughter" (QO, 68) such a concept may inspire, Cavell, however, in order to develop his sense that "there is a life and death of the world, dependent on what we make of it" (ibid), turns to several authors, among them Coleridge, Heidegger, John Wisdom, and Wordsworth.

While aiming to demonstrate that Coleridge's *Biographia Literaria* testifies to a strong interest in Kant and the problem of skepticism, Cavell's interest in this representative of romanticism centers on *The Rime of the Ancient Mariner*, and in particular the famous sequence describing the Mariner's shooting of the albatross.[21] In a perverse act of free will, reminiscent of the spiritual implications of the Fall, the Mariner, being disappointed with his knowledge of the bird, forfeits, through the act of shooting, his responsibility to establish a connection with it. Rather than sustaining an interest in the bird, which would include feeding it, caring for it, and perhaps even talking to it, as people do to their pets, the Mariner "may just have wanted at once to silence the bird's claim upon him and to establish a connection with it closer, as it were, than his caring for it: a connection beyond the force of his human responsibilities, whether conventional or personal, either of which can seem arbitrary" (IQO, 60). Like the other-minds skeptic who cannot tolerate his separation from the other, and who therefore rationalizes his failure to know others as a metaphysical problem, thus turning the other into a complete enigma, the Mariner, in desiring an absolute connection, ends up creating the opposite: an absolute distance, allegorized as death. But Coleridge's dream-poem does more than dramatize this dialectic of death: it also hints at an alternative to the "desert-sea of skepticism" (IQO, 65). For in so far as the shooting may be seen not only as the killing of another, but also as a form of suicide, a denial of one's connection with others (to be spelled out as an agreement or attunement in criteria) in favor of a death-bearing privacy, any redemption of the world must equally involve a redemption of the perpetrator. On Cavell's reading, another character, the Wedding-guest, teaches the Mariner to accept his aloneness: for, as in marriage, the only way to achieve intimacy is through the willingness, however unassured, to continue to be responsive to the particularity of the other's expressions of herself.

In his account of Heidegger's late essay "The Thing," of 1950, Cavell considers the idea that redeeming the things of the world requires a redemption of humans from themselves: "The redemption of the things of the world is the redemption of human nature, and chiefly from its destructiveness of its own conditions of existence" (IQO, 66). In Heidegger, this destruction is viewed in terms of an alleged (modern) dominance of technological mastery and control, leading to an impoverished conception of experience. For a thing to be a thing (or, as Heidegger puts it, "the thing in itself") it is not sufficient that it satisfies, as in Kant's Copernican turn, the conditions of human knowledge: rather, for us to be who we are, we must "satisfy the conditions of there being things of the world – whatever accordingly these turn out within philosophical thought to be" (IQO, 66). Whereas philosophy may attempt to systematize these conditions, it is poetry that is ultimately capable of bringing them into expression. While eschewing technological thinking, poetry, if constantly in search of its own possibility, "is the possibility of human life": just as Thoreau's prose reaches a state of absolute seriousness, so in bearing absolute responsibility for each and every computation of words, poetry redeems human nature from the grip it has of itself. Moreover, in "Thinking of Emerson," Cavell detects similar expressions of such a turning of the Copernican turn in Heidegger's conception of thinking as receiving, as opposed to Kant's positing or active synthesis.[22] Echoing both Emerson's "sacred affirmative" ("The Preacher") and Nietzsche's "sacred Yes" (*Thus Spoke Zarathustra*), Heidegger conceives of genuine thinking as a form of thanking, a grateful response to that which calls for thinking.[23]

While acknowledging Heidegger's distinct contribution to the romanticist call for a reanimation of the world, a worry may arise about its capacity to elicit a serious philosophical response. "The thing stays – gathers and unites – the fourfold. The thing things the world."[24] Are such propositions rationally justifiable? Do they clarify, rather than obscure, the central romantic dialectic of a self-imposed life and death of the world? In order to further his thoughts on the issue of animism, Cavell turns to John Wisdom, an analytical philosopher, initially a student of Wittgenstein, whose article "Gods" provokes the question of what Wisdom calls the hypothesis of minds in flowers and trees.[25] On considering a

skeptic's response to the question "Do flowers feel?" Wisdom imagines a context in which someone's caring for flowers elicits from
an observer the assertion, "You believe flowers feel." Inevitably,
however, the attribution in this case of a specific belief suggests that
the skeptic finds the person's treatment of flowers to be inappropriate, perhaps even slightly crazy, which is how Wisdom's discussion gets started. If, on the other hand, the explanatory hypothesis
about *believing* that flowers are animate is suspended in favor of
being struck simply by the actions themselves, by how flowers
happen to be treated, at least by certain people, then the skeptic
might be provoked to *consider* what flowers are and what he takes
to be appropriate in our treatment of them. Such a consideration
would perhaps include observations about how we arrange
flowers, whether lovingly or not, and on how we meet them, say
by seeking their odor, rather than saying hello. Whereas the attribution of belief (that flowers feel) invites the suspicion of a pathetic
fallacy, an investigation into how we permit certain objects to *count*
for us as flowers can be viewed as a way of recounting the criteria
by means of which the application of the concept of "flower" is
regulated. By focusing on the apparent absurdity of *believing* that
flowers are animate, Wisdom's skeptic repudiates in advance the
shared conditions for anything to count as a flower. So Cavell is not
claiming, contrary to commonsense belief, that flowers do feel; his
point is rather that we ought to reflect on the significance of our
way of dealing with them, and realize that flowers, like all other
things, demand, or require, a specific form of response for them to
be what they are.

Turning, finally, to Wordsworth's "Intimations of Immortality
from Recollections of Early Childhood," Cavell again explores the
issues of birth and death, and how the poet's speech may be heard
as seeking to "re-seduct" his readers and thus renew their interest
in the world.[26] Yet seduction and, hence, life are bought at a price:
there is no natality, no second birth, without abandonment and loss:
"Our birth is but a sleep and a forgetting."[27] As opposed to the
eternal re-enactment of the past that marks the nostalgia of many
of Freud's patients, a successful rebirth of the subject, while imaginatively participating in and recollecting the enchantment and cre-
ativity of childhood, involves an acceptance of the child in us as
gone. It thus requires a relinquishment of the wish to avenge oneself
on the passing of time – in short, a process of mourning whereby
the subject, however painful it might be, "recathects" desire so as
to achieve freedom. To some, this spiritual teaching may seem

implausible or even fraudulent. To others, it may seem over-whelmingly evident. Apart from our own reactions and commit-ments, whether or not we aim at taking possession of our own experience, nothing will insure its teachability. Such are the risks and satisfactions of perfectionist writing – of Cavell's bold claim that philosophy is a journey of the soul from sickness to health.

Epilogue

Looking back over the development of Cavell's thinking, it can hardly be doubted that it represents a highly distinct and rewarding contribution to contemporary "post-analytical" philosophy. Not only has Cavell succeeded brilliantly in defending and renewing the Austinian heritage of ordinary language philosophy, but he has also extended his reflections to a vast array of extra-philosophical areas of intellectual and imaginative engagement, thus producing a complex and challenging pattern of critical interventions that together make up the substance of his work. The increasing number of conferences and publications devoted to his thought speaks for itself of its academic prominence – not just in philosophy but in fields such as feminism, film studies, and literary theory. At the heart of his enterprise, as it has been interpreted in this book, is a foundationless philosophy in which our shared form of life, our sharing of judgments, and our constant everyday willingness (or not) to expose ourselves to our others and acknowledge them constitute the fundamental fabric of human experience and likewise the key to the unraveling of the fundamental problems of philosophy, at least as Cavell construes them. While combining a strong non-foundationalist bias with an equally emphatic modernism centered on the idea of self-authorization, Cavell's work might be seen as offering a kind of contemporary Hegelianism, one liberated from metaphysical aspirations of totality and ready to address the open-endedness of the modern world in all its complexity and ambiguity.

Yet while Cavell has been tremendously accomplished as a professional philosopher, it is nevertheless largely the case, as we have seen, that his work, both rhetorically and existentially, seeks to resist a quick and easy accommodation to the demands of professional philosophy. Few if any of the key issues we have encountered – self-knowledge, the ordinary and ordinary language, questions of style and self-presentation, self-transformation and friendship, the dialectic of reading and being-read – are likely to resonate with the concerns of current academic philosophy. It is true, of course, that Cavell has never explicitly taken leave of traditional (analytic) philosophy. In view of the intellectual environments – at Berkeley and Harvard, but also American philosophy more generally – that have dominated his entire academic career, he considers such an act of discarding to have been dishonest. Moreover, his work, while utilizing a more extensive range of rhetorical devices than is common in the profession, has seldom, if ever, showed signs of eschewing its standards of rigor and argumentation altogether.

Significant as this may be, however, his keen sense (echoing Heidegger and Wittgenstein) that what is at stake in philosophy exceeds the boundaries of its secure professionalization, and indeed that its main impulse will tend to come from "out of school," has driven him to inhabit an unassured position of perpetual reflection and local response, one rather different from the typical practices of the academically accredited experts one would usually find in a major philosophy department. Cavell's primary goal has been less to *solve* certain meta-scientific problems and puzzles than to authorize his own voice (and hence existence) within a field of experience marked by our shared commitments to the logic(s) of ordinary language. Like language or linguistic articulation itself, the potential for philosophical reflection is for him inherently democratic; its temptations, disappointments, and insights are equally distributed among all speakers who take an interest in their own experience.

But does Cavell ever advocate the view that philosophy somehow is illegitimate, and that its entry into the extracurricular areas of film, biography, opera, and so on ultimately ought to spell the end of philosophy as a distinct discipline or *Fach*? It is revealing, in this respect, to compare Cavell to Richard Rorty, arguably the most influential contemporary proponent of a post-philosophical culture. According to Rorty, professional philosophy, in the tradition from Kant to Frege, Russell, and beyond, has conclusively failed, and should be left to the historians. In his account, the professionalization of philosophy went hand in hand with an almost exclusive interest in epistemology. Central to the epistemological project was the belief that responsibility for the correctness of our claims means to be in touch with "a 'hard', nonhuman reality."[1] But as the very idea of representing reality as it *really is*, apart from the way our historically shaped vocabularies allow us to solve problems internal to our practices, can be shown to be misguided, the emphasis on epistemology ought to be replaced with a pluralist, non-foundationalist vision of intellectual engagement. In such a culture, philosophy, while at best continuing to articulate the fallacies of representationalism, has no role to play as an autonomous discipline; it is a culture in which freedom and solidarity, the explicit commitment to human commonality, and the avoidance of cruelty are valued higher than truth.

Direct exchanges between Rorty and Cavell have been few and far between. In the recent *Rorty and His Critics*, Rorty dismisses Cavell's thinking as "an unfortunate throwback to pre-Hegelian attempts to find something ahistorical to which philosophers may pledge allegiance. The Ordinary," he argues, "strikes me as just the latest disguise of the *ontos on*."[2] Moreover, in his review of *The Claim of Reason*, while applauding the literary and experimental style of Part IV, Rorty views the first three parts as expressive of an outmoded and ultimately vain obsession with traditional problems of epistemology.[3] After all, Cavell *solves* none of the problems he so effectively lays out for analysis. Rather than flogging dead horses, it would be better, Rorty concludes, to reinvent the discourse completely, thus leaving the tradition behind rather than recapturing it.

Rorty's attempt to split *The Claim of Reason* in two and offer diametrically opposed assessments of each half seems ill-founded. Although it is true, as I have mentioned, that the final sections of *The Claim of Reason* are written in a more extravagant style than the rest, it hardly follows that Cavell here is somehow more ready to take leave of academic epistemology than he is elsewhere. If anything, what we find in "Skepticism and the Problem of Others" is a philosopher who, while acutely aware of the existential difficulty of presenting philosophical insights involving the self, essentially frames his discussion by means of an epistemological vocabulary. More significantly, however, as should by now have become clear, Cavell does not so much intend to block or rebut skepticism as to diagnose and locate it in the economy of human knowing; thus Rorty's objection about a presumptive regress to foundationalism fails to hit the mark. In whichever way it achieves articulation, the ordinary never takes on the ahistorical appearance of the *ontos on* of foundationalist, Platonic epistemology. Nor is it a reservoir of fundamental truths from which the philosopher, in her privileged discourse, can draw. Rather, if thought of in terms of criteria in the Wittgensteinian version recommended by Cavell, it invites, and indeed may even nourish, the skeptical impulse. Our shared agreement in judgments, while the source of all intelligibility, is forever to be repudiated by our wish to sublime language. To construe the ordinary as the *ontos on*, as Rorty does, would effectively be tantamount to its denial.

Cavell agrees with Rorty that the notion of philosophy as a distinct, specialized, and professional discipline should be questioned. And like Rorty, who in the final chapter of *Philosophy and the Mirror of Nature* introduces the concept of edification in order to designate the task of philosophy, he thinks that philosophy is best understood as an advanced form of cultural self-reflection, an "education of grownups" (CR, 125). Both thinkers advocate a vision of philosophy as a stimulus for human change, not just natural growth. To engage in philosophy means to allow oneself to be challenged, to be ready for personal transformation.

Unlike Cavell, however, Rorty thinks that the activity of self-transfiguration should be strictly limited to the private sphere. While for Cavell the culture will be confronted "along the lines in which it meets in me" (ibid), for Rorty a culture can only be criticized in the name of universal interest and impersonal justice: the sublime experiences of private man should be of no consequence in public life. The lines whereby culture and individuality intersect, in so far as they encourage a view of the society as illegitimate from the standpoint of the deviant individual, should, according to Rorty, simply be repressed. Ultimately, this means that self-transforming philosophy, though of great personal interest, will have nothing to say on matters of intersubjective concern such as, for example, justice; thus the Cavellian anxiety of self-authorization, of not knowing, like children or seriously engaged teachers, what ground we may occupy and recognize as ours does not arise for Rorty. On the contrary, in Rorty's work the *we*, the community of interpreters, form the final context of validity; thus the individual can only be right or justified in so far as her utterances are acceptable to her peers. Truth, then, becomes a compliment we pay to those of our assertions that can find communal assent.

For Cavell, though individuals agree in forms of life and hence in judgments, the authorization of one's (political, aesthetic, philosophical, etc.) judgment is far from simply a matter of conforming to social authority relations. Indeed, for Cavell, unlike Rorty, epistemic authority is never just a given fact about someone; rather, it must be earned. The conversations Cavell takes inspiration from thus involve a continuous and often heartbreaking or dangerous search for entitlement, where all parties, in order to speak for themselves, will risk both being rebuffed and having to rebuff others. While philosophy has no right to intervene in such exchanges from an a priori standpoint, the most promising way of thinking about the role and function of philosophy would be as agents for the promotion of dialogue, and indeed, as Emerson would say, of provocation. By turning his back on philosophy, as if the problems it poses can simply be left behind as relics of a flawed and therefore illegitimate tradition, Rorty renounces the education of humans, the way in which they themselves, each one of them, must find their voice and assert authority. And since this, for Cavell, is the only way of individualizing ourselves before the other(s), and thus of making ourselves known, it follows that a genuine community would not be one in which communal agreement is taken for granted, but one in which the nature and content of consent would allow for, and indeed also invite, disputes. By dividing the individual into the private and the public man, the first being unresponsive to the community, the second just a function of communal norms, Rorty ends up siding with the skeptic's repression of voice, and hence of existence.

In Cavell's work, in short, what is affirmed is not at all a set of theoretical propositions but rather the ability of individuals to authenticate their lives before themselves and others. Ultimately, whether this counts as the continuation of philosophy or as its final overcoming is a matter of one's own response. Yet Cavell's writings do not culminate either in postmodern complacency or modernist despair but, rather, with the demand, based on an acknowledgment of our finitude, that we bring ourselves into existence. Faced with a task like that, this seems like an appropriate moment at which to end this book.

Notes

Preface

1 Among the most significant volumes of commentary on Cavell's work are Timothy Gould, *Hearing Things: Voice and Method in the Writing of Stanley Cavell* (Chicago: University of Chicago Press, 1998); Stephen Mulhall, *Stanley Cavell: Philosophy's Recounting of the Ordinary* (Oxford: Oxford University Press, 1994); Michael Fischer, *Stanley Cavell and Literary Skepticism* (Chicago: University of Chicago Press, 1989); Richard Fleming, *The State of Philosophy: An Invitation to a Reading in Three Parts of Stanley Cavell's "The Claim of Reason"* (Lewisburg: Bucknell University Press, 1993); Richard Fleming and Michael Payne (eds.), *The Senses of Stanley Cavell* (Lewisburg: Bucknell University Press, 1989); Ted Cohen, Paul Guyer, and Hilary Putnam (eds.), *Pursuits of Reason: Essays in Honor of Stanley Cavell* (Lubbock: Texas Tech University Press, 1993).

Chapter 1   Ordinary Language Philosophy

1 See James Conant, "An Interview with Stanley Cavell," in Richard Fleming and Michael Payne (eds.), *The Senses of Stanley Cavell* (Lewisburg: Bucknell University Press, 1989), p. 36.

2 See Herbert Marcuse, *The One-Dimensional Man: Studies in the Ideology of Advanced Industrial Society* (London: Routledge, 1964), p. 173: "Austin's contemptuous treatment of the alternative to the common usage of words, and his defamation of what 'we think up in our armchairs of an afternoon'; Wittgenstein's assurance that 'philosophy leaves everything as it is' – such statements exhibit, to my mind, academic sado-masochism, self-humiliation, and self-denunciation of the intellectual whose labor does not issue in scientific, technical or like achievements."

3   See John Austin, *Sense and Sensibilia* (Oxford: Oxford University Press, 1962).

4   See POP, 82: "It is not possible . . . to re-create the climate in which positivism was pervasive and dominant in the Anglo-American academic world, from the mid-1940's through the 1950's and beyond, almost throughout the humanities and the social sciences – a hegemonic presence more total, I believe, than that of any one of today's politically or intellectually advanced positions. Positivism during this period was virtually unopposed on any intellectually organized scale."

5   See Cavell, "Existentialism and Analytical Philosophy," in TOS, p. 209.

6   See Benson Mates, "On the Verification of Statements About Ordinary Language," in V. C. Chappell (ed.), *Ordinary Language* (Englewood Cliffs, NJ: Prentice Hall, 1964), pp. 64–74.

7   John Austin, "A Plea for Excuses," in PhP, 181.

8   See Gilbert Ryle, *The Concept of Mind* (Chicago: University of Chicago Press, 1984), p. 69.

9   See Stephen Toulmin, *The Uses of Argument* (Cambridge: Cambridge University Press, 1974).

10   See Immanuel Kant, *Critique of Pure Reason*, trans. N. K. Smith (London: Macmillan, 1986), B25: "I entitle *transcendental* all knowledge which is occupied not so much with objects as with the mode of our knowledge of objects in so far as this mode of knowledge is to be possible *a priori*."

11   Kant, *Critique of Judgement*, trans. J. H. Bernard (New York: Hafner Press, 1951), p. 47.

12   For a further elaboration of this point, see Richard Eldridge, "'A Continuing Task': Cavell and the Truth of Skepticism," in *The Persistence of Romanticism: Essays in Philosophy and Literature* (Cambridge: Cambridge University Press, 2001), p. 198.

13   Ibid, p. 50: "We may see now that in the judgment of taste nothing is postulated but such a *universal voice*, in respect of the satisfaction without the intervention of concepts, and thus the *possibility* of an aesthetical judgment that can, at the same time, be regarded as valid for everyone."

14   David Pole, *The Later Philosophy of Wittgenstein* (London: The Athlone Press, 1958).

15   For a useful elucidation of the intrinsic link between self-recognition and communal practices, see Richard Eldridge, "The Normal and the Normative: Wittgenstein's Legacy, Kripke, and Cavell," *Philosophy and Phenomenological Research* 36, 4 (1986), pp. 555–75.

16   Saul Kripke, *Wittgenstein on Rules and Private Language* (Cambridge, MA: Harvard University Press, 1982).

17   Ibid, p. 62.

18   Ibid, p. 90.

Chapter 2   Skepticism: Criteria and the External World

1   Stephen Mulhall, *Stanley Cavell: Philosophy's Recounting of the Ordinary* (Oxford: Oxford University Press, 1994). For a critical discussion of Mulhall's view for which I am indebted at this juncture, see Steven G. Affeldt, "The Ground of Mutuality: Criteria, Judgment, and Intelligibility in Stephen Mulhall and Stanley Cavell," *European Journal of Philosophy*, 6 (1998), pp. 1–31. See also Mulhall's response to Affeldt in his "The Givenness of Grammar: A Reply to Steven Affeldt," *European Journal of Philosophy*, 6 (1998), pp. 32–44.

2   Mulhall, *Stanley Cavell*, p. 80.

3   Ibid, p. 152.

4   Ibid, p. 171.

5   Affeldt, "The Ground of Mutuality," p. 7.

6   Roger Albritton, "On Wittgenstein's Use of the Term 'Criterion'," in George Pitcher (ed.), *Wittgenstein* (London: Macmillan, 1968), pp. 231–50; Norman Malcolm, "Wittgenstein's *Philosophical Investigations*," in ibid, pp. 65–103.

7   See PhP, pp. 76–116.

8   René Descartes, *Meditations on First Philosophy*, trans. D. A. Cress (Indianapolis: Hackett, 1979).

9   See Barry Stroud, "Reasonable Claims: Cavell and the Tradition," *The Journal of Philosophy*, 77 (1980), pp. 731–44.

10   Ibid, p. 743.

Chapter 3   The Other

1   See, for example, Paul Churchland, "Eliminative Materialism and the Propositional Attitudes," *The Journal of Philosophy*, 78 (1981), pp. 67–90.

2   See John Cook, "Wittgenstein on Privacy," in George Pitcher (ed.), *Wittgenstein* (London: Macmillan, 1968), pp. 286–323.

3   See George Pitcher, *The Philosophy of Wittgenstein* (New Jersey: Prentice Hall, 1964), p. 300.

4   See Alan Donagan, "Wittgenstein on Sensation," in George Pitcher (ed.), *Wittgenstein* (London: Macmillan, 1968), pp. 324–351.

5   See the important remarks in MWM, 263–4.

6   See Wittgenstein, *Remarks on the Philosophy of Psychology*, vol. I, trans. G. E. M. Anscombe; vol. II, trans. C. G. Luckhardt and M. A. E. Aue (Oxford: Blackwell, 1980) and *Last Writings on the Philosophy of Psychology*, vols I and II, trans. C. G. Luckhardt and M. A. E. Aue (Oxford: Blackwell, 1982).

7   See Stephen Mulhall, *Being in the World: Wittgenstein and Heidegger on Seeing Aspects* (London: Routledge, 1990), p. 79: "The error involved is stated . . . explicitly . . . when Cavell says: ' "Seeing something as something" is what Wittgenstein calls "interpretation" ' (CR, 354); for it is one of the fundamental aims of Wittgenstein's treatment of aspect

perception to show that aspect-dawning and continuous aspect perception are a matter of seeing *rather than* interpretation (cf. PI, 212d). . . . In employing the notion of interpretation to characterize our relation to other people Cavell is therefore using a concept which, as defined by Wittgenstein in this context, can only help to draw the reader away from one of the key insights which emerges from Wittgenstein's treatment of this issue; and the misleading connotations ramify beyond this initial stage."

8   See Peter Winch, "'Eine Einstellung zur Seele'," *Proceedings of the Aristotelian Society*, 81 (1980–1), p. 10.

9   For an excellent account of Merleau-Ponty's anti-skepticism in comparison with Cavell and Wittgenstein, see Marie McGinn, "The Real Problem of Others: Cavell, Merleau-Ponty and Wittgenstein on Scepticism about Other Minds," *The European Journal of Philosophy*, 6 (1998), pp. 45–58.

10   See Hans Blumenberg, *The Legitimacy of the Modern Age*, trans. Robert M. Wallace (Cambridge, MA: MIT Press, 1983).

11   Cf. Sigmund Freud, "Mourning and Melancholia," in *The Penguin Freud Library*, vol. 11, trans. and ed. J. Strachey (Harmondsworth: Penguin, 1984), pp. 251–68.

12   Ibid, p. 253.

13   DK, 13.

14   See Freud, "From the History of an Infantile Neurosis," in *The Penguin Freud Library*, vol. 9, pp. 227–366, esp. pp. 259–80.

15   Cavell's reading of Nietzsche is at this point indebted to Heidegger, *What Is Called Thinking*, trans. J. Glenn Gray (New York: Harper and Row, 1968).

Chapter 4   Art and Aesthetics

1   See David Hume, "Of the Standard of Taste," in Hume, *Selected Essays*, ed. Stephen Copley and Andrew Edgar (Oxford: Oxford University Press, 1993), pp. 133–54.

2   Ibid, p. 148.

3   Cavell adopts this idea from Clement Greenberg. For Greenberg's most programmatic defense of modernism, see his "Modernist Painting," in *The Collected Essays and Criticism*, vol. 4, ed. John O'Brian (Chicago: University of Chicago Press, 1993), pp. 85–93.

4   In a recent essay, "The World as Things: Collecting Thoughts on Collecting," in Yve-Alain Bois and Bernard Blistene (eds.), *Rendezvous: Masterpieces from the Centre Georges Pompidou and the Guggenheim Museums* (New York: Abrams, Harry N Inc, 1988), pp. 64–89, Cavell seems to have become more sympathetic toward pop art than he was in the 1960s. Like the unrestricted sincerity of modernist painting, Andy Warhol's *The Twenty Marilyns* "declares the issue of a painting's facing us" (p. 81).

5 Cavell is here indebted to Michael Fried, *Three American Painters* (Cambridge, MA: Harvard University Press, 1965).

6 Erwin Panofsky, "Style and Medium in the Moving Pictures," in Daniel Talbot (ed.), *Film* (New York: Simon and Schuster, 1959), p. 31.

7 See André Bazin, *What is Cinema?*, trans. Hugh Gray (Berkeley: University of California Press, 1967); Siegfried Kracauer, *Theory of Film* (New York: Oxford University Press, 1960).

8 Bazin, *What is Cinema?*, p. 19.

9 Martin Heidegger, "The Age of the World View," trans. Marjorie Grene, *Boundary*, 4 (1976), pp. 341–55.

10 I borrow this example from Douglas P. Lackey, "Reflections on Cavell's Ontology of Film," *Journal of Aesthetics and Art-Criticism*, 32 (1973), p. 272. See also H. Gene Blocker's discussion of Cavell's film aesthetics in "Pictures and Photographs," *Journal of Aesthetics and Art-Criticism*, 36 (1977), pp. 155–62.

11 See Martin Heidegger, *What Is Called Thinking?*, trans. J. Glenn Gray (New York: Harper and Row, 1968).

12 In Cavell's account, the central women of both the comedies and melodramas in question may be seen as descendants of Ibsen's Nora. While the demand for education and the concomitant creation of the self relates the woman of comedy to Nora, the inability of Helmer, her husband, to provide such an education, thus making remarriage impossible, anticipates the fate of the women of melodrama. It should be noted, though, that Cavell predominantly tends to associate Ibsen's *A Doll's House* (along with Shakespeare's *The Winter's Tale*) with the comedies. His lack of consistency in these matters as well as the overwhelming fact of Nora's refusal to remarry will serve to justify, I hope, my own use of Ibsen's play in order to highlight features of melodrama.

13 René Descartes, *Meditations on First Philosophy*, trans. D. A. Cress (Indianapolis: Hackett, 1979).

14 See Jaakko Hintikka, "Cogito, Ergo Sum: Inference or Performance?" *The Philosophical Review*, 71 (1962), pp. 3–32.

15 Sigmund Freud, "The Neuro-Psychoses of Defence," in *Standard Edition of the Complete Psychological Works of Sigmund Freud*, vol. 3, edited and translated in collaboration with Anna Freud (London: Hogarth Press, 1966), p. 50.

16 Cavell, "Something Out of the Ordinary," *The Proceedings and Addresses of the American Philosophical Association*, 71 (1997), p. 36. See also the extensive discussion of opera in POP, pp. 131–69.

Chapter 5   Ethics and Politics

1 See Jürgen Habermas, *Moral Consciousness and Communicative Action*, trans. Christian Lenhardt and Shierry Weber Nicholson (Cambridge, MA: MIT Press, 1990).

2 See CR, 266.
3 See Arthur N. Prior, *Logic and the Basis of Ethics* (Oxford: Clarendon Press, 1949).
4 See David Hume, "Of the Original Contract," in Hume, *Selected Essays*, ed. Stephen Copley and Andrew Elgar (Oxford: Oxford University Press, 1993), pp. 274–92.
5 Ibid, p. 276.
6 Jean-Jacques Rousseau, *The Social Contract and Discourses*, trans. G. D. H. Cole (London: Everyman, 1973), p. 181: "Man is born free; and everywhere he is in chains."
7 Ralph Waldo Emerson, "Self-Reliance," in Emerson, *Selected Essays*, ed. Larzer Ziff (London: Penguin, 1985), p. 175.
8 Ibid, p. 99.
9 See Cavell, "The Uncanniness of the Ordinary," in QO, pp. 153–78.
10 Emerson, "An Address Delivered Before the Senior Class in Divinity College, Cambridge," in *Selected Essays*, p. 112.
11 Sigmund Freud, "An Outline of Psychoanalysis," in *The Penguin Freud Library*, vol. 15, ed. James Strachey (London: Penguin, 1993), p. 408.
12 Ibid, p. 409.
13 See John Rawls, *A Theory of Justice* (Cambridge, MA: Harvard University Press, 1971), pp. 325–32.
14 Ibid, p. 325.
15 Cavell, "What is the Scandal of Skepticism? Moments in Schopenhauer and Levinas," presented at the ASCA conference on skepticism and interpretation, Amsterdam, June 2000.
16 Emmanuel Levinas, *Totality and Infinity: An Essay on Exteriority*, trans. Alphonso Lingis (Pittsburgh: Duquesne University Press, 1969); *Otherwise than Being, or Beyond Essence*, trans. Alphonso Lingis (The Hague: Martinus Nijhoff, 1981).
17 For a promising attempt to criticize this premise in Levinas, see Simon Critchley, *Very Little . . . Almost Nothing: Death, Philosophy, Literature* (London: Routledge, 1997), pp. 73–83.
18 See MWM, 163–79.
19 Levinas, *Otherwise than Being, or Beyond Essence*, p. 123.

Chapter 6   Between Philosophy and Literature: Deconstruction and Romanticism

1 Several commentators have argued that deconstruction is essentially a skeptical enterprise, among them Michael Fischer, *Stanley Cavell and Literary Skepticism* (Chicago: University of Chicago Press, 1989), pp. 7, 140; Charles Altieri, *Act And Quality* (Amherst: University of Massachusetts Press, 1981), p. 27; Christopher Norris, *Deconstruction: Theory and Practice* (London: Methuen, 1982), p. xii.
2 Stanley E. Fish, *Is There a Text in This Class? The Authority of Interpretive Communities* (Cambridge, MA: 1980), p. 108.

3 Ibid, p. 242.
4 Paul de Man, *Allegories of Reading: Figural Language in Rousseau, Nietzsche, Rilke, and Proust* (New Haven, CT: Yale University Press, 1979), p. 131.
5 Ibid, p. 9.
6 Ibid.
7 See Jacques Derrida, *Speech and Phenomena, and Other Essays on Husserl's Theory of Signs*, trans. David B. Allison (Evanston: Northwestern University Press, 1973).
8 Derrida, "Signature Event Context," in *Limited Inc*, trans. Samuel Weber and Jeffrey Mehlmann (Evanston: Northwestern University Press, 1990), pp. 1–23.
9 See Alfred J. Ayer, *The Foundations of Empirical Knowledge* (London: Macmillan, 1963).
10 Derrida, *Speech and Phenomena*, p. 99.
11 Euripides, *Hippolytus*, trans. Robert Bagg (London: Oxford University Press, 1974).
12 John L. Austin, *How To Do Things With Words* (Cambridge, MA: Harvard University Press, 1962), p. 10.
13 Derrida, "Signature Event Context," p. 14.
14 Ibid, p. 15.
15 TCR, 369–89.
16 For a well-known expression of this tendency, see Friedrich Schlegel, "Critical Fragments," in *Friedrich Schlegel's* Lucinde *and the Fragments*, trans. Peter Firchow (Minneapolis: University of Minnesota Press, 1971), §115: "The whole history of modern poetry is a running commentary on the following brief philosophical text: all art should become science and all science art; poetry and philosophy should be made one."
17 For an excellent account of these issues and how they bear on modern philosophy, in particular that of Wittgenstein, see Richard Eldridge, *Leading a Human Life: Wittgenstein, Intentionality, and Romanticism* (Chicago: The University of Chicago Press, 1997), esp. pp. 56–85.
18 See PI, §122:

> A main source of our failure to understand is that we do not *command a clear* view of the use of our words. – Our grammar is lacking in this sort of perspicuity. A perspicuous representation produces just that understanding which consists in "seeing connexions." Hence the importance of finding and inventing *intermediate* cases.
>
> The concept of a perspicuous representation is of fundamental significance for us. It earmarks the form of account we give, the way we look at things. (Is this a "Weltanschauung"?)

19 Cavell refers to Jürgen Habermas, *The Philosophical Discourse of Modernity*, trans. Frederick G. Lawrence (Cambridge, MA: MIT Press, 1987), pp. 185–210.

20 NYUA, 20. See also Philippe Lacoue-Labarthe and Jean-Luc Nancy, *The Literary Absolute: The Theory of Literature in German Romanticism*, trans. Philip Barnard and Cheryl Lester (Albany: State University of New York Press, 1988).

21 Samuel Taylor Coleridge, *The Rime of the Ancient Mariner and Other Poems* (New York: Dover, 1992), p. 7. See also Coleridge, *Biographia Literaria*, ed. J. Shawcross (Oxford: Oxford University Press, 1949).

22 See also "Night and Day: Heidegger and Thoreau," in James E. Faulconer and Mark A. Wrathall (eds.), *Appropriating Heidegger* (Cambridge: Cambridge University Press, 2000), p. 32, where Cavell refers to Heidegger's formulation of awakening "as 'letting whatever is sleeping become wakeful,' where this 'letting' names the relation to being that forms a world, the distinct privilege of the human."

23 SW, 132. See also Heidegger, *What Is Called Thinking?*, trans. J. Glenn Gray (New York: Harper and Row, 1968).

24 See Heidegger, "The Thing," in *Poetry, Language, Thought*, trans. Albert Hofstadter (New York: Harper and Row, 1971), p. 181.

25 John Wisdom, "Gods," in *Philosophy and Psychoanalysis* (New York: Barnes and Noble, 1969), pp. 149–68.

26 See William Wordsworth, "Ode: Intimations of Immortality from Recollections of Early Childhood," in *Selected Poems*, ed. Walford Davies (London: J. M. Dent and Sons, 1975), p. 107.

27 Ibid.

Epilogue

1 See Richard Rorty, *Contingency, Irony, and Solidarity* (Cambridge: Cambridge University Press, 1988), p. 4.

2 Rorty, "Response to Hilary Putnam," in Robert B. Brandom (ed.), *Rorty and His Critics* (Oxford: Blackwell, 2000), p. 90.

3 Rorty, "From Epistemology to Romance: Cavell on Skepticism," *Review of Metaphysics*, 34 (1981), pp. 759–74. (Reissued in *Consequences of Pragmatism* (Minneapolis: University of Minnesota Press, 1982).)

Bibliography

Works by Stanley Cavell

The Cavell Reader, ed. Stephen Mulhall. Oxford: Blackwell, 1996.

The Claim of Reason: Wittgenstein, Skepticism, Morality, and Tragedy. Oxford: University of Oxford Press, 1979.

Conditions Handsome and Unhandsome: The Constitution of Emersonian Perfectionism. Chicago: The University of Chicago Press, 1990.

Contesting Tears. The Hollywood Melodrama of the Unknown Woman. Chicago: University of Chicago Press, 1996.

Disowning Knowledge. In Six Plays of Shakespeare. Cambridge: Cambridge University Press, 1987.

In Quest of the Ordinary. Lines of Skepticism and Romanticism. Chicago: University of Chicago Press, 1988.

Must We Mean What We Say? A Book of Essays. Cambridge: Cambridge University Press, 1976.

"Night and Day: Heidegger and Thoreau," in James E. Faulconer and Mark A. Wrathall (eds.), *Appropriating Heidegger*. Cambridge: Cambridge University Press, 2000.

Philosophical Passages: Wittgenstein, Emerson, Austin, Derrida. Oxford: Blackwell, 1995.

A Pitch of Philosophy. Autobiographical Exercises. Cambridge, MA: Harvard University Press, 1994.

Pursuits of Happiness. The Hollywood Comedy of Remarriage. Cambridge, MA: Harvard University Press, 1981.

The Senses of Walden. Chicago: The University of Chicago Press, 1992 (expanded edition).

"Something Out of the Ordinary," *The Proceedings and Addresses of the American Philosophical Association*, 71 (1997), pp. 23–37.

Themes Out of School: Effects and Causes. Chicago: University of Chicago Press, 1988.

This New Yet Unapproachable America. Lectures after Emerson after Wittgenstein. Albuquerque, New Mexico: Living Batch Press, 1989.

"What is the Scandal of Skepticism? Moments in Schopenhauer and Levinas," unpublished paper presented at the ASCA conference on skepticism and interpretation, Amsterdam, June 2000.

"The World as Things: Collecting Thoughts on Collecting," in Yve-Alain Bois and Bernard Blistene (eds.), *Rendezvous: Masterpieces from the Centre Georges Pompidou and the Guggenheim Museums*. New York: Abrams, Harry N Inc, 1998, pp. 64–89.

The World Viewed. Reflections on the Ontology of Film. Cambridge, MA: Harvard University Press, 1971.

Other Works

Affeldt, Steven. "The Ground of Mutuality: Criteria, Judgment, and Intelligibility in Stephen Mulhall and Stanley Cavell," *European Journal of Philosophy*, 6 (1998), 1–31.

Albritton, Roger. "On Wittgenstein's Use of the term 'Criterion'," in George Pitcher (ed.), *Wittgenstein*. London: Macmillan, 1968.

Altieri, Charles. *Act and Quality*. Amherst: University of Massachusetts Press, 1981.

Austin, John. *How To Do Things With Words*. Cambridge, MA: Harvard University Press, 1962.

——. *Sense and Sensibilia*. Oxford: Oxford University Press, 1962.

——. *Philosophical Papers*. Oxford: Oxford University Press, 1970.

Ayer, Alfred J. *The Foundations of Empirical Knowledge*. London: Macmillan, 1963.

Bazin, André. *What is Cinema?*, trans. Hugh Gray. Berkeley: University of California Press, 1967.

Blocker, H. Gene. "Pictures and Photographs," *Journal of Aesthetics and Art-Criticism*, 36 (1977), 155–62.

Blumenberg, Hans. *The Legitimacy of the Modern Age*, trans. Robert M. Wallace. Cambridge, MA: MIT Press, 1983.

Churchland, Paul. "Eliminative Materialism and the Propositional Attitudes," *The Journal of Philosophy*, 78 (1981), 67–90.

Cohen, Ted, Paul Guyer, and Hilary Putnam (eds.). *Pursuits of Reason: Essays in Honor of Stanley Cavell*. Lubbock: Texas Tech University Press, 1993.

Coleridge, Samuel Taylor. *Biographia Literaria*, ed. J. Shawcross. Oxford: Oxford University Press, 1949.

——. *The Rime of the Ancient Mariner and Other Poems*. New York: Dover, 1992.

Conant, James. "An Interview with Stanley Cavell," in Richard Fleming and Michael Payne (eds.), *The Senses of Stanley Cavell*. Lewisburg: Bucknell University Press, 1989.

Cook, John. "Wittgenstein on Privacy," in George Pitcher (ed.), *Wittgenstein*. London: Macmillan, 1968.

Critchley, Simon. *Very Little . . . Almost Nothing: Death, Philosophy, Literature*. London: Routledge, 1997.

De Man, Paul. *Allegories of Reading: Figural Language in Rousseau, Nietzsche, Rilke, and Proust*. New Haven, CT: Yale University Press, 1979.

Derrida, Jacques. *Speech and Phenomena, and Other Essays on Husserl's Theory of Signs*, trans. David B. Allison. Evanston: Northwestern University Press, 1973.

——. *Limited Inc*, trans. Samuel Weber and Jeffrey Mehlmann. Evanston: Northwestern University Press, 1990.

Descartes, René. *Meditations on First Philosophy*, trans. D. A. Cress. Indianapolis: Hackett, 1979.

Donagan, Alan. "Wittgenstein on Sensation," in George Pitcher (ed.), *Wittgenstein*. London: Macmillan, 1968.

Eldridge, Richard. "The Normal and the Normative: Wittgenstein's Legacy, Kripke, and Cavell," *Philosophy and Phenomenological Research*, 36, 4 (1986), 555–75.

——. *Leading a Human Life: Wittgenstein, Intentionality, and Romanticism*. Chicago: University of Chicago Press, 1997.

——. *The Persistence of Romanticism: Essays in Philosophy and Literature*. Cambridge: Cambridge University Press, 2001.

Emerson, Ralph Waldo. *Selected Essays*, ed. Larzer Ziff. London: Penguin, 1985.

Euripides, *Hippolytus*, trans. Robert Bagg. London: Oxford University Press, 1974.

Fischer, Michael. *Stanley Cavell and Literary Skepticism*. Chicago: University of Chicago Press, 1989.

Fish, Stanley E. *Is There a Text in This Class? The Authority of Interpretive Communities*. Cambridge, MA: Harvard University Press, 1980.

Fleming, Richard. *The State of Philosophy: An Invitation to a Reading in Three Parts of Stanley Cavell's "The Claim of Reason."* Lewisburg: Bucknell University Press, 1993.

Fleming, Richard and Michael Payne (eds.). *The Senses of Stanley Cavell*. Lewisburg: Bucknell University Press, 1989.

Freud, Sigmund. *Standard Edition of the Complete Psychological Works of Freud*, 24 vols, ed. and partial trans. Anna Freud. London: Hogarth Press, 1966.

——. *The Penguin Freud Library*, 15 vols, trans. and ed. James Strachey. Harmondsworth: Penguin, 1984.

Fried, Michael. *Three American Painters*. Cambridge, MA: Harvard University Press, 1965.

Gould, Timothy. *Hearing Things. Voice and Method in the Writing of Stanley Cavell*. Chicago: University of Chicago Press, 1998.

Greenberg, Clement, *The Collected Essays and Criticism*, vol. 4, ed. John O'Brian. Chicago: University of Chicago Press, 1993.

Habermas, Jürgen. *The Philosophical Discourse of Modernity*, trans. Frederick G. Lawrence. Cambridge, MA: MIT Press, 1987.

——. *Moral Consciousness and Communicative Action*, trans. Christian Lenhardt and Shierry Weber Nicholson. Cambridge, MA: MIT Press, 1990.

Heidegger, Martin. *Being and Time*, trans. J. Macquarrie and E. Robinson. Oxford: Basil Blackwell, 1962.

——. *What Is Called Thinking?*, trans. J. Glenn Gray. New York: Harper & Row, 1968.

——. *Poetry, Language, Thought*, trans. Albert Hofstadter. New York: Harper and Row, 1971.

——. "The Age of the World View," trans. Marjorie Grene, *Boundary*, 4 (1976), 341–55.

Hintikka, Jaakko. "Cogito, Ergo Sum: Inference or Performance?" *The Philosophical Review*, 71 (1962), 3–32.

Hume, David. "Of the Original Contract," in Stephen Copley and Andrew Edgar (eds.), Hume, *Selected Essays*. Oxford: Oxford University Press, 1993.

——. "Of the Standard of Taste," in Stephen Copley and Andrew Edgar (eds.), Hume, *Selected Essays*. Oxford: Oxford University Press, 1993.

Ibsen, Henrik. "A Doll's House," in *Complete Major Prose Plays*, trans. and ed. Rolf Fjelde. New York: New American Library, 1965.

Kant, Immanuel. *Critique of Pure Reason*, trans. Norman Kemp Smith. London: Macmillan, 1929; reprinted 1986.

——. *Critique of Judgement*, trans. J. H. Bernard. New York: Hafner Press, 1951.

Kracauer, Siegfried. *Theory of Film*. New York: Oxford University Press, 1960.

Kripke, Saul. *Wittgenstein on Rules and Private Language*. Cambridge, MA: Harvard University Press, 1982.

Lackey, Douglas P. "Reflections on Cavell's Ontology of Film," *Journal of Aesthetics and Art-Criticism*, 32 (1973), 271–3.

Lacoue-Labarthe, Philippe and Jean-Luc Nancy. *The Literary Absolute: The Theory of Literature in German Romanticism*, trans. Philip Barnard and Cheryl Lester. Albany: State University of New York Press, 1988.

Levinas, Emmanuel. *Totality and Infinity: An Essay on Exteriority*, trans. Alphonso Lingis. Pittsburgh: Duquesne University Press, 1969.

——. *Otherwise than Being, or Beyond Essence*, trans. Alphonso Lingis. The Hague: Martinus Nijhoff, 1981.

Malcolm, Norman. "Wittgenstein's *Philosophical Investigations*," in George Pitcher (ed.), *Wittgenstein*. London: Macmillan, 1968.

Marcuse, Herbert. *The One-Dimensional Man: Studies in the Ideology of Advanced Industrial Society*. London: Routledge, 1964.

Mates, Benson. "On the Verification of Statements about Ordinary Language," in V. C. Chappell (ed.), *Ordinary Language*. New Jersey: Prentice Hall, 1964.

McGinn, Marie. "The Real Problem of Others: Cavell, Merleau-Ponty and Wittgenstein on Scepticism about Other Minds," *The European Journal of Philosophy*, 6 (1998), 45–58.

Mulhall, Stephen. *On Being in the World: Wittgenstein and Heidegger on Seeing Aspects*. London: Routledge, 1990.

——. *Stanley Cavell: Philosophy's Recounting of the Ordinary*. Oxford: Oxford University Press, 1994.

——. "The Givenness of Grammar: A Reply to Steven Affeldt," *The European Journal of Philosophy*, 6 (1998), 32–44.

Nietzsche, Friedrich. *Thus Spoke Zarathustra*, trans. Walter Kaufmann. New York: Penguin, 1978.

Norris, Christopher. *Deconstruction: Theory and Practice*. London: Methuen, 1982.

Panofsky, Erwin. "Style and Medium in the Moving Pictures," in Daniel Talbot (ed.), *Film*. New York: Simon and Schuster, 1959.

Pitcher, George. *The Philosophy of Wittgenstein*. New Jersey: Prentice Hall, 1964.

Pole, David. *The Later Philosophy of Wittgenstein*. London: The Athlone Press, 1958.

Prior, Arthur N. *Logic and the Basis of Ethics*. Oxford: Clarendon Press, 1949.

Rawls, John. *A Theory of Justice*. Cambridge, MA: Harvard University Press, 1971.

Rorty, Richard. *Philosophy and the Mirror of Nature*. Princeton: Princeton University Press, 1979.

——. "From Epistemology to Romance: Cavell on Skepticism," *Review of Metaphysics*, 34 (1981), 759–74.

——. *Consequences of Pragmatism*. Minneapolis: University of Minnesota Press, 1982.

——. *Contingency, Irony, and Solidarity*. Cambridge: Cambridge University Press, 1988.

——. "Response to Hilary Putnam," in Robert B. Brandom (ed.), *Rorty and His Critics*. Oxford: Blackwell, 2000.

Ross, William D. *Foundations of Ethics*. Oxford: Clarendon Press, 1949.

Rousseau, Jean-Jacques. *The Social Contract and Discourses*, trans. G. D. H. Cole. London: Everyman, 1973.

Ryle, Gilbert. *The Concept of Mind*. Chicago: University of Chicago Press, 1984.

Schlegel, Friedrich. *Friedrich Schlegel's* Lucinde *and the Fragments*, trans. Peter Firchow. Minneapolis: University of Minnesota Press, 1971.

Shakespeare, William. *Othello*, ed. Alvin Kernan. London: Signet Classic, 1963.

——. *King Lear*, ed. Kenneth Muir. London: Methuen, The Arden Shakespeare, 1972.

——. *The Winter's Tale*, ed. J. H. P. Pafford. London: Methuen, The Arden Shakespeare 1978.

——. *Hamlet*, ed. Harold Jenkins. London: Methuen, The Arden Shakespeare, 1982.

Stevenson, Charles. *Ethics and Language*. New Haven: Yale University Press, 1944.

Stroud, Barry. "Reasonable Claims: Cavell and the Tradition," *The Journal of Philosophy*, 77 (1980), 731–44.

Thoreau, Henry David. *Walden and Civil Disobedience*. New York: Penguin, 1986.

Toulmin, Stephen. *The Uses of Argument*. Cambridge: Cambridge University Press, 1974.

Winch, Peter. "Eine Einstellung zur Seele," *Proceedings of the Aristotelian Society*, 81 (1980–1), 1–14.

Wisdom, John. "Gods," in *Philosophy and Psychoanalysis*. New York: Barnes and Noble, 1969.

Wittgenstein, Ludwig. *Philosophical Investigations*, trans. G. E. M. Anscombe. New York: Basil Blackwell, 1958.

——. *On Certainty*, trans. G. E. M. Anscombe. New York: Basil Blackwell, 1979.

——. *Remarks on the Philosophy of Psychology*, vol. I, trans. G. E. M. Anscombe, vol. II, trans. C. G. Luckhardt and M. A. E. Aue. Oxford: Basil Blackwell, 1980.

——. *Last Writings on the Philosophy of Psychology*, 2 vols, trans. C. G. Luckhardt and M. A. Aue. Oxford: Basil Blackwell, 1982.

Wordsworth, William. *Selected Poems and Prefaces*, ed. Jack Stillinger. Boston: Houghton Mifflin Company, 1965.

Index